Date Due			
Oct 13 69			
Apr 26 79			
Feb 18 80			
	PRINTED	IN U. S. A.	

THE DESIGN OF THE SCRIPTURES

BOOKS BY ROBERT C. DENTAN

Preface to Old Testament Theology
The Holy Scriptures: A Survey
The Apocrypha, Bridge of the Testaments
The Design of the Scriptures

THE DESIGN
OF THE
SCRIPTURES

A First Reader in Biblical Theology

ROBERT C. DENTAN

McGRAW-HILL BOOK COMPANY, INC.
New York   Toronto   London

The Design of the Scriptures

Library of Congress Catalog Card Number: 60-15254

First Edition

The material in this book first appeared as articles in *The Living Church* and *Episcopal Churchnews*. Used by permission.

16404

For Lawrence Rose
with affection and gratitude

CONTENTS

Part Two: *DOCTRINE*

Part Three: *LIFE*

INTRODUCTION

The purpose of this book is to set forth the teaching of the Bible in such a way as to illustrate the consistency and organic unity of biblical thought: the harmony which underlies the all-too-obvious differences between the two Testaments, the threads of interrelationship which tie together their separate parts in a complex and fascinating design. The diversity in point of view between the Testaments and among their various books and authors has been exploited frequently enough; the aim of this book is to show that underneath these differences there is a fundamental unity with respect to the questions with which they deal, the solutions which they offer, and the historical and literary images which are the basic vocabulary with which they speak.

It is not, of course, suggested that this is the only way in which the Bible should be read. There are many other valuable approaches—by books, by sources, by personalities, by rearrangement of the literary material in chronological order, even by perusal from cover to cover—and for each of them some special advantage may be claimed. It is undoubtedly important to learn as much as possible about the background, thought-patterns and literary style of the various authors who have contributed to the Bible and to understand the intricate process by which the present canon of scripture developed. But each of these methods of study is defective in some way and most of them have certain defects in common. Purely literary and historical study tends to concentrate the reader's attention either upon the various elements of which the Bible is composed, thus reducing the Book to a collection of fragments, or else upon the complex procedure by which these elements were fused into books and later into the completed canon, which tends to make the genetic process seem more significant than the end result. The common alternative to this kind of critical study is that of simply reading the Bible through from Genesis to Revelation, a method which, in the case of the ordinary unprepared reader, is likely to be more productive of confusion and frustration than edification.

The present book, it must be clearly understood, presupposes the "assured results" of biblical criticism, but is itself concerned with critical methods only rarely and incidentally. Its interest is in the Bible as a finished product and in its meaning for faith and life. For the Christian Church—as for the Jewish Church before it—the Bible is a unity, a collection of books bound together by a common outlook and a common spirit (though we should be more faithful to Christian convictions if we capitalized the word Spirit). If this unity is a fact and not merely a fancy born of ecclesiastical tradition, it should be possible to demonstrate it by actual observation and make it evident to the common reader as well as to the professional theologian. Such is the intention of this book. Whether that intention has been successfully realized is a question which the reader will have to answer for himself. The author can claim no more than that he is personally convinced of the validity of this approach and has earnestly tried to make its validity apparent to others also. It is his conviction that there is—as faith has always maintained—an overall pattern or design to the Bible which makes its total meaning something greater than the meaning of even the greatest of its parts.

The subtitle describes this book as *A First Reader in Biblical Theology*. Biblical theology, as I attempted to show in a small book published some years ago,[1] is the branch of biblical studies which treats the religious ideas of the Bible systematically—i.e., not from the point of view of their historical development, but from that of the structural unity of biblical religion. The applicability of this definition to the present book will be evident from what has previously been said. The word "Reader" in the subtitle is used advisedly, since this is not a treatise on biblical theology, but a guide to reading the Bible in order to discover what biblical theology is. The Bible text is primary. The book is intended to provide a simple commentary on the passages selected rather than a collection of texts chosen to support the opinions of the author. It is called a "first" reader in order to indicate the elementary character of the task proposed. The author's purpose has been to introduce the reader to a method of studying the Bible and thinking about it which, it is hoped, he may then pursue by himself at greater length and in greater depth.

Something should be said, briefly, about the arrangement of the book and the point of view from which it is written. There have been many treatises on biblical theology (or Old Testament, or New Testament, theology) and many different opinions expressed concerning the way in which its subject matter should be arranged. It is, for example, a popular view today that biblical theology is merely a recital of "the acts of God." Here I can only say, without arguing the thesis at length, that this seems

[1] R. C. Dentan, *Preface to Old Testament Theology*. Yale University Press, 1950.

to me an inadequate conception of the task (although I appreciate the profound truth about the nature of biblical religion which the proponents of this view wish to emphasize). While it is evident that God's mighty acts in history for us men and for our salvation are the ultimate theme of Holy Scripture, only certain portions of the Bible are devoted to an explicit account of them. The major part of the Bible is concerned with the history of the *people* of God and the implications for life and thought of the fact that their God has shown Himself to be the kind of God He is. This means, to say the least, that the structure of the Bible and the theology which is implicit in it is far more complex and subtle than the formula "biblical theology is a recital of the acts of God" would suggest. In the book mentioned above, I defended the use of the classical rubrics of dogmatic theology—Doctrine of God, Doctrine of Man, Doctrine of Salvation—as the most useful subject headings for organizing a treatise on biblical theology, and I have arranged the contents of the doctrinal part of this book according to that basic scheme. But it has become increasingly clear to me that this alone does not provide a satisfactory account of the theological content of the scriptures. What the Bible contains is not simply the story of God's dealings with the world and His chosen people, nor merely an implicit body of doctrine. It contains, rather, a *body of doctrine* (or, if one prefers, a set of convictions) founded upon a *story* and issuing in a distinctive *manner of life*. Each of these elements is organically related to the others; taken together they constitute the framework of biblical theology and provide three basic categories under which the smaller units in the pattern or design of the scriptures can be arranged. The three divisions of this book are, accordingly: *history* (the story of God's people and His dealings with them), *doctrine* (the

abiding assertions about the nature of God and His relation to man to which this history gave rise), and *life* (the
forms of piety and of personal and corporate existence
which belief in the story and acceptance of the doctrine
necessarily imply).

The term "history" as used in this connection has a
somewhat special sense. In the study of biblical theology
we are not so much concerned with mere events in their
chronological sequence as with the *theological meaning*
which those events acquired in the total perspective of
biblical thought. To give just one example: in this book
our interest in Abraham will be less in the shadowy historical figure who may have lived in the first part of the
second millenium B.C. than in Abraham as the ideal man
of faith who appears to us in later Jewish and Christian
tradition, especially in the writings of St. Paul and the 11th
chapter of the Epistle to the Hebrews. The history with
which this book is concerned is not secular or even "religious" history, but rather theological or sacred history
(what the Germans call *Heilsgeschichte*). This is not to
say that it is false or merely legendary history (although
it includes, as all history does, some legendary elements),
but only that it is history viewed from a special theological point of view and in the light of our interest in historical events as the principal media of redemption and
revelation.

A word also needs to be said with regard to the vantage
point from which we attempt to grasp the design—the
artistic shape and fashion—of the scriptures. The form
which the Bible takes to our mind will be at least in part
determined by the angle from which we view it. It is evident, for instance, that the ultimate meaning of the Old
Testament will be drastically different for those who view
it from within the Christian community rather than from

within the fellowship of Judaism. This does not mean that the Christian will have a different understanding of every verse in the Old Testament, or even very many of the verses, but the fact that he sees Old Testament history as reaching its logical terminus in the New Testament rather than in the Talmud will determine his view of the overall significance of the Hebrew scriptures and therefore influence his interpretation of some crucial passages. A Christian cannot help believing that the New Testament gives the clue to the meaning of the Old Testament at its deepest level. The present book is written frankly, and in all its parts, from the Christian perspective. To define its vantage point more precisely, it may be said that it attempts to view the whole Bible, not merely from some point within the New Testament itself, but from that somewhat indefinite point in early Christian history when the sacred writings of the Old and New Testaments became, in approximately their present form, the Church's canon of scripture.

Since this is merely an introductory work, no attempt has been made to include all conceivable topics or make use of every text which might be brought to bear upon any particular subject. The treatment is intended to be illustrative rather than exhaustive. The only deliberate attempt at comprehensiveness has been in the use of the books of the Bible. Every book of the Old and New Testament has been referred to at least once, as have the four most important books of the Apocrypha.[2] As far as possible the selections given for reading are extended passages

---

[2] The section entitled Apocrypha, which is printed in some editions of the Bible, contains certain important books on ancient Jewish literature which are valuable for understanding developments between the Testaments. Separate editions of the Apocrypha are published by the Oxford University Press, Harper & Brothers, and Thomas Nelson & Sons. General information about these books will be found in R. C. Dentan, *The Apocrypha—Bridge of the Testaments* (Seabury Press, 1954) and B. M. Metzger, *An Introduction to the Apocrypha* (Oxford University Press, 1957).

rather than isolated verses, it being the author's conviction that the Bible is not to be treated as a collection of "proof-texts," even for the study of biblical theology, but is a body of literature, in which the order, shape and flow of a writer's thoughts may be as significant as his final, categorical judgments. In the case of narrative selections, the need for this procedure is self-evident.

Because the comments in the various chapters of this book are intentionally brief, the reader would do well to have at hand a complete Bible commentary to clear up incidental questions which may arise and are not discussed here. The one-volume commentaries edited by Charles Gore (The Macmillan Company, 1929), by Frederick C. Eiselen, Edwin Lewis, and David G. Downey (Abingdon Press, 1929), and W. K. L. Clarke (The Macmillan Company, 1952) would be quite satisfactory for this purpose, as would also *The Interpreter's Bible* (12 vols., Abingdon Press, 1950–56). A good dictionary of the Bible, such as *Harper's* (Madeleine S. and J. Lane Miller, 1952), would be another valuable tool.

The scriptural quotations, with only a few exceptions, are taken from the King James Version (KJV), because this is still the most generally familiar and available. The reader should, however, become acquainted also with the Revised Standard Version (RSV), which is both more accurate and more immediately intelligible.

In conclusion, I wish to express my appreciation to the editors of *Episcopal Churchnews* and *The Living Church* in whose columns most of this material appeared in its original and unrevised form (under the title of "Searching the Scriptures") and by whose courtesy it is reproduced here.

ROBERT C. DENTAN

General Theological Seminary
New York

PART ONE: *HISTORY*

I. PARADISE LOST

Genesis 2:4b–3:24; Matthew 4:1–11; Luke 22:39–44;
I Corinthians 15:21–22, 45–49

Biblical history starts with Adam and the garden, where man begins to react as a free agent to the world in which God has placed him. The preceding material in Genesis (1:1–2:4a, which is by another and later hand) is concerned solely with the activity of God; although in narrative form, it is doctrine rather than history.

The story of the garden is, in reality, the story of Everyman. It is not concerned with events which happened once for all in a far-off mythical time, but with what has happened, and is happening, in the lives of all men everywhere. The very name Adam suggests that this is the proper interpretation of the story, since in Hebrew it means simply "man." This account of man's defection from his Maker is not placed at the beginning of Bible history because there really was a time when snakes could speak and trees bore fruit capable of conferring immortality or secret knowledge, but because there is no other story in the world's literature which pictures so clearly the essential human situation. Here we see mankind both in its high dignity and pitiful distress. We see man created for the noblest of destinies, called to serve God and live in fellowship with Him, but reduced instead to the status of an outcast, a sinner and a slave to sin, in desperate need of redemption from bondage to his sins and to his own corrupt self-centeredness.

3

As is true with many other stories, the point of it is clearest when we look first of all at the conclusion. In Genesis 3:16–19 we find a description of actual human life as we know it and as the ancient Hebrews also knew it. The passage deliberately ignores the happier aspects of life and concentrates on the sorrow and frustration which the author sees as the more basic facts of human existence. It takes only a slight effort of the imagination to realize that the description is accurate. These are the things, furthermore, which need to be explained. If God is good, one is not surprised to find goodness in His world. But how can one explain the world's agony and grief? This is the greatest of life's enigmas and our story gives the biblical answer to it.

When we now turn back to the beginning of the narrative we see what God intended man's life to be. The language and the conceptions are those of ancient Hebrew myth, but these are not the essence of the story. What the Bible seeks to tell us in this way is what God intended us to be and what in fact we have become. God created man for happiness. He put him in a garden called Eden (in Hebrew, "pleasantness"), provided with all he needed for daily life and with immortality within his grasp (2:9). Here man was intended to live a happy and useful existence, doing God's work (v. 15), master of the lower creation (19), living in friendly converse with his own kind (18, 21–25).

But in order that man might learn to be free, able to make moral decisions and to give his God a love that was entirely unconstrained, he was given the power to observe or not to observe the single restriction that was placed upon him. It was God's clearly expressed will that he should not eat of the tree of "the knowledge of good and evil" (2:16–17). Scholars have discussed at great length the meaning of this term, but it is unnecessary to go into it here, since the tree itself is not really significant. It is merely the symbol of man's area of free moral choice. But here we must notice one other important figure in the tale —the serpent, the Tempter. He is the symbol of a dark, mysterious power, not ourselves, which makes for evil in the world. We cannot perhaps satisfactorily explain his existence, but we know he is here. He can be felt all too plainly in the tensions and temptations of our modern world. And when men are left to themselves, they tend to make friends with the Tempter rather than with God. When the test came, both the man and the woman failed. They listened to the Tempter and determined to do their own will instead of God's.

This, says the writer, is the source of all the tragedy of human existence. We do not have to look far to recognize the man and the woman in this story, for it is the story of every human life, the story of our preference for *our* will instead of God's, of our childish readiness to listen to the flattering voice of the Tempter who pretends that our natural destiny is not to serve the God who made us, but to become little gods ourselves (3:5). And the story also tells us that "we have no power of ourselves to help ourselves." The garden gates are closed and the way back is barred. Perhaps we should prefer to say that not God but we ourselves have closed the gate and barred the way. Man cannot return at his own volition. Only God by His grace can restore to us the paradise we have lost and the hope of everlasting life we have forfeited.

Unable by his own strength to bring order into his disordered world, man must wait in patient faith and hopeful trust for God to act and restore to him the full measure of his forfeited inheritance. The rest of the Bible story is essentially the story of how God has done this.

From this sad beginning we now move on to trace "the history of our salvation."

This is also the moment to look ahead into the distant future and catch at least a glimpse of the goal toward which that history was moving. If we turn to Matthew 4:1–11 we read of another temptation which ended as triumphantly as this did disastrously. And if we then turn to Luke 22:39–44 we come upon another scene in a garden where what Adam lost was won for us again by Jesus, who, confronted by a far more agonizing decision, set his Father's will above his own. And, finally, in a few brief verses in I Corinthians 15:21–22, 45–49 we find the Apostle Paul telling his readers that the story which began in Eden has now reached its proper end and that we who are so obviously children of Adam, the man of earth, can become like Christ, the man of heaven.

II. THE COVENANT OF FAITH

Genesis 12:1–4; 15; 22:1–19; Hebrews 11:8–12;
Galatians 3:7–8, 26–29

The first eleven chapters of Genesis are composed, for the most part, of stories drawn from ancient Hebrew myth or folklore. They are tales told by the men of Israel around the campfire or at evening by the city gate, partly no doubt for entertainment, but chiefly to try and provide some explanation for the otherwise insoluble mysteries of the world in which they found themselves. Some of the material, such as that in Genesis 1, is the product of late theological reflection, but most of it consists of stories, simple and naive in form, which can frequently be paralleled in the literature of neighboring peoples, although none of the parallels begins to approach the biblical stories in the loftiness of their conception of God and the profundity of their understanding of the human situation. The theological and moral superiority of the Bible stories seems to show that God Himself was at work among the people who told them. These simple stories picture to us, as could be done in no other way, the majesty and righteousness of God the Creator and the sad state of man, reduced by sin to a pitiable caricature of his true self. The stories of the Fall, of Cain and Abel, of the Flood and the Tower of Babel, all show some aspect of the havoc man has made of his world.

But these opening chapters are only the prologue to the story the Bible really has to tell. They set the stage and show the immense gulf which now separates our fallen, perverted human nature from the goodness of its Maker. The essential Bible story, the story of the bridging of the gulf, the reversing of man's downward trend, begins in Genesis 12, and the first character to appear on the scene is Abraham. From a literary standpoint, the story of Abraham marks the transition from the sphere of myth to that of quasihistorical legend. While we cannot be sure that Abraham was a real historical figure, yet in broad outline the story of his life is one that *might* have happened. The historical setting can be identified and the local color is in many cases remarkably accurate. Scholars are much less skeptical than they were a generation ago about the possibility of there being at least a core of genuine folk memories behind the stories of the patriarchs.

But the importance of Abraham is not tied down to

his existence as an historical figure; it lies rather in the place he occupies as a symbol of God's special relationship to the people of Israel. The men of both the Old and New Testaments were convinced that God long ago had chosen Israel to be His own people, to serve Him in a special way. (This is what is called, in biblical language, the doctrine of Israel's *election*.) Just as God makes use of special persons—great teachers and leaders—to be His agents and messengers, so He once chose a special nation, Israel, and prepared it to be a source of "light to the Gentiles" (Isa. 42:6; 49:6; Luke 2:32). In biblical tradition the figure of Abraham is regarded as marking the point at which God's election of Israel began.

The first of our selections (Gen. 12:1–4) tells how God called Abraham to leave his ancestral home in the broad plain of Mesopotamia and cross the desert to live in a new and unfamiliar land. His unhesitating obedience shows him to possess the one quality required above all others in a true man of God, the quality of perfect *faith*. The two stories told of him in Genesis 15 and 22:1–19 give further illustrations that the kind of faith he had—and the kind which is required of men today—was not mere blind acceptance of unprovable propositions and promises, but rather a complete trust in the kindly purposes of God and an entire willingness to place the direction of life in the hands of a Heavenly Father. The great teachers of the Bible, from Isaiah to St. Paul, insist that faith, of the quality of Abraham's, is the one indispensable ingredient of the religious life, the first and basic condition for establishing a right relationship with God. If we now turn to the passage in Hebrews (11:8–12) we shall be ready to appreciate the almost poetic beauty of the unknown author's description of Abraham as the chief of the heroes of faith.

Because Abraham believed in God's promises, God "counted it to him for righteousness" (Gen. 15:6) and entered into a covenant with him, a permanent relationship of friendship and mutual obligation. In the biblical view, man's relationship to God is always within the framework of a particular covenant; but the way of entrance into the covenant is, as St. Paul so clearly demonstrated for both the Testaments, the way of faith, the kind of faith dramatized in the story of Abraham. The covenant of which we read in Genesis 15:18 was made with Abraham and his descendants, but its blessings were intended, from the beginning, for "all the families of the earth" (Gen. 12:3). Israel's covenant with God was not established as a means of self-glorification (though she sometimes forgot this), but as an instrument by which the whole of humankind might be restored to God in love and obedience. This purpose was at last realized in the coming of Christ, when the national limitations of the covenant were done away with and its blessings became ours too, for we are Christ's and therefore also "Abraham's seed, heirs according to the promise" (Gal. 3:7–8, 26–29).

III. THE COVENANT OF LAW

Exodus 3:1–17; 14:15–31; 19:1–6; 20:1–17; Romans 7:7–14; John 1:17

Abraham is important largely as a symbol of Israel's chief article of faith, that God had chosen her for Himself and had made a covenant with her. But if Abraham is

mainly a legendary and symbolic figure, there can be little
doubt that Moses was a truly historical one. Abraham was
the traditional father of the nation and therefore the one
with whom, ideally, the covenant was conceived to be
made; Moses was its actual, historical mediator. With these
passages about Moses we emerge from the dim mists of
prehistoric times onto the stage of genuine history in the
secular sense of the term. In the four brief selections from
Exodus we learn the crucial facts about Moses' career and
his significance for the history of his people.

First of all there is the familiar story of the burning
bush and the revelation of God which came to Moses as he
tended the flocks of his father-in-law on the slopes of Mount
Horeb (Exod. 3:1–17). Although some details of the story
are plainly legendary, there lies back of it a profound and
soul-shaking experience which convinced Moses that God
had chosen him for a special mission, to be the teacher
of his people and to rescue them from slavery. Central in
this experience was the revelation of a new name for God.
Before Moses' day, the Hebrews had worshiped many gods
under many different names, but now they were to learn
that the older gods—of Abraham, Isaac and Jacob—were
merely manifestations of their one true God, who was
from this time on to be worshiped under the name of
Jehovah (or Yahweh), a mysterious name which later
writers understood to mean "He Who Is" (vv. 14–16).
Thus Moses' first gift to his people was a new and profounder understanding of the nature of God.

The second selection from Exodus relates the story
of Israel's departure from Egypt. Some generations before,
a few Hebrew families, insignificant and unorganized, had
settled there during a famine in the desert, an event
frequently paralleled in Egyptian history. In the course
of time their status, originally honorable, deteriorated un-

til they became mere slaves of the Egyptian crown, exploited to help with building operations in the Delta. When Moses returned from the desert with his amazing story, they rallied gratefully behind him and under his leadership escaped from their oppressors. The account of their deliverance in Exodus 14:15–31 represents the traditional form in which the tale was told at the annual commemoration of the event—the Passover. In its present shape fact is clearly intertwined with legend, but the fact is sure. Israel's history began when she escaped from slavery in Egypt, and she knew it could not have happened except that God was with her. From the beginning, the God of Israel and the Bible is a Redeemer God who is both willing and able to save His people.

In Exodus 19:1–6 the tribes have at last arrived at Sinai (or Horeb) and there, in a solemn ceremony the nature of which we can only dimly see, Israel accepted Yahweh as her God and thus became His own possession, "a kingdom of priests and a holy nation" (vv. 5f). In this way Moses, inspired of God, founded the nation of Israel. But we must notice that right from the start it was not merely a nation like other nations, but a spiritual community, a Church. This is the actual beginning of the Church of God, the Church of the Old Israel, which would one day expand into the Church of the New Israel.

The basis of the covenant which now came into being was the Law of God, to which Israel promised faithful obedience. The Ten Commandments, found in one form in Exodus 20:1–17 (also in Deut. 5:6–21), may be taken as typifying the essential requirements of the Law. As the community grew and lived under new conditions, it is natural that the number of her laws increased and old laws were adapted to meet the needs of an altered situation. The collections of laws which now follow in Exodus, Leviticus and Numbers mostly come from much later times, but all bear witness to the conviction of Israel that there is a law of right and wrong and that the first duty of God's children is to obey it.

If we now turn to the New Testament passages, we may find ourselves in difficulty, for the selection from Romans (7:7–14) is not an easy one. But it is an important passage and not so difficult once one grasps the central thought. Paul is trying to show that both in common sense and in the providence of God man had first to be introduced to the Covenant of Law before he could understand the Covenant of Grace in Christ. Until men have been confronted with God's demands in the Law, they cannot know that they are sinners. And until they have tried to keep the Law and failed, they cannot realize that they are helpless and in need of the grace which only Christ can give. So, says Paul, it was necessary that God should have led Moses to establish the Covenant of Law, for only in this way could men become conscious of their fallen state and their need for God's redemptive work in Christ. This chapter is not a mere academic exercise in speculative theology, but is obviously in large measure autobiographical, and passionately so. In his own experience Paul, as a pious Pharisee, had found it impossible to live up to the Law's majestic demands. But it was this very sense of failure which opened his heart to the Gospel, and he was sure this was exactly why the Law had been given and was "holy and righteous and good."

The little verse from John (1:17) nicely summarizes the nature of the covenants and strikes the proper affirmative note on which to end this chapter.

IV. THE PROMISED LAND

Joshua 6; 11:23; Micah 4:1–5; Hebrews 4:1–11; 11:13–16

By accepting the covenant of the Law at Sinai, the people of Israel had become an organized community—potentially, at least, a nation. But they were not yet a nation in the fullest sense of the word because they had no land of their own.

The selection from Joshua (6; 11:23) tells of the way in which they acquired the land of Canaan and made it the land of Israel. How important the idea of "the land" has been in their tradition is shown by the fact that in our own day hundreds of thousands of Jews have gone back to the land of their fathers and have once more given the name "Israel" to a part of it. It is difficult for us today to read the story of Joshua with much sympathy, since the invasion it describes is likely to seem bloody, barbarous and morally unjustified. One need only read Joshua 6:21 with imagination to realize how horrible the story actually is, and it makes it only the more sickening to realize that these things were supposedly done in God's name.

There would be something wrong with our religious and moral sense if we did not feel some sense of revulsion. Nevertheless, certain facts may help to moderate our feelings. First of all, modern scholarship suggests that the conquest was probably not as thoroughgoing, and therefore not as savage, as the Book of Joshua represents it. It is likely that the capture of cities such as Jericho and the subse-

quent extermination of their inhabitants was a compara-
tively rare event. The actual "invasion" was for the most
part a peaceful infiltration in which the Hebrews began
by occupying unsettled parts of the country and only
gradually gained dominion over their Canaanite neighbors.
The story of a single war of conquest in the Book of Joshua
is the product of later tradition which simplified the complexities of actual history and took pride in exalting the
military prowess of the nation's ancestors.

No doubt there were some bloody battles and barbarous massacres, but in thinking of them one must judge
the Hebrews by the standards of their time, not of ours.
Such events were common to the ancient world, and the
Canaanites had no doubt originally established their claim
to the land in just this way. Further, we should note that
from the standpoint of objective history the conquest of
the Canaanites by the Hebrews was the conquest of a
highly civilized but morally debased people by a people
who were relatively uncultured but gifted with a moral
sense and a spiritual vitality higher than that of any other
nation the world has known. From the standpoint of later
history, including our own, it would have been a disaster
if the Hebrews had failed to conquer Palestine.

The most familiar of the stories in Joshua (6), that of
the battle of Jericho, has been selected for reading simply
because it is typical of the stories in this book. As one can
see by looking at a physical map of Palestine, Jericho had
to be taken by the Hebrews if they were to control the
country, since it is the gateway from Transjordan and
the desert lands to the east. Undoubtedly the capture of
the city was accomplished by more conventional means
than the present story suggests. As it now stands, the narrative is less a precise historical record than an expression of

the faith of later Israel that her victories were won by the power of God rather than by her own military skill.

Verse 17 refers to a strange and (to us) horrifying practice whereby the besieged city was vowed to God as a holocaust; every article was to be destroyed, every living thing killed. While to the modern, Christian mind such a vow is inexpressibly cruel and contrary to all that is known of God, yet it was not illogical in the context of ancient "holy war" since it demonstrated that the warriors were fighting for some ideal purpose, and not for personal gain in the form of slaves and plunder.

The hero of the story—and of the book—is Joshua, but he remains a shadowy figure of whom little can be said beyond the obvious fact that he was reputed to be a great military leader. Joshua 11:23 summarizes the story of the whole book and shows the place which Joshua came to occupy in the late tradition about these earliest days in Canaan.

Since it is often supposed that the battle-ethics of the Book of Joshua are typical of the whole Old Testament, it is well at this point to turn to the idyllic picture of a later Hebrew seer who thought it was the ultimate destiny of Israel and her land to be a center from which peace and good will should flow to the nations of the earth (Mic. 4:1–5). A comparison of this gentle and attractive poem with the sanguinary tales of Joshua makes it evident that God's Spirit was at work in the hearts of His people during the long centuries which intervened.

Finally we turn to the New Testament, to a passage in the epistle to the Hebrews where the author argues (in somewhat complicated fashion) that, while God always intended that His faithful people should share with Him "the rest"—the sense of completion, fulfilment and joyous achievement—which He experienced on the seventh day of creation (Gen. 2:2f), this intention was not, as many seemed to think, finally realized by Joshua's conquest of Canaan. The proof, he says, is that a psalm (95; v. 11) written years later could still speak of the "rest" as future. There still "remains a sabbath rest for the people of God" (Hebrews 4:9 RSV); the Promised Land still lies before us. By such reasoning the experiences of Israel in the desert, the crossing of the Jordan, and the conquest of Canaan ceased to be mere facts of ancient national history and became instead symbols of the triumphant progress of the human spirit toward its divinely appointed destiny.

In 11:13–16 the same author pictures the ancient men of faith as all of them pilgrims whose journeys, unknown to themselves, were directed toward that true and heavenly Promised Land.

V. THE FOUNDING OF
THE KINGDOM

I Samuel 11:1–11, 15; 18:5–12; 31; Acts 22:6–21

Saul is the first character who emerges from the Old Testament story with a clearly defined personality. Earlier figures are either legendary or else our information about them is fragmentary and we are unable to form any clear picture of the kind of human beings they really were. But when we come to the age of Saul and David the historical sources become so full and, for the most part, so clearly authentic, that we feel we know the leading figures as real persons like ourselves. None of them is likely to touch us more deeply than Saul, the founder of the kingdom of Israel and the most genuinely tragic figure in the Bible.

The founding of the kingdom was another of the important turning points in the developing history of the people of God. Before Saul's time, Israel had been a loosely organized confederation of tribes bound together by the worship of a common God. But in the 11th century B.C. a crisis arose which made it necessary for them either to unite more closely or to perish. The Philistines, who had settled along the coast about the same time the Hebrews were infiltrating the highlands, had begun to push eastward and, with the advantage of more compact organization and superior weapons, were threatening the independence of the Israelite tribes. Great crises frequently produce great men and Saul was the man for this one. It was he who changed the scattered forces of Israel into an army and took the first energetic steps to drive out the invader, and he was the first to whom the people of Israel gave the title of King.

There are several stories and legends in I Samuel which have to do with the rise of the monarchy, but the one in 11:1–11, 15 is obviously the closest to the facts. It tells of an attack on the Israelite town of Jabesh-Gilead by the neighboring Ammonites, who threatened to put out the right eye of every inhabitant of the city. In vv. 4f we read how news of this came to Saul the farmer as he returned to his home in Gibeah from plowing in the field. The next verse tells of his characteristic response. A manic rage, which his countrymen ascribed to "the Spirit of God," fell upon him and he sent a grim summons to all the tribes to join him in saving Jabesh. So impressed were the people by his military skill and vigorous leadership that, after his defeat of the Ammonites, they made him king of Israel (v. 15) (vv. 12–14 are not part of the original story).

Later chapters describe the beginning of the war with the Philistines and in the course of them we are introduced to David, who was destined to be Saul's successor. Now the dark side of Saul's nature began to appear. The story becomes tragic in the strict sense of the term, which refers properly to the downfall of a great man for a single fatal weakness. Saul was a great man—a genius with volcanic energy—but like many geniuses he was emotionally unstable and jealousy was his fatal flaw. When the king saw his handsome and personable protégé, David, enjoying the popularity which had once belonged to him, the surging river of his energies began to turn inward instead of outward, darkening his mind and reducing him to periodic madness. We read of this in 18:5–12, although what is there attributed to "an evil spirit from God" we should today explain in terms of psychopathology.

The drama reaches its inevitable end in chap. 31 when Saul kills himself after his defeat by the Philistines at the battle of Gilboa. The full measure of the tragedy becomes evident when we realize that the Old Testament tells of only two other genuine suicides. The Hebrews were too healthy-minded a people for self-destruction to present itself as a normal possibility. Yet the story does not altogether end in darkness, for the last episode describes how the men of Jabesh, mindful of the debt they owed to Saul, went by night at peril of their lives and rescued his body from desecration. Their gratitude is final evidence of his essential greatness and goodness.

Saul has no theological significance like Abraham and Moses, and his name is rarely mentioned later. But it was Saul who founded the kingdom of Israel, and it is from the idea of the kingdom of Israel that eventually there came the idea of "the kingdom of God," one of the key

concepts of the Bible. It is true that the name later associated with the perpetuation of the kingdom was that
of David, and the future Messianic King is always called the
Son of David, not the son of Saul, but it was Saul who laid
the foundation upon which David built and it was he, a
truly royal though tragic figure, who first seemed great
enough to his own people to bear the name of King.

Although there is only one tiny incidental reference to
Saul in the New Testament, it is well to remember that he
was not entirely forgotten. More than a thousand years
after his time a young man, also of the tribe of Benjamin,
was named for him and, though no king himself, he also
helped to build a kingdom. There is some evidence that
he too was emotionally unstable—he was at least of a highly
sensitive temperament—but when the Lord took possession
of him on the Damascus road the vigorous stream of his
energies began to move, not inward, but outward and became a source of blessing to the world. This is the story
of Acts 22:6–21.

VI. DAVID—THE MESSIAH KING

II Samuel 1:17–27; 5:1–10; 11; 12:13–25; Jeremiah 23:5–6;
Luke 2:8–11; Mark 11:8–11

The connection between David and the idea of the
Messiah is far more direct than the connection between
Saul and the idea of the Kingdom of God. Saul merely
happened to be the first Hebrew king, but, for later generations of Israel, David was the ideal and perfect ruler who

provided the pattern for the ideal king of the future and from whose descendants the Messiah would one day come. Indeed, it is not quite accurate to distinguish between David and the Messiah, since "messiah" was actually one of his titles, as it was of every king of Israel and Judah. The word messiah in Hebrew means merely "the anointed one" and, since all the kings were anointed at their coronation, all were entitled to the name. It was only after the earthly monarchy had fallen and men's hopes were directed toward the establishment of the Kingdom of God in the future that the name Messiah, in a new and special sense, came to be applied to the Son of David who would reign in those latter days.

As one reads the story of David (and we are fortunate in having more information about him than about any other character of the Old Testament) it is easy to see why he laid such hold upon the popular imagination. With all his faults, which were many and serious, his people loved him. They loved him first of all because he was himself a man who loved deeply. Nothing shows this more clearly than the lament he composed when he heard that Saul and Jonathan were dead (II Sam. 1:17–27). There is no reason to doubt the sincerity of his feeling in spite of the long estrangement between himself and his former master, for Jonathan was his friend and Saul was a sick man against whom he could hold no grudge. Nothing in David's character is more attractive than this constant readiness to understand and to forgive, a quality which seems especially remarkable against the background of a rude and warlike age which regarded revenge not only as a right, but as duty (cf. for example the behavior of Joab in II Sam. 3:27).

Such gentleness is often the mark of an artistic temperament, and one is not surprised to find that David the warrior was also a poet and musician. His lament over

Saul is one of the oldest, as well as one of the finest pieces of Hebrew literature which has come down to us from antiquity. It was David's skill as a poet, along with the obvious sincerity of his religious faith, which ultimately gave rise to the tradition that he was also the author of the book of Psalms.

But, if people loved David for his warm heart, they also loved him for his achievements. Where Saul had been a tragic failure, David was an overwhelming success. David finished the job Saul had begun—that of unifying the nation and driving out the Philistines—and did something Saul would never have dreamed of attempting, for he created an Israelite Empire which ruled the surrounding peoples. II Samuel 5:1–10 gives just a hint of the magnitude of his accomplishments when it says, "And David became greater and greater, for the Lord, the God of Hosts, was with him." This chapter also has a special interest for it tells how he captured the ancient Canaanite city of Jerusalem and made it the capital of his kingdom. As David was to become the earthly symbol of One infinitely greater than himself, so Jerusalem was to become a symbol of the goal of every man's desire, a fact of which we are reminded every time we sing "Jerusalem the golden" or read the shimmering description of the New Jerusalem in Revelation 21.

The author of Chronicles, writing 700 years after David's time, expurgated the story of David and attempted to present him as a kind of unblemished Tennysonian hero; but the older sources make no attempt to do this. They show us all of David, the light and the dark alike. He was a great man who in most respects towered far above his age, but he was also a great sinner, as the story in II Samuel 11 and 12:13–25 all too plainly tells us. It is a revolting tale, only slightly alleviated by our knowledge that it comes to us from an unrestrained and violent age, but we are grateful for the honesty of the Bible which permits us to see David in full perspective. It is obvious that his people did not love him blindly, but in spite of his sins and weaknesses.

No later king was gifted with David's remarkable combination of brilliance and personal charm. Most of them were mediocrities or worse. So, it is not surprising that men began to dream of the return of David or of one who would be like him. Out of this hope—born of present disappointment joined to a firm faith in God's power and His good will toward His people—came the expectation of the Messiah, the ideal King whom God would send one day. After the final destruction of the Davidic monarchy, belief in the Messiah gradually became a fixed element in the creed of many of the greatest spiritual leaders in Israel. The brief passage in Jeremiah 23:5f is just one expression of this hope.

And at last the Messiah came. The gospel story (Luke 2:8–11) tells that his birthplace was Bethlehem, the town where David himself had been born, and in Mark 11:8–11 we read of his royal entry into David's capital. He was not like David in his weakness, but he was like him in his strength. Like him, he was a truly royal figure, reigning upon a throne, although it was a cross; he won a mighty victory on Easter Day; and he created a spiritual Empire, the universal Church.

VII. SOLOMON IN ALL HIS GLORY

I Kings 2:10–12; 4:20–30; 6:37–7:1; 10:1–10;
Jeremiah 22:13–16; Acts 7:47–50; Matthew 12:42; 6:25–29

Solomon's claim to "glory" is far more valid than his claim to wisdom. His reputation for wisdom is a result of the natural tendency of tradition to magnify the figures with which it deals and was made possible in this particular case because the ancient Hebrews had a broader conception of wisdom than our own. For example, they sometimes used the word to designate a certain superficial cleverness of hands or brain. And if mere agility of mind is wisdom, then no one doubts that Solomon was a wise man.

The word could also be used to designate roughly what we should call "culture," a concern for the arts and sciences and a capacity to dabble in them. In this sense, also, Solomon was a wise man. It was under him that Israel first became a cultured nation. Before his time the Israelites had been a rude, almost barbaric people—at least when compared with their neighbors—and the arts of war had been the chief concern of their rulers. But with Solomon's long, peaceful reign, the culture of the surrounding world —its philosophy, poetry and architecture—began to filter in; the royal court became a center for scholars, artists and men of letters, and the king himself, enjoying the leisure made possible by the wealth of his inherited domains, acted the part of the magnificent dilettante as well as patron of all the arts.

Because Solomon had "wisdom" in this limited and rather shallow sense it was possible for later generations to attribute to him also the profounder wisdom which consists in knowing the true meaning of life and the principles which should govern human conduct. They liked to think of him as an ideal monarch, whom God had endowed with all the gifts desirable in a ruler. Nevertheless it is evidence of the healthy good sense of the Hebrews that Solomon was never taken to be the pattern of the Messiah. They might picture him as the philosopher-king who wrote profound books such as Proverbs and Ecclesiastes (not to mention the apocryphal Wisdom of Solomon, written in Greek near the beginning of the Christian era!), but he was too soft and self-indulgent to be the Hero-King of the future.

As we read the story of Solomon's reign with modern eyes, we are more impressed by his folly than by his wisdom. We can see that it was his policy of government which destroyed the empire David had created. Subject peoples had already begun to break away in Solomon's time and at his death the kingdom of Israel broke apart, never to be united again. To uncritical eyes the reign of Solomon was bathed in glory, as we can see from the description of the luxury of his court in I Kings 4:20–30; but its glory was that of gold that glitters, not the Glory of God shining in the hearts of men.

There were no external wars, and wealth flowed into the royal coffers from trade, industry and, especially, from heavy taxes on the people. This made possible the enormous building program Solomon undertook, a program designed to exhibit in visible and permanent form the magnificence of his rule. He occupied seven years in the building of a temple for his God and—significantly—thirteen years in constructing a house for himself (I Kings 6:37–7:1). In later years the temple became a center of

devotion for the whole people of Israel, the chief focus
of their spiritual life, but this was scarcely Solomon's intention. For him it was a palace chapel, comparable in
modern terms to the chapel of the English kings at Windsor
Castle.

Although Solomon introduced an insidious poison
into the life of his people—the love of luxury and mere
display—the authentic spirit of old Israel continued to live
in the minds of her great religious leaders. In later times
we find them frequently, and sometimes violently, opposed
to the policies of kings who endeavored to follow in Solomon's footsteps. Jehoiakim was such a king and when we
read Jeremiah's criticism of him in Jeremiah 22:13–16,
we might almost imagine the words had been written about
Solomon himself. The glory of the Old Testament is not
the glory of Solomon, but the glory which consists in a
passion for justice and righteousness and a concern for the
poor and needy. As Jeremiah says (v. 16) the true knowledge of God—which is only another way of saying true
wisdom—consists in being concerned for the things with
which God is concerned. Neither Solomon nor Jehoiakim
possessed *this* kind of wisdom.

The three references which the New Testament makes
to the achievements of Solomon range in tone from out-
right condemnation to mildly unfavorable comparison.
Stephen in the great speech he made at his trial criticizes
Solomon for having tried to confine God in a temple: "The
Most High dwelleth not in houses made with hands" (Acts
7:47–50). In Matthew 12:42 Jesus expresses his sorrow at
the failure of his generation to hear the Gospel, whereas
in ancient days the Queen of Sheba traveled from the ends
of the earth to hear the wisdom of Solomon, which was
of far less value. And finally, in Matthew 6:25–29, we note
our Lord's striking use of a comparison between the glory

of Solomon and the beauty of a single wild flower (vv. 28f).
The true spirit of the prophets and of ancient Israel continues to speak through Jesus. He makes us see the shabbi-
ness of Solomon's attempts at a man-made and man-
centered magnificence when compared with the glory
which every man can enjoy but only God can create.

VIII. A HOUSE DIVIDED

I Kings 12:1–20; Ezekiel 37:15–28; John 17:20–23

The history of the kingdom of Israel is a success
story in reverse. The only great days it ever knew, in the
worldly sense, were the days of David and Solomon. Then,
for a brief space of time, Israel was the greatest of the nations in its own little world. But after the death of Solomon Israel's history takes the form of a descending line.

The first disaster was the break between North and
South which produced two kingdoms where there had been
only one before. The northern kingdom was destroyed by
invading armies two centuries later and the southern kingdom lasted only another century and a quarter after that.
No nation ever had brighter dreams than Israel did in the
days of David, but no people ever saw its hopes for material grandeur more completely frustrated in the end.

The immediate cause of the disruption of the kingdom is evident enough from reading the story of Solomon's
reign. The glory of his kingdom was built on rotten foundations. His temple, his palace, the luxury of his court were

made possible only by the exploitation of the people, and at last they rebelled. The North had always been somewhat restive under the rule of David and Solomon, who were Southerners, and even before Solomon's death rumblings of revolt had been heard. His son Rehoboam, who had neither David's genius for war and politics nor his father's flair for the grandiloquent gesture, was totally incapable of dealing with the crisis in which he found himself. The result was the loss, forever, of two-thirds of his territory and an even larger proportion of his people.

The sad story is told in I Kings 12:1–20. When Rehoboam came to Shechem to be recognized as king by "all Israel" (which means here the tribes of the North as contrasted with the tribe of Judah to which the king belonged) he was confronted with a petition for the redress of grievances. The story tells how the older men advised him to meet the demands of the people and so win their gratitude and loyalty. But he preferred to listen to the young hotheads who were close to him and who recommended a policy of repression and violence. In every society, including ours, there are some who think that generosity and a spirit of compromise are signs of weakness. So Rehoboam not only refused to make any conciliatory move, but actually threatened to increase the people's burdens.

Israel always had a strong democratic tradition which regarded kings as, at best, a necessary evil and the whole ethos of the nation was opposed to the claims of Divine Kingship made by Solomon and his imitators. Since this tradition was especially strong among the northern tribes, no serious observer could doubt how they would react to Rehoboam's stupidity and arrogance. They raised the old battle cry of rebellion, which had been heard even in David's days (II Sam. 20:1)—"What portion have we in

David? We have no inheritance in the son of Jesse!"—and expelled the Davidic dynasty, decisively and finally, from their territory.

Jeroboam, the hero of the revolt, was consecrated king over the tribes of the North. His dynasty was soon to be exterminated in blood, as were most of the dynasties of the northern kingdom, but at least for his own lifetime he was securely enthroned as king over most of the land of Israel. It is important to keep in mind that, during the two centuries that followed, the northern kingdom (Israel) was the greatest of the two and most of the important events in the history of the period transpired there. But it is also important to remember that it was the people of the little, relatively insignificant, kingdom of Judah (the "Jews") who were to survive the catastrophes of later times and preserve for the world the incalculable treasure of God's revelation. Here we see one of the persistent patterns of God's working in history. He chooses the most im-probable agents (judged by human standards), "the weak . . . and the base . . . and the things that are despised" (I Cor. 1:27f), for the accomplishment of His mighty pur-poses.

One of the unchanging convictions of biblical religion is that God desires the unity of His people. The permanent separation of the Hebrew kingdoms was certainly not in accord with God's will, though it may have been necessary under the circumstances of the time. We can see that it resulted from human sin rejecting the purpose of God for Israel. This first great schism in the household of faith, like every later one, was the result of arrogance and a selfish love for power. But the great spiritual leaders of Israel were confident that God had both the will and the might ultimately to overrule the wills of sinful men and would one day restore to His people "the witness of visible unity." This assurance is beautifully and pathetically expressed by the prophet Ezekiel (37:15–28) in words which gain added poignance from the realization that when they were spoken the northern kingdom had already been gone for over a century and the southern was at that moment lying in ruins.

The problem of the unity of God's people is still with us in both the political and ecclesiastical life of our modern world. So, as we conclude our study of the disruption of the ancient community of faith, it is well to remind ourselves of the prayer for the unity of his people which the Fourth Gospel places upon the lips of Jesus (John 17:20–23).

IX. ELIJAH—THE TROUBLER OF ISRAEL

I Kings 18:16–40; 21:1–22; II Kings 2:9–12; Malachi 4:5–6; Luke 1:5–17

The prophet Elijah appears upon the stage of Israel's history with the suddenness of a thunderclap. The final editor of the Book of Kings introduces him, without the slightest preparation, as a full-grown man pronouncing God's judgment upon the reigning house of Northern Israel. In I Kings 15–16 the author has obviously been quoting from the accurate, but almost painfully dull official records of the kingdom. Suddenly with the opening verse of chap. 17, the mood of his narrative changes.

One can see that he is no longer dependent upon the pro-saic chronicles of the court but is using a popular biography of one of Israel's great national heroes. We sense the excitement in his tone when he begins to relate the tale: "And Elijah the Tishbite, who was of the inhabitants of Gilead, said unto Ahab, As the Lord God of Israel liveth, before whom I stand, there shall not be dew nor rain these years, but according to my word. . . ."

With the figure of Elijah we stand at the beginning of the apostolic succession of prophets, the men who were to be the hearts and minds and consciences of the people of Israel in the centuries ahead. The prophets had two functions to perform: on the one hand they would be the "troublers of Israel" (I Kings 18:17), dedicated to awakening the spiritual and moral sensibilities of the people by pointing out their sins and the judgment which must necessarily follow. But also, especially in later times, they were the comforters of Israel, who showed the nation in times of discouragement that God's ultimate purpose is not judgment but redemption and reconciliation. In all the dark times of later years they would be like shining lights reminding the Chosen People that their God is the Lord of History who rules the nations by the moral law and is guiding all history toward the realization of His purposes. In Elijah we see only the troubling, not the comfort. But this is natural, for neither men nor nations are prepared to receive the gospel of redemption until their consciences have been disturbed and a realization of their sinfulness has brought them to understand the need for God's help.

The immediate stimulus to Elijah's work was the growth of the spirit which Solomon had introduced in Israel—manifested by the increasing claims of royal power, a willingness to compromise the pure religion of the fathers by introducing the worship and debased morality of other gods, and a growing contempt for the rights of little, "unimportant" people. Ahab, the ruling head of the northern kingdom, was a living embodiment of this apostate spirit and had brought Israel's affairs to a crisis through his marriage to Jezebel, a strong-minded Phoenician princess who was determined to make the nation conform to the pattern of other oriental kingdoms. Elijah, with that clear intuition which is always the property of a truly great man, saw that the policy of Ahab and Jezebel meant the end of Israel as a unique people and the loss of the spiritual treasure which had been committed to her. So the whole of his tremendous energy and that of his disciple Elisha after him was directed toward a war to the death with the royal family and all it stood for.

The battle was fought on two fronts, as we can see from the two long readings from Kings. The first was that of winning men's exclusive allegiance to the God of Israel. In I Kings 18:16–40 there is a stirring narrative which epitomizes this phase of the conflict. As we read it we shall probably feel that the story has grown somewhat in the telling. It has all the excitement and relish of a folk tale and certainly includes legendary elements, as do all the stories of the Elijah and Elisha cycle. But one also feels that it is an authentic reflection of the long and finally victorious struggle of Elijah and his followers with the forces of paganism.

The other incident, the one recorded in I Kings 21:1–22, illustrates the second aspect of Elijah's struggle, his championing of social justice and the rights of small men. The religion of Israel had always been democratic in spirit and would always remain so in the teaching of the prophets. One of the major concerns of all Israel's prophetic leaders was to defend the poor and those who had no one else to help them. In the present story, Naboth was entirely within his rights in refusing to cede his small plot of land to the king. The scheme of Jezebel was part of a larger plan to alter the distinctive character of Hebrew society and destroy the religious principles on which it rested. Without the opposition of Elijah, she would undoubtedly have succeeded.

When one considers Elijah's stormy character and tempestuous career it is not surprising that later generations believed that he had not died a natural death, but had been swept up to heaven in a whirlwind (II Kings 2:9–12). Still later it was believed (as it is even now by orthodox Jews) that he would return one day to prepare men for the coming of the Lord (Mal. 4:5–6).

Men of the New Testament quite naturally saw the promised return of the great "troubler of Israel" in the awe-inspiring figure of John the Baptist (Luke 1:5–17; cf. Matt. 11:14). ("Elias" in KJV is the Greek form of Elijah.) Those who accepted Jesus as Messiah could hardly fail to see in John, the prophet who prepared his way.

X. ELISHA AND THE GREAT REVOLT
II Kings 5; 9:1–7, 30–37; Hosea 1:4; Luke 4:24–30

Life can give to a teacher no greater gift than a disciple who is able to carry on his work. Elijah, alone among the prophets of the Old Testament, had this satisfaction. Other prophets had followers who collected their sayings and kept their memories fresh, but only Elijah had a pupil whose temper and ability made it possible for him to pick up his master's work and carry it through to completion.

The career of Elisha is the direct continuation of that of Elijah and the lives of the two men were so closely interrelated that it is impossible to think of one without the other. Even ancient Hebrew tradition had some difficulty in keeping them apart and it is clear from the Bible that stories told originally about one might easily come to be told about the other also.

Nevertheless, the two men were distinct and their personalities were quite different. Elijah was a solitary, hermitlike figure, while Elisha was a gregarious man living in close association with other prophets. Elijah was essentially a man of prayer, who lived near to God and depended upon his awesome proclamation of the Word of God to achieve his ends. Elisha was more the man of action and did not hesitate to use worldly and political means to arrive at results he considered morally justified. On the whole, Elijah is a remote and grandiose figure, while Elisha is more human and accessible. Yet with all their differences, the two were animated by a common purpose—a passionate resolve that the pure metal of Israel's faith should not be contaminated by the alloy of pagan religion and pagan morality.

The story of Elisha's call and his accession to Elijah's dignity is told, for those who care to look it up, in I Kings 19:19–21 and II Kings 2:1–15. We shall here consider only two stories from his later career. Each shows him under a different, but typical, aspect. In the first (II Kings 5) we see him in the role of minister to men's bodily needs, a role frequently attributed to him and one which no doubt reflects something of the natural warm humanity of his character. In this chapter the breadth of his sympathies and the power of his God are shown by the fact that the man to whom he ministers is not an Israelite, but a foreigner, the victorious general of an enemy king. Naaman is said to have been a leper (although this may refer to some milder disease than the one now called leprosy). The story of his healing has come down to us through later disciples of the prophets who told it in such a way as to illustrate two basic principles of prophetic thought: the necessity of unquestioning obedience to God's commands, and the requirement of pure disinterestedness in those who would serve Him. Naaman objects to what seems to him the silly command to bathe in the Jordan River (vv. 10–12), but his servants point out that one who is prepared to obey in great matters should also be ready to obey in small (13). Convinced, and perhaps somewhat ashamed, he does what he has been told and is rewarded by perfect restoration to health (14). The second principle, the need for disinterestedness in God's service, is illustrated by the story of Elisha's servant, Gehazi, who tried to capitalize on his master's act of kindness (20–24), but was rewarded for his greed and the betrayal of his trust by becoming a leper himself (25–27).

The other story (II Kings 9:1–7, 30–37) illustrates the political side of Elisha's work and its final, somewhat horrifying, result. Although Ahab, Elijah's enemy, now was dead, his family still ruled and the Queen-Mother Jezebel was the most powerful figure in the land. We see Elisha deliberately stirring up an armed revolt against them and associating with himself the sinister figure of Jehu, a bloody-minded rogue and adventurer if there ever was one, in order to achieve the overthrow of the ruling house (vv. 1–7). The story of Jezebel's death (30–37) is one of the most shocking and yet dramatic tales in the Old Testament. Ahab's dynasty was exterminated; Jehu became king, and Israel was saved from the danger of national apostasy. The program of Elijah and Elisha was, for the moment at least, fully realized.

Although we sympathize fully with the program, we can only regret the means which Elisha chose to carry it out. The pure religion of the Bible, both Old Testament and New, repudiates the resort to "the arm of flesh" to accomplish God's purposes. God is quite able to take care of Himself, as the later prophets never wearied of telling their hearers (though sincere religious leaders of modern times have occasionally forgotten this). Just a hundred years after Elisha's time, another prophet cursed the house of Jehu, which was still on the throne, for the blood that was shed in this revolt (Hos. 1:4).

In Luke 4:24–30 two stories telling of Elijah's and Elisha's ministry to foreigners are used to illustrate the principle that "no prophet is accepted in his own country." But a greater principle is involved than just this, for a prophet who is repudiated by his own people has the opportunity of taking his message to the larger world. This seemed to have been true of Elijah and Elisha and was certainly true of Jesus and his Gospel. We are meant to understand that a mission to all the world, not merely to the Jews, was implicit in our Lord's ministry from the very beginning. The two stories of Elijah and Elisha illustrate the fact that God's power and love are never limited by national boundaries. The world-embracing Gospel of Christ is the final expression of this basic biblical truth.

XI. AMOS AND HOSEA— HERALDS OF JUDGMENT

Amos 2:6–16; 5:21–27; Hosea 6:4–6; 11:1–7; II Kings 17:1–6; Luke 3:1–9; Matthew 9:10–13

The first great function of the prophets was to bring to Israel the solemn consciousness of sin. Up to this point, in spite of the disruption of the kingdom and a series of revolutions, the dominant temper of the nation had been one of optimism and even smug self-satisfaction. In the middle of the 8th century B.C. this mood seemed justified by the great prosperity which both kingdoms were temporarily enjoying. But men of spiritual insight could see that this apparent well-being was only a mask concealing a deeply rooted sickness of soul which could lead the nation nowhere but to disaster and death.

It was at this period that the "literary" prophets began to appear. These are the men who give their names to the prophetic books of the Bible, but the modern reader must remember that the books were not actually written by them but are collections of brief addresses which were originally delivered orally and only later written down, either by themselves or by their disciples. To get the full impact of the prophetic discourses one should picture them as spoken, spontaneously and vehemently, before an audience gathered in the courtyard of some sanctuary on a feast day.

All the early prophets really had but one basic theme:

"Because of her sins, Israel is about to be destroyed." God would gladly have saved His people from reaping the harvest they had sown, because He is a God of love as well as of righteousness, but if they would not repent and change their ways there was no escape from the judgment which must inevitably come. If the prophets often seem almost brutal in their predictions of doom, it is because of their despair. They could see that the nation's spiritual disease had reached the point where repentance and restoration were impossible.

The prophets were the first to realize how incurably sick is the heart of man. They understood that sin is not an occasional minor disorder of the human personality, but a basic disorientation of man's whole being. Ultimately they would come to see that God in His wisdom and goodness must have a plan for the healing of His people. But this point had not yet been reached by the earliest prophets. Their mission was only to preach the reality of sin and the imminence of judgment. In doing so, they were of course helping to "prepare the way of the Lord," since the Gospel of redemption in Jesus Christ could have no meaning except for a world convinced of its spiritual sickness and its need for help.

The first two prophets, Amos and Hosea, both appeared in the northern kingdom (in the reign of Jeroboam II) just before its fall. Both spoke of the sins of the nation, but attacked the subject from different points of view. All sin has two aspects and involves two relationships: man's relation to his fellow man and his relation to God. Amos was concerned with the first of these; Hosea with the second.

Amos was a solitary man of the desert, a laborer, no professional huckster of religion (as he boasts in the familiar words of Amos 7:14f). He had been revolted by the evidence of man's inhumanity to man as he saw it everywhere in the cities of Israel, by the selfish luxury of the rich and the unheeded misery of the poor, by the corruption of judges who "sold the righteous for silver and the poor for a pair of shoes" (Amos 2:6–16). God's primary demand, he said, is not temples and feasts and fine religious music, but that men should "let judgment (better translated "justice"—RSV) roll down as the waters and righteousness as a mighty stream" (5:21–27).

Hosea, on the other hand, was chiefly concerned with the people's lack of loyalty to God. The prophet himself had suffered from the disloyalty of a faithless wife (as we learn from the rather obscure personal narrative in Hos. 1–3). Although the people professed to serve the God who long ago had made a covenant with Abraham and Moses, they seemed to have no knowledge of the kind of God He was. They worshiped other gods whenever it suited their purposes and acknowledged no responsibility to learn His will or return His love. All God really expected, they thought, was an occasional sacrifice or burnt offering (Hos. 6:4–6). To the prophet this was infinitely pathetic in view of the love God had always shown them and, since love cannot be rejected with impunity forever, they must prepare themselves for the blow that was about to fall (11:1–7).

Amos and Hosea had correctly diagnosed the condition of the people. The whole moral life of Israel was deeply infected by injustice toward men and disloyalty toward God. Such a nation, the prophets insisted, could not survive. And in II Kings 17:1–6 we read the story of its end. The kingdom of Israel, to which they preached, was destroyed by the Assyrian invader and vanished forever from among the nations of the earth.

When we turn to the New Testament we find that the

main emphases of prophetic teaching are renewed both by John the Baptist and by Jesus. John came, as Amos did, prophesying judgment and calling for repentance (Luke 3:1–9). He seems to have chiefly stressed just and kindly relations among men. Jesus, like Hosea, seems rather to have dwelt on the need for an inner transformation of character by means of a right relationship with God. It is, of course, Hosea whom Jesus quotes in his rebuke to the Pharisees in Matthew 9:10–13.

XII. ISAIAH—PROPHET OF FAITH

II Kings 15:1–7; Isaiah 6:1–7:16; 9:1–7; Matthew 1:18–23

The writers of the historical books in the Bible do not always make it easy for modern readers to follow the story. They were, of course, writing for people of their own time to whom the proper names and the general course of events were far more familiar than they are to us. For this reason it is almost essential that a Bible reader of today have at his elbow a good one-volume Bible commentary and a good Bible dictionary (see Introduction, p. xvii).

This need is well illustrated by the passage from II Kings (15:1–7) which gives the historical setting of Isaiah's call to prophesy. Without some assistance from the outside the reader could hardly be expected to know that King Azariah, mentioned there, is the same person as the "Uzziah" whose name occurs in v. 13 and in the opening verse of Isaiah 6.

The long and prosperous reign of this king in Judah was roughly contemporaneous with that of Jeroboam II in the northern kingdom. The movement of "literary" prophecy began in both kingdoms at about the same time, which was for both of them a time of great, although temporary, prosperity. Times of security and ease have even more need of the proclamation of God's Word than times of trouble. The Anglican Prayer Book wisely bids men to pray, "in all time of our prosperity . . . Good Lord deliver us!"

The 6th chapter of Isaiah is the classic account of the call of a prophet. In his own words Isaiah tells us how the call came to him in the courtyard of the temple while he was worshiping God on some great feast day in the year of Uzziah's death. The barrier which normally divides the seen from the unseen was suddenly removed and Isaiah seemed to be looking into the mysterious veiled inner sanctuary of the temple where the majestic Lord of Israel sat enthroned in the midst of His heavenly host. Isaiah's first reaction was a sense of overwhelming unworthiness (v. 5). This is the inevitable result of a true and valid experience of God. Only those who do not really know God are satisfied with themselves; those who are most conscious of their sins and inadequacies are the saints and prophets who are closest to Him. But God never leaves His children in despair, and Isaiah is illustrating the typical course of man's spiritual life when he tells us how his sense of personal unworthiness was taken away by the gracious forgiving act of God (6f). In this experience is undoubtedly to be found the germ of the great doctrine of Faith in God which was Isaiah's most important contribution to his people and to the world. Finally there came the call to serve God by becoming a messenger of His Word (8–13). There are several things in this part of the chapter which are difficult to understand, but this much at least is clear: Isaiah, like Amos and Hosea, was to be a prophet of doom and prepare the people for the catastrophe which their selfishness and disloyalty were bringing upon them. Furthermore, he was not to cease his preaching or become discouraged, however unresponsive they might seem to be.

But if Isaiah was like Amos and Hosea in his message of coming doom, he eventually came to speak with another voice which is scarcely found in them at all, at least in their unquestionably authentic utterances—the voice of hope and encouragement. Chap. 7 tells how this came about. More than ten years after Isaiah's call, in the reign of Ahaz, Judah was threatened with war by two powerful neighbors, Israel and Syria, and the heart of the people shook "as the trees of the forest shake before the wind" (v. 2 RSV). In this crisis, Isaiah was inspired to become the strengthener rather than the "troubler" of Israel. "Take heed, and be quiet; fear not . . ." he said. "If ye will not *believe,* ye shall not be established" (4, 9).

There are some difficulties in this chapter, not least in v. 14. Obviously this is not a prophecy of the birth of Christ many centuries later, since the promised sign was one which Ahaz himself was to see. (The use made of the verse in Matt. 1:22f is symbolic and poetic, rather than literal and historical.) But whatever the passage means and whoever the promised child may have been, the heart of Isaiah's message lies in the name which was to be given him, Immanuel, which in Hebrew means "God is with us." This was the essence of Isaiah's teaching. The people might desert God, but God would not desert them. Even if disaster came, He would somehow fulfill His purpose and redeem His promise.

One of the ultimate results of the faith which Isaiah

preached was the hope for the coming of a Messianic king. There are a number of passages in his book (we are thinking here only of chaps. 1–39) which speak of the coming of such an ideal figure. Chapter 9:1–7 is just one example. Whether it is actually by Isaiah we do not know, but there can be no doubt that it is a product of the kind of faith Isaiah taught.

The final vindication of Isaiah's faith is, of course, to be found in the New Testament, and Matthew 1:18–23 reminds us that the full force of the words "God is with us" became evident only with the coming of Jesus Christ. He was the Messiah of whom Isaiah's pupils dreamed, but also the very God in whom Isaiah trusted. In him the name Immanuel became a statement of fact and not merely an affirmation of faith.

XIII. JEREMIAH AND THE NEW COVENANT

II Kings 22:1–13; 23:1–5; Jeremiah 1; 7:1–15; 31:31–34; I Corinthians 11:23–25; Hebrews 8

About a hundred years after the time of Isaiah there came to the throne of Judah a king who seemed the perfect embodiment of the prophetic ideal. Josiah was noted for his goodness, his fair dealing and his loyalty to the God of Israel. The fine qualities of Josiah's rule were all the more striking because of the contrast they presented to the reign of Manasseh who, for over fifty years, just before Josiah's time, had terrorized the loyal worshipers of Jehovah and forced the party of the prophets to become a kind of political underground.

The story of Josiah's reign begins in II Kings 22:1–13. It must have seemed to those who lived through his early days that the Kingdom of God was at hand and that all the dreams of the prophets were about to be realized. The temple of God which had been long neglected, was restored to its former magnificence (vv. 3–7) and in the course of the renovation a book was discovered which set forth in legal style the requirements of Israel's God as the prophets understood them (8–13). No sooner had the book been brought to the king's attention, than he ordered it to be publicly read and accepted formally as the law of the land (23:1–5).

But admirable as Josiah's intentions were and fine as was the law which he imposed (commonly thought to be a part of our present Book of Deuteronomy), the Kingdom of God did not arrive. As a matter of fact, Judah was standing at this moment on the edge of disaster. Josiah's life was to end in tragic defeat; the Babylonian Exile was drawing near; the great reform was only the bright glow before the sunset. The people of God had begun to learn the meaning of sin; they still had to learn the meaning of suffering and hopelessness.

All through these strange and discouraging times there was one man who kept his head, the prophet Jeremiah, the most human and attractive of all the great figures of the prophetic tradition. He was not swept away by enthusiasm for Josiah's well-intentioned, but superficial, reform; and he did not fall into despair when the kingdom was destroyed and Israel's worldly hopes were shattered. He knew that true reform has to begin with the hearts of men and not with the laws under which they live. When things were darkest, he was sure that God is in control of things, and that He is at work through all the devious windings of human history to reclaim the souls and minds of men.

We read the story of his call in the first chapter of his book. It tells of a country boy, quiet and introspective by nature, whom God called to His service and sustained by His grace through forty years of loneliness and violent opposition. Jeremiah had none of the natural qualities of a hero, but because he knew that God was with him he became "a fortified city, and an iron pillar, and brazen walls" (vv. 18f). The account makes it evident that the burden of his preaching, in the beginning, was to be the imminence of judgment. "Out of the north an evil shall break forth upon all the inhabitants of the land" (14). Jeremiah felt the inner corruption of the nation, in spite of external evidences of reformation, and he knew she would still have to pass through the fire.

The precise counts in Jeremiah's indictment of Israel are summarized in his Temple Sermon in chap. 7:1–15, where he accuses the people of trusting in the sticks and stones of the House of God to protect them, whereas they should have put their trust in steadfast loyalty to God and in just dealing "between a man and his neighbor" (vv. 4–7). Because they had not done this, God was about to destroy Solomon's magnificent temple, which meant so much to them (14), and bring the kingdom to an end (15).

But the message of Jeremiah was by no means entirely a message of doom. He lived to see his predictions come true and, when that happened, the nature of his preaching changed. The most remarkable of his prophecies, and perhaps the most important in the Old Testament, is the one in which he foresaw the establishment of a New Covenant (31:31–34), a covenant which would be based on an inner and personal communion with God rather than on external obedience to a written code of laws. In many ways the thought of Jeremiah rises above the limitations of his own day to find points of contact with both the remote past and the remote future—with the religion of the patriarchal age, symbolized for us by the covenant with Abraham, and with the religion of the New Testament, embodied in the New Covenant in Christ. Recent studies in the Old Testament have shown that the religion of Israel's ancestors in the days before Moses was a much more personal thing than it became after the Israelite community was established. This is shown by the references in the Pentateuch to the God of Abraham, Isaac and Jacob (Gen. 26:24; 28:13; Exod. 3:15), and by the intimacy with which their relationship to God is described. The mind of Jeremiah seems to have a deeper affinity for this kind of religion than for the more legalistic type which was associated with the name of Moses, and which had so recently, and fruitlessly, been revived by the reforms of Josiah. So he looks forward into the future and sees a time when the covenant of laws will be done away and a new order established in which God would rule directly in men's "inward parts . . . and in their hearts" (v. 33).

The very existence of a book called the New Testament (which means New *Covenant*—see the title page in the RSV) is evidence that the hope of Jeremiah was fulfilled. The selected passages from the New Testament underline this fact. In St. Paul's account of the Last Supper (I Cor. 11:23–25—the earliest we have), Jesus speaks of the shedding of his blood as the means by which the New Covenant would come into being. Every communion a Christian makes is both a pledge and a renewal of this covenant. The passage from Hebrews (chap. 8) is a splendid as well as a solemn affirmation of its final validity and adequacy.

XIV. EZEKIEL AND THE EXILE

II Kings 25:1–12; Ezekiel 34:1–16; 37:1–14; John 10:1–16

At last the great disaster came. For a hundred and fifty years the prophets had been announcing the imminence of doom, but little heed was given them. There were, of course, individuals who could see that things were not right and that Israel's self-centeredness and disloyalty to God were destroying her only reason for existence. But it takes more than the conversion of a few individuals to heal a deep-seated disease in the body of a nation.

To continue the medical analogy, we might say that surgery alone could help. The Exile was a terrific surgical operation which separated the people from their land and destroyed their existence as an ordinary nation. But like every good bit of surgery it destroyed one part of the nation's life only to give another and more important part opportunity to function healthily. Israel ceased to be a nation like other nations in order that she might become what God had always intended her to be: a spiritual fellowship, "a nation of priests," a *Church*. It was during the Exile that this change began and that it happened was partly due to the healing and encouraging activity of the spiritual leader of the exiled community, the prophet Ezekiel.

Toward the end of the seventh century, the kingdom of Judah had been quietly absorbed by the rising Babylonian Empire. But no nation is ever long content to be ruled by foreigners, and twice (in 597 and 587 B.C.) the Jews rose up in armed rebellion against their new masters. On the second occasion, described in II Kings 25:1–12, the Babylonians resolved to make a third attempt impossible. They tortured and deposed the king, destroyed Jerusalem and many of the other cities of Judah, and carried away a large part of the population into Babylonia. Thus the Exile began.

Already in 597 some of the Jews had been taken to Babylon and the prophet Ezekiel was among them. It is unfortunate that Ezekiel's true greatness is obscured for modern readers by the difficulty and monotony of his style and the harshness of his personality. It requires a real effort at sympathy to read his book. We shall not concern ourselves here with the early oracles contained in chaps. 1–24 or the oracles against foreign nations in 25–32. Most of these were delivered before the last attack on Jerusalem in 587 and merely repeat in Ezekiel's own characteristic way the threats of doom found in the older prophets. In chap. 33 the mood of the prophet changes and the rest of the book consists of oracles of deliverance. When these prophecies were spoken, Jerusalem had already been reduced to a heap of rubble and the people of God no longer had temple, country or king. It is a remarkable and thought-provoking fact that the prophets always preached in opposition to the prevailing mood. In days of material prosperity and universal optimism they had been heralds of doom. But now that the doom had come and the popular mood was one of complete despair, they began to picture the future in glowing terms and their message became one of evangelical hope and encouragement.

So, in chap. 34:1–16, one of the rare places where Ezekiel seems to exhibit anything in the nature of tender emotions, he speaks of the contrast between the days of the old kings who had once reigned on the thrones of Israel and Judah, exploiting the people for their personal advantage, and the new time of the future when God Himself would be the King of Israel and feed His people and heal their wounds (vv. 11–16). This chapter reflects the ancient oriental custom of speaking of kings as "shepherds." If we remember that, to men of the Bible, the word shepherd suggested the thought of a king, we shall not today be in danger of sentimentalizing the idea of the shepherd as is so often done in devotion and religious art.

The other chapter we have chosen from Ezekiel, the 37th (vv. 1–14), is more characteristic of the man's weird and sometimes gruesome genius, and is undoubtedly one of the most impressive single bits of imaginative discourse in the Old Testament. In a vision the prophet sees the nation of Israel as a defeated and slaughtered army of long ago, the whitened bones of its soldiers covering all the surface of a plain. "Can these dry bones live?" comes the skeptical question everyone was asking. Ezekiel's answer was that what is impossible for man is possible for God. He sees in his vision the divine breath blowing across the valley and quickening the bones to life. "The breath came in them, and they lived, and stood up upon their feet, an exceeding great army" (v. 10). In the same fashion, says Ezekiel, God will one day take his broken people Israel and make of them again a great nation.

As we shall see in our next set of readings, the dream of Ezekiel was partly realized by the return of the exiles to Palestine and the rebuilding of their national life in the land of their fathers. But in a far more profound and significant sense it was fulfilled in the Christian Church, the final flowering of the tree of Israel. There, indeed, we find "an exceeding great army." And the promise of the Good Shepherd is fulfilled, as all can see, in the person of Jesus

Christ. This is the point of the familiar and beautiful parable in John 10:1–16.

XV. SECOND ISAIAH AND THE RETURN FROM EXILE

Isaiah 40:1–11; 52:1–10; 55; Luke 3:1–6

For nearly fifty years the people of God remained a captive and helpless nation. Ezekiel's encouraging message of reconstruction seems to have made little impression upon them, which is not to be wondered at since the slow passing of the years brought no change in the objective political situation.

But finally the wheel of history began to turn in their favor. A great new power appeared upon the scene and it became obvious that the days of the Babylonian Empire were numbered. From the mountains to the east and north of the Babylonian plain rumors began to filter in even to the common people that Cyrus, king of the Persians, was on the march and older nations seemed unable to withstand him. People also began to hear of his generosity toward captured nations and his policy of tolerance toward the religion and customs of the subject races of his empire.

To the cynic this might seem to be merely evidence of the fickleness of fate, which whimsically raises up kings and empires only to destroy them. But there was at least one man in Babylon, the last of the great prophets, who saw, in the onward march of Cyrus, the hand of God at work to redeem His unhappy people and restore them to their ancient home. For him, Cyrus was the "shepherd" of the Lord, His "anointed" servant, chosen to carry out the mighty purposes of the God of Israel (Isaiah 44:28; 45:1).

Strangely enough we know almost nothing about this prophet beyond the fact that he lived in Babylon in the days just before and after the Persian conquest. Even his name is unknown and we call him Second Isaiah merely because an accident of literary history caused his oracles (Isaiah 40–55) to be attached to a collection of the oracles of Isaiah, who lived about two hundred years before his time. (A recent novel by Sholem Asch, *The Prophet,* is an interesting attempt at a fictional reconstruction of his career.)

It is one of the paradoxes of the Bible that this prophet, of whom we know less than almost any other, is in many ways the greatest of them all. No other speaks so directly, and with such immediate appeal, to the heart of the modern Christian. He is the great theologian of the Old Testament; but also the great singer, whose themes are the universal themes of high religion: love, joy and confidence; the Glory, Power and Mystery of God.

The opening lines of the first oracle (Isa. 40:1–11) set the tone for the whole of his prophecy: "Comfort ye, comfort ye my people." One can hardly imagine a greater contrast than the one between this message and that of older prophets such as Amos. By the time of Second Isaiah, Israel had come to know all too well the God of righteousness; she was now ready to learn that God's righteousness and justice are only aspects of His love. It was the special mission of Second Isaiah to proclaim the redeeming love of God. As he saw the fall of Babylon drawing near and the way being opened for the return of God's people to the land of the covenant, his poetic imagination overflowed and, without a trace of sentimentality, he began to picture the God of Israel—the only God who is—as One who would feed His flock like a shepherd and gather the lambs in His arm (v. 11).

In the second of the passages (52:1–10) the poet summons Jerusalem, lying in ruins far away across the desert, to awake from a long and horrible nightmare to greet her God who now returns to her in love and mercy. "How beautiful upon the mountains are the feet of him that bringeth good tidings!" (v. 7). The prophet's contemporaries, who first heard his message, must have greeted him in almost precisely these words.

The third passage (chap. 55) is one of the high water marks of Old Testament scripture. Originally it was addressed to the Jews of Babylon inviting them to accept the opportunity which Cyrus had offered of returning to their homeland. Curious as it may seem, many were reluctant to do so, since they had already established themselves in profitable businesses in Babylon and had no desire to face a new existence in what would, for them, be essentially a pioneer country. The prophet urges them to remember that life has rewards to offer which are far more valuable than anything which money can buy (v. 2). Security seemed to them the greatest of life's values, but true security comes only to those who hear the voice of God and gladly obey His call (3–5). As so frequently happens, the opportunity comes only once, never to return again (6). The ways of God may seem mysterious (8), but His promises are sure (10ff). Although spoken so long ago, the words of the prophet are as meaningful for men of our own materialistic, security-conscious age as they were for the Jews of ancient Babylon.

The vision of Second Isaiah was far too great to be realized within the framework of the political history of

Israel and it is not surprising that Christians have always seen in his words an anticipation of the redeeming work of Christ and the glories of his kingdom. Lessons chosen from Second Isaiah are particularly familiar to members of liturgical churches from hearing them read with this application in the Christmas and Epiphany seasons. In our last passage (Luke 3:1-6) the evangelist uses some of the prophet's most familiar words as a magnificent over-ture to the opening scene in the story of our Lord's public ministry.

XVI. AFTER THE RETURN— NEW TROUBLES AND NEW HOPES

Ezra 1:1-2; 2:1-2, 64-70; 5:1-2; Haggai 1; Nehemiah 8:1-8; Zechariah 9:1-10; Matthew 21:1-5

The historical records of Israel from the end of the Babylonian Exile to the beginning of the Christian Era are exceedingly meager. In contrast to the detailed and consecutive history which tells the story of the Hebrew monarchy from the time of Saul to the fall of Jerusalem, the history of post-exilic Israel comes to us only in the form of a few highlighted stories separated from each other by decades and even centuries of which we know absolutely nothing.

The whole story of this long period—over five hun-dred years—is contained in the books of Ezra and Nehe-miah (and, outside the canonical Old Testament, in I-II

Maccabees and the histories of Josephus). The first reading suggested above from Ezra (1:1–2; 2:1–2, 64–70) tells
briefly of the return of some of the Jews to Palestine in
response to Cyrus' decree and introduces us to Zerubbabel
and Joshua, the leaders of the little post-exilic community
in Jerusalem. Joshua was the high priest, while Zerubbabel, a member of the royal family who is listed in the
New Testament as one of the ancestors of Jesus (Matt.
1:12), was civil governor in the Persian administration.

The first important achievement of the returned
exiles was the rebuilding of the ruined temple. Ezra 5:1f
tells very briefly how this was brought about. Fortunately
we are able to supplement this inadequate account by
turning to the book of Haggai (chap. 1) and to Zechariah
1–8, which contain the actual pronouncements of the two
spiritual leaders chiefly responsible for getting the work
started. During the first years after the return from Babylon, the people had been too busy building houses for
themselves (Hag. 1:4) and trying to cope with the discouraging economic situation (v. 6) to give much thought
to the building of a temple, but Haggai convinced them
that their selfish disregard of God's glory was a major
source of their troubles (8–11). The prophet's arguments
are admittedly not on the highest religious plane and may
seem to us a little oversimple, but at least they were effective, for the new temple was begun in 520 B.C. (12–15) and
completed four years later.

The rebuilding of the temple did not result in any
sudden, miraculous improvement in the material condition of the people, but it did at least provide Israel once
more with a center for her spiritual life. The great love
which later Jews were to feel toward Jerusalem and the
house of God really grew up in connection with this second temple, architecturally insignificant though it was,

rather than with the older and more imposing temple of Solomon. It was for this temple that many, perhaps most, of the Psalms were composed; and the Book of Psalms was assembled to be used as its hymnal.

Postexilic Israel never amounted to much as a nation (except during a brief period in the second and first centuries B.C. when she was ruled by the descendants of the Maccabees). Most of the time Palestine was only an unimportant province of some great world empire, inhabited by people who were economically and culturally poor and famous only for what seemed to the rest of the world certain strange ideas about religion and a fanatical devotion to their God.

One result of the narrowing and impoverishing of Jewish life was an increased devotion to the traditional written Law. Lacking a king and all the other external signs of nationhood, it was only natural that strict observance of the Law should come to seem the very essence of being a Jew. In Nehemiah 8:1–8 we find the story of a solemn public ceremony in which the Law (some part of the Pentateuch) was read to the people by Ezra, the great religious hero of postexilic Judaism, and enthusiastically accepted by them. Much as we must sympathize with the Jews in these difficult times and honor them for the tenacity which enabled them to survive at all, Christians cannot but regret the narrowing of Israel's horizons which necessarily resulted from this concentration on mere legalistic observance, this growing emphasis upon the Covenant of Law rather than upon the more basic Covenant of Faith.

For the most part the story of the last five centuries before the Christian era is a sad and uninspiring one. It almost seems as though Israel's creative spiritual force had exhausted itself in the exalted thoughts and magnificent language of Second Isaiah. But in spite of the general depression of these times there were many who dreamed more fervently than ever of the time when God would show His power and goodness by establishing His kingly rule on earth. Indeed the worse times became, the brighter the hope sometimes seemed to flourish, as in the latter part of Daniel, written during the most desperate crisis of the age.

Typical of these postexilic expressions of faith is the idyllic portrait of the future King of Peace found in an anonymous oracle now attached to the book of Zechariah (9:1–10). "Shout, O daughter of Jerusalem, behold thy king cometh unto thee . . . lowly and riding upon an ass" (v. 9). It was to this hopeful and forward-looking aspect of Judaism that our Lord attached himself by his actions on the first Palm Sunday (Matt. 21:1–5).

The Old Testament ends inconclusively, on an unresolved chord; the conclusion of the story and the resolution of the chord are found in the New Testament, to which, after a brief interlude with the Apocrypha, we now must turn.

XVII. THE AGE OF THE MACCABEES

I Maccabees 1:1–10, 41–64; 4:28–59; II Maccabees 12:43–45; Daniel 11:20–21, 28–32; 7:7–8, 23–25; Matthew 24:15–18; John 10:22–23; Revelation 13:1–10

Between the Old Testament and the New in many Bibles there is a section called the Apocrypha which consists, for the most part, of books written in the intervening period. There has always been considerable discussion with regard to the canonical authority of these books, but there can be none with respect to their historical importance. They throw indispensable light upon one book of the Old Testament and upon many passages of the New. (See Introduction, p. xvi, footnote 2.)

The most significant event in the nearly four hundred years which elapsed between the events narrated in the Old and New Testaments was the ferocious persecution of the Jews which broke out in Palestine under the rule of Antiochus Epiphanes, one of the later Greek rulers of what we now call the Middle East. In order to unify his empire and secure his southern boundaries, he decreed the abolition of the Jewish religion, which he felt made the Jews, alone amongst all his subject peoples, an absolutely intractable and unassimilable group. This was probably the first persecution ever to be directed purely at a religion. Jews who were willing to conform to Antiochus' decree—and there were many of them—were unaffected by it, but those who refused to give up the traditional beliefs and practices of their people were subjected to torture and death. That the historic faith of Israel was not entirely lost was largely due to the heroism of Jewish guerilla fighters who, under the leadership of Judas Maccabeus and his brothers, finally defeated the forces of Antiochus and the kings who succeeded him.

This is the story which is told in the two Books of Maccabees (two partly parallel accounts of the same events, written from somewhat different points of view). The selections from these books, necessarily rather long, are chosen to illustrate the high points of the narrative. The first (I Macc. 1:1–10, 41–64) puts the events in the setting of general history (vv. 1–10) and tells of Antiochus' actions to destroy the Jewish religion (41–53), culminating in the erection of a pagan altar, "the abomination of desolation," in the temple of Jerusalem (54f) and the merciless persecution of the faithful (56–64).

The next selection (I Macc. 4:28–59) describes a great victory of Judas and his forces some three years later (vv. 28–35) which led to the recapture of the temple, its reconsecration to the worship of the God of Israel (36–58) and the institution of a permanent feast (called "Hanukkah" in Hebrew) to celebrate the event (59).

Finally, a brief selection from II Maccabees (12:43–45) illustrates a significant addition to the religious creed of many in Israel which resulted from the sufferings of the faithful in the Maccabean age: a new and firm belief in the resurrection of the dead and in the efficacy of prayers and sacrifices on their behalf. It was this which made possible and natural Martha's unhesitating affirmation of faith in the resurrection in John 11:24.

The Book of Daniel in the canonical Old Testament is a product of this same period, as one can readily see from a reading of 11:20f and 28–32, which evidently contain a cryptic account of the conduct of Antiochus Epiphanes (the "contemptible person" of v. 21) and his erection of "the abomination that maketh desolate" (31).

Chapter 7 is, theologically, the most important in the book. Later, in another connection, we shall have occasion to look at vv. 9–14. Here, for the moment, we are concerned only to note that in vv. 7f there is an even more cryptic picture of Antiochus (the "little horn" in v. 8), which is, however, interpreted in more intelligible terms in 23–25. It is of incidental interest to note that it is only in Daniel of all the books of the Old Testament that the doctrine of a resurrection from the dead is plainly taught (12:1–3). (Isa. 26:19 is a minor and unimportant exception to this statement.)

The terrible events of the Maccabean Age created a new spirit in Israel: an expectation of future persecutions, a sense of glory in the possibility of martyrdom for the faith, and a sense of assurance in God's victory over the forces of evil and His power to raise even the dead to share in His triumph. There was a tendency to see the final events of human history as following the pattern of events in the days of the Maccabees and to use the language and images of that age to describe them.

We see our Lord Himself using this now traditional language in such a passage as Matthew 24:15–18 where he speaks of a future trial of the faithful and the erection of another "abomination of desolation" in the holy place.

In John 10:22f we see Jesus in the temple, joining with his countrymen in celebrating the feast of Dedication, "Hanukkah." The reference to winter is a reminder that Hanukkah is observed at approximately the same time as our Christmas.

Finally, in Revelation 13:1–10 we have a picture of the future tribulations of the Church ("the saints" of v. 7) in which the persecutor, one of the Roman Emperors, is described in terms which are borrowed wholesale from Daniel 7. The Book of Revelation belongs to the type of "apocalyptic" literature which first became widely current in the Maccabean Age and of which Daniel is the first great example. The influence of this type of thinking can be traced in many other parts of the New Testament and is perhaps of more basic significance than is ordinarily supposed.

XVIII. JESUS AND THE GOSPEL OF THE KINGDOM

Isaiah 33:17–24; Mark 1:9–15; Luke 13:18–30; 18:15–30; Acts 14:21–22; 19:8; Revelation 11:15

More than twelve centuries had passed since Moses heard the call of God and the people of Israel began their long spiritual pilgrimage. There had been many turnings in the road and, for many, it must have seemed to lead nowhere at all. From prosperity and power under David and Solomon they had descended to the impotence of the divided monarchies and the final disaster of the Exile. As a narrative of human achievement one could easily think of Israel's story as a tragic farce, a bitter commentary on the futility of human effort and the fatuity of human pride.

But we do not read the Old Testament simply as human history; it is not a story of man's failure, but of God's success. Underneath the superficial crosscurrents of political success and failure one can feel the ground swell of God's purpose moving tirelessly forward. He had intended Israel to be a prophetic and priestly nation dedicated to bringing the knowledge of God to all the families of the earth. The spiritual leaders of Israel, the creative minority, understood this and looked forward in eager confidence to the time when the divine intent would be fulfilled and the earth would "be full of the knowledge of the Lord, as the waters cover the sea" (Isa. 11:9). Few as they were, these men were the real Israel and knew that the destiny of their people was not to be realized in a future kingdom of Israel, but only in the Kingdom of God.

Isaiah 33:17–24, composed by some unknown prophet of postexilic times, is just one expression of this assurance of the Kingdom which kept the heart of Israel alive during long years of spiritual depression, but it is a singularly beautiful one. Although the language in some places is obscure, it is not difficult to trace the main outlines of the prophet's picture. In the Kingdom of God, he says, there will be no oppression, no battleships, no sickness, but only beauty, peace, and the forgiveness of sins. Many different images are used in these late passages of the Old Testament to describe the Kingdom, but all are merely various ways of making vivid the conviction that God had not failed, but would one day cause His will to be done on earth as it is in heaven.

It is this faith which unites the Old and the New Testaments. The climax of the Old Testament story is not to be found in the Old Testament itself nor in the infancy narratives of Matthew and Luke, but in the first chapter of Mark (the earliest of the gospels to be written). In its dramatic account of the opening scene of our Lord's ministry (Mark 1:9–15) it picks up the thread of the Old Testament story in a verse which tells that, when John was imprisoned, "Jesus came into Galilee preaching the kingdom of God, and saying, 'The time is fulfilled, and the kingdom of God is at hand: repent ye, and believe the gospel' (*meaning*, 'good news.')" (Mark 1:14f).

To understand our Lord's teaching, one must grasp first of all the centrality of the idea of the Kingdom. Jesus did not come primarily to teach a new doctrine of God or new moral principles. He came to declare that the reign of God was beginning to break in upon the world and that the powers of the Kingdom were already available to those who were prepared to use them. The final establishment of the Kingdom might be centuries in the future, but its foundations were laid and the energies necessary for its completion were already at work.

In Luke 13:18-30 we find several descriptions of the Kingdom. In one (vv. 18-21) it is compared to a grain of mustard seed or a bit of leaven, both of which are so small as to be almost imperceptible at first and yet are capable of growing to prodigious dimensions. So the Kingdom as first seen in the fragile body of Jesus appears almost contemptible and yet is one day destined to cover the earth.

In vv. 24-30 Jesus pictures the universal scope of the Kingdom. It is intended not merely for the ancient people of God, but for all the world: east, west, north and south (29). Though the gate is broad enough to admit men of all nations, it is too narrow to permit the passage of the careless and the arrogant. Citizenship in the Kingdom is for those of deep and humble faith (24-28). This was a rebuke to those who rejected the teaching of their own prophets and thought that Jewish birth was sufficient to guarantee acceptance into the Kingdom. As we shall see later, membership in the Kingdom involves a certain quality of life. If men will not live the life, they cannot hope to find the Kingdom.

The same note of warning is to be heard in Luke 18:15-30. God's Kingdom has no room for the proud and self-satisfied, for those who are wise in their own conceits or are tied down to material possessions or merely worldly values. It is open only to those who, like little children, are humble, open-hearted, unsophisticated and teachable.

These were the things that Jesus said as he began his ministry in Galilee, inaugurating not only the New Testament story, but the last and final chapter in the history of a fallen race. These things were also the burden of the first

Christian missionaries, as we see from Acts 14:21f; 19:8. And despite the altered terminology of later times, the essential faith of the Church is still best expressed in such words as those of the little hymn of the Kingdom in Revelation 11:15.

XIX. JESUS—HIMSELF THE KING

Isaiah 11:1–5; Matthew 7:24–29; Mark 2:1–12; 8:27–29; 9:2–8; Revelation 19:11–16

The essence of Old Testament faith in the Kingdom of God was that one day God would overcome the forces of evil and show on earth the fullness of His power. Just how this would happen and what the precise form of the Kingdom would be were matters on which there was a considerable variety of opinion. Some thought God would do it by a sheer act of His will without the help of any human agent; but the more common view was that He would send a human individual to act as His representative and rule in His behalf. Since the greatest of Israel's kings had been David, it was natural for this future king to be thought of as one of his descendants; and since the kings of Israel were all anointed at their coronation, it was natural that he should be called the Anointed One (in Hebrew, "The Messiah"; in Greek, "The Christ"). The most appealing picture of the Christ to come is the familiar one in Isaiah 11:1–5.

As we saw in our last set of readings, the chief burden

of Jesus' message was that the promises of God were at last being fulfilled and the Kingdom of God was at hand. In the present series, we see that he was not only the herald of the coming Kingdom, but was himself to be the King.

At the beginning Jesus did not proclaim his kingship, but only the fact of the Kingdom. He allowed his followers to discover for themselves his own peculiar relationship to it. No doubt those who first began to follow him did so because they saw him as the last and greatest of the prophets, come to declare the imminence of God's rule; but as they came to know him better, they saw that the category of prophet was inadequate to explain him. While in many respects he was like other religious teachers of Israel in the past and present, certain qualities set him sharply apart from all of them. The most striking was the *authority* with which he spoke and acted.

The tone of authority was evident in both major areas of his public ministry: his teaching and his healing. In Matthew 7:24–29, one sees the impression made by his teaching. The passage is the conclusion of the "Sermon on the Mount" (actually a collection of addresses drawn from many different occasions). Later in our study we shall be concerned with the content of his teaching as it is recorded here, but at the moment we are interested only in the effect which it had on those who heard him. "The people were astonished at his doctrine: For he taught them as one having authority, and not as the scribes" (v. 28f).

The prophets of old had spoken merely as God's messengers and the scribes spoke only as the guardians and expositors of a body of teaching already given to Israel in complete and definitive form. But Jesus spoke as one who had authority in his own person. He could criticize the traditional law (as in Matt. 5:31f) and add his own commandments to it (as in 33ff) and speak of his words as the solid rock on which every human life must be built (7:24–27). It is little wonder that the people were surprised at his manner. Nor is it strange that he aroused the antagonism of the official teachers of religion, although in personal character he was the mildest and gentlest of men.

The same note of authority was as much apparent in the things he did as in the things he said—in his seeming mastery of nature and the mysterious forces which disturb the human spirit. It was said that he could command demons and make them obey and had been known to still a raging storm. No doubt some of the stories are legendary (like those of the Apocryphal Gospels) and some have been embellished by tradition, but all testify to the aura of royalty and even divinity which surrounded him. The story of the healing of a paralytic in Mark 2:1–12 is a good example of the power of his person and the effect he created.

One can easily imagine the growing change these experiences brought about in the minds of his disciples. At last the time seemed ripe for getting a mature and final judgment from them as to who he was, and at Caesarea Philippi, Jesus asked them bluntly what they thought (Mark 8:27–29). Perhaps they had never previously faced the question in just this way, but once it was put there was only one possible answer. Peter, acting as spokesman for the twelve breathlessly, almost incredulously, gave the reply: "Thou art the Christ!" The full force of his response becomes evident to us only as we remember that Christ means "king." Peter was not so much approving the claim of a teacher to be heard as of a monarch to be obeyed. The conviction that, in the Kingdom of God, Jesus himself is King is the foundation of New Testament faith.

A few days later, their eyes opened by their new-found faith, the disciples saw the glory of his Kingship

(Mark 9:2–8). One cannot say just what happened on the mountain, for the story tells of an indescribable experience which belongs to the order of the spirit rather than to external, objective history. But one thing is certain: Those who had known Jesus as a prophet now saw him, briefly, clothed in royal dignity as the Christ of God. In Revelation 19:11–16, a later writer, in more florid language, describes a similar vision—the same vision the Church holds before men's eyes today.

XX. THE CRUCIFIED MESSIAH

Mark 8:31–33; 10:35–45; Isaiah 52:13–53:9; Mark 15:22–39; I Corinthians 1:18–24; Philippians 2:5–11

The great obstacle to our Lord's being accepted by his own people was the fact of the crucifixion. They did not object to his claims to kingship so much as they objected to a king who either could not or would not vindicate his claims. A true king, they felt, should be like David, a ruler of nations and a winner of victories, not an impractical dreamer incapable of saving even himself. Their idea of the coming King—the Christ, the Messiah—was that of a conquering soldier, whereas from the very beginning Jesus had no other ideal than that of a humble servant of God, destined to fail, to suffer and to die.

In our last readings we heard the words of Peter acknowledging Jesus as the long-expected King of Israel. "Thou art the Christ." But as we continue the story in the first of the present selections (Mark 8:31–33) we can see how far Peter was from understanding what kind of King Jesus intended to be.

The same conflict of ideals is dramatized in the story of two of Jesus' other disciples, James and John, who asked him for the privilege of being the leading members of his cabinet when the Kingdom finally arrived (Mark 10:35–37). He chided them gently (vv. 38–40) and then made use of the opportunity to expound his own conception of kingship. Unlike the kingdoms of the pagan world, where authority and greatness rest upon the exercise of power, God's kingdom would be established on the principle that the highest honors go to those who give unselfishly of themselves to serve their fellows (42–44). And by this same rule the King must win his crown. "For even the Son of man came not to be ministered unto, but to minister, and to give his life a ransom for many" (45).

Where did this ideal come from? Was it a totally new conception, brought into the world by Jesus, or was there any foreshadowing of it in the ancient scriptures of his people? For the most part the Old Testament pictures the coming Kingdom and its King in language drawn from political life, but there is one passage which speaks of God delivering His people in quite different terms, where the word kingdom never occurs and the deliverer is not called a king, but a "servant." It was in this passage, Isaiah 53, that our Lord apparently found the pattern of his life. In Mark 10:45 he summarizes the thought of the whole chapter in a single verse.

The passage (which really begins in 52:13) is one of the poems of Second Isaiah, composed in Babylon for the congregation of the Exiles. It is generally believed by scholars that Second Isaiah was thinking of Israel itself as the Servant, or at least of the little inner core of the faithful, and of the shame and humiliation they had undergone. The prophet was sure their sufferings could not be punitive (for they had received of the Lord's hand "double for all their sins"—40:2) and in a flash of spiritual insight he glimpsed the possibility that in some mysterious way God was making it possible for them to bear the sufferings of others. By suffering as they did they were actually serving mankind and making the world a better place for other men to live in.

The vision of the prophet was greater than he knew. It was too great to be realized by the people of Israel and, indeed, they soon forgot that it had ever been intended to apply to them. The ideal of human life which it embodies has never been realized anywhere but in the person of Jesus Christ. While he did not refuse the ancient title of King, he seems to have based his understanding of the function and dignity of kingship entirely upon the figure of the suffering servant of Isaiah 53.

We now turn briefly to the story of the crucifixion itself (Mark 15: 22–39), reminding ourselves that in reading the Bible we are concerned not with fine theories but with historical facts, not with splendid ethical ideals manufactured in academic isolation but with the actual living of human life. Jesus did not come merely to teach the noblest way to live; he lived it. He saw the painful path God meant Him to walk and followed it unswervingly to the end—although the end was Golgotha. There they crucified him and placed above his head the mocking, but unconsciously prophetic words, "Jesus of Nazareth, the King . . ." (John 19:19).

As Paul tells us, the earliest preachers of the Gospel did not find many who were receptive to the message of the Cross (I Cor. 1:18–24). It was hard for either Jew or Gentile to accept for their Lord and King a man who had been executed as a common criminal. Yet the very essence of the Christian mission lay in the preaching of a *crucified* Messiah; and, in spite of the "stumbling block" and the "foolishness" men have not been able to escape the fascination of "that strange man upon his cross." Herod, Pilate and Tiberius Caesar died and the Roman Empire passed from history long ago, but the crucified King continues to reign on his piteous and awful throne. Paul, in his letter to the Philippians (2:5–11), pictures the final triumph and reminds his readers that a Christian is one who not only admires the cross, but follows in the steps of the Crucified. "Let this mind be in *you* . . ."

XXI. THE RISEN LORD

Isaiah 53:10–12; I Corinthians 15:3–8; Luke 24;
Romans 6:4–11

No part of the mysterious 53rd chapter of Isaiah is more difficult to interpret than the concluding verses (10–12), but in spite of all its uncertainties the chapter plainly ends upon a note of victory. The death of the Servant was not a tragic and pointless defeat; it was the fulfillment of God's purpose. By means of it the sins "of many" were taken away and "many" were justified. But, more than that, the death of the Servant was followed by his triumph: "he shall prolong his days, and the pleasure of the Lord shall prosper in his hand" (v. 10). Whatever the ancient prophet may have meant by these words, they could have only one meaning once they were understood to refer to the death of an individual—they could only be a prophecy of his resurrection.

So when Jesus came to see in this chapter the pattern of his own life and death, he must have seen there the dawn of Easter as well as the gathering shadows of Good Friday. This would help to explain why even the first prediction of his passion (Mark 8:31) ended with a promise of his rising to life again.

The apostles, who apparently had not anticipated his death, naturally had no hope of his resurrection. What Jesus had said about these things seems to have remained a complete enigma to them. Up to the moment of his arrest, they still expected him to turn the tables on his enemies by supernatural means and gloriously ascend the throne of David, so the actual trial of Jesus and his subsequent execution meant nothing less than the extinction of their hope and the momentary end of their little world.

No event in history is more amazing than the reversal of attitude which took place in the minds of the apostles in the few days which followed the crucifixion. Their cowardice turned into courage and their despair into confidence. The change was brought about by a series of events which convinced them that Christ had left his tomb and had destroyed forever the power of sin and death. His grave was reported to be empty; women said they had met him on the road; he had appeared to many of his followers, sometimes singly and sometimes in groups; various disciples told that they had talked with him and even had him for their guest at table.

The stories could not even then all be reconciled with each other and it is impossible today to arrange those that remain in any kind of strict logical order, but all bear uniform witness to one central and inescapable fact—Jesus rose from the dead. This fact is the cornerstone of the Gospel and of the Church which proclaims it. On the basis of their experience of the resurrection, that little group of eleven discouraged men became the nucleus of a mighty army which finally conquered even Caesar's legions and outlasted every human institution of the ancient world.

The earliest account of the resurrection appearances is the one in I Corinthians 15:3–8. Paul is here reminding the Christians at Corinth of the story of the resurrection as they had heard him tell it and as he in turn had heard it from the original eyewitnesses. According to this account the first appearance was to Peter. Later, Christ showed himself to all the apostles, and another time (not mentioned in the Gospels) to more than five hundred people at once. Paul also mentions an otherwise unrecorded appearance to James ("the brother of the Lord") and, interestingly enough, includes his own vision of Christ on the road to Damascus along with the other resurrection appearances.

The last chapter of Luke contains not only a version of the story of the empty tomb (24:1–12), but also the most beautiful of all the stories of the resurrection, that of the walk to Emmaus (vv. 13–32). Its particular appeal lies partly in the fact that it is a parable of the experience of the Church in later centuries. As our Lord was made known to two disciples "in the breaking of bread" (30, 35), so he continues to manifest himself to his followers in the sacramental bread of the Eucharist. The next incident (36–49) emphasizes that the appearance of the risen Christ was not a mere hallucination, but the objective manifestation of a tangible reality (39). It also makes clear that it was only after the resurrection that the disciples came to know the true nature of Jesus' Messiahship and learned that, as his witnesses, they were to preach the good news of his victory and the beginning of God's Kingdom to all the world (47). The chapter concludes with an account of the ascension (50–53), which was the concluding act of the resurrection drama. This was the day when the resurrection appearances ceased and the disciples knew that Jesus Christ was no longer the humble prophet or suffering servant of the Lord, but the King of Creation reigning forever in heaven as well as in the hearts of his people. As the immediate sequel to this chapter (Acts 1:9–11) relates, their gaze was no longer to be directed sadly toward the unhappy events of the immediate past or the deprivations of the present, but hopefully toward a future day when he would return and make his royal dignity manifest in the eyes of the world.

The last selection, Romans 6:4–11, reminds us that the resurrection is intended to be part of the life of every Christian. In baptism each one of us is made to share Christ's resurrection experience. As he was buried in the earth and rose again, so we are buried in the waters of baptism and raised again. (The image is, of course, clearer when we think in terms of total immersion, as it was practiced in St. Paul's day.) Christians have all received the power of the risen Christ to rise from the death of sin to a new life in him.

XXII. THE BIRTH OF THE NEW ISRAEL

Isaiah 10:20–22; Joel 2:28–32; Acts 2:1–42;
Romans 9:6–8, 24–28; 11:1–5

Although the history of the people of Israel was so largely a story of rebellion against God's will for them, the prophets never doubted that God would find some way to accomplish His purposes. One form which this conviction sometimes took was "the doctrine of the remnant," which taught that even though the nation as a whole might become apostate and perish, there would always be a small group of the faithful, like the 7000 in the days of Elijah who did not bow their knees to Baal (I Kings 19:18), whom God could use as the nucleus of a new and better Israel. The classical statement of this doctrine is Isaiah 10:20–22.

When Jesus the Messiah was repudiated by his own people, his twelve apostles became the whole of this faithful remnant. The next chapter in the Bible story tells of the renewal of Israel's life which began with the apostles on the day of Pentecost. The number twelve is itself significant, for it is the number of the tribes of Israel and suggests immediately that the apostles were already Israel in miniature—the fresh sprout of an old tree, from which a new and more imposing plant would grow. As we have already learned, the new Israel was to be based upon a new and more spiritual covenant and would be open to all the nations of the world. By his death and resurrection,

Jesus Christ had burst not only the bonds of death, but also the shackles of Law and national pride.

The prophets had told of many signs which would accompany the beginning of the Kingdom of God. All the descriptions are poetical and some merely fanciful, but amongst the pictures they drew one of the most remarkable is that of the outpouring of the Spirit of God upon great numbers of people, so that the gift of prophecy (i.e., of eloquent speech in the name of God) would no longer be the possession of a small professional class, but of many simple and untrained persons: ". . . your sons and your daughters shall prophesy, your old men shall dream dreams, your young men shall see visions." (Joel 2:28–32)

This oracle provides the principal text for Peter's speech in Acts 2 (note verse 16). A short time after the resurrection and ascension of our Lord, the apostles assembled in a room in Jerusalem, presumably to celebrate the Jewish feast of Pentecost. While they were there, perhaps engaged in prayer and singing and in discussing the marvelous events which had recently transpired, there came over the whole group a tremendous sense of the presence of the Holy Spirit of God. It was a sudden dramatic experience which could be compared only to "a rushing mighty wind" and to "cloven tongues like as of fire" sitting upon them (vv. 2f).

Immediately they went out and began to speak to the crowds which had gathered in Jerusalem for the festival from all over the world and spoke with such fervor and conviction that 3000 persons are said to have joined the Church that day (41). So the Christian, the universal, the *Catholic* Church began—the new Israel which was intended to bring God's saving power to "Parthians and Medes and Elamites" and all the peoples of the world (9–11). The Holy Spirit was to be the Church's permanent possession; baptism was to be the means of entrance into it (38); fidelity to apostolic teaching and continuity in apostolic life the chief marks of its character; and Holy Communion the principal act of its common worship (42).

Readers naturally ask, "Did the apostles actually speak foreign languages at Pentecost?" It would be presumptuous simply to answer "No," as though such things are impossible, but it is true that elsewhere in the New Testament there is evidence that "speaking with tongues" ordinarily meant highly emotional, even unintelligible, discourse rather than speaking a foreign language (those who are interested might read Paul's discussion of the subject in I Cor. 14:1–33). The phenomena described in Acts 2:4–11 are best understood this way and the statement that "every man heard . . . in his own language" as the author's attempt to picture in a dramatic way the future proclamation of the Gospel in all the languages of the world. The story of Babel in Genesis 11:1–9 is a parable of the way in which sin had destroyed the unity of the human race; Acts 2:11 is a parable of the restoration of that unity through the gift of the Holy Spirit.

The fragmentary readings suggested from Romans 9–11 (9:6–8, 24–28; 11:1–5) are intended to show how Paul pictured the relationship of the Old and the New Israel. This whole section of Romans is devoted to the theme and it is worth reading for those who have the time and a commentary to help them understand it. The fragments are enough however, to show that Paul saw in the Christian Church the true heir and successor of Israel. Christians are "the children of promise" (9:8); they now are God's "people" and His "beloved" (9:25); they are "the remnant" of which the prophet spoke (9:27; 11:5).

Lest we should be tempted to feel smugly superior as we read these words, it might be well to read the rest of chapter 11 too and see how Paul warns his Christian readers against spiritual arrogance, especially toward the Jews. God still loves His ancient people, and the followers of Christ must also regard them with affection as their own spiritual brethren. *All* men are sinners and subject to judgment, the Christian no less than the Jew. Although the Jewish people seem temporarily estranged from Christ, they have their part to play in God's plan and Paul feels sure He will one day bring them into His fold (vv. 25–32).

XXIII. THE CHURCH AT JERUSALEM

Deuteronomy 24:17–22; Acts 4:32–37; 5:12–42; 6:8–15; 7:55–60; I Corinthians 16:1–4

God's demand for a spirit of brotherhood was a cardinal element of Old Testament faith. Ideally, Israel was intended to be so organized that the poor could always count on the help of their wealthier brethren. This ideal was, of course, never attained in actual practice, and throughout most of its history the nation's life was characterized by callous disregard for the rights of the weak and helpless. The prophets never ceased to denounce this as rebellion against the Divine Law and declared that when God passed final judgment upon His people, the greed of their ruling classes and the spirit of selfishness which pervaded the community would be a major count against them. We have already seen a good example of this kind of prophetic preaching in Ezekiel 34:1–16. The present

passage, from Deuteronomy (24:17–22), shows in a different way how seriously the religious leaders of the old Israel
attempted to incorporate essential principles of social justice into the basic law of the nation.

It is not surprising that when the disciples of Jesus
organized the first community of the *new* Israel, in Jerusalem, they tried to make it conform to the law of brotherhood by putting all property into a common fund and
having the church assume responsibility for the fundamental needs of all its members (Acts 4:32–37). Since later
churches were not organized in this way, it is obvious that
the experiment did not work out in practice, but the
example of the Jerusalem church remains as an incentive
to Christians of today to seek the same end in more practical ways, and as a continual rebuke to members of the
church who feel no sense of responsibility for human
beings less fortunate than themselves.

The Church, as the continuing organ of Christ's work
on earth (the "body" of Christ) felt the obligation of continuing his activities of healing and preaching. Our second
passage from Acts (5:12–42) illustrates this phase of the
Church's work and the success which seems generally to
have attended it. We see how the fame of the apostles'
healing power spread (vv. 12–16) and how there grew up
even a superstitious veneration for the wonder-working
gifts of Peter, the head of the Jerusalem church (15). The
spread of the Gospel was not due so much to the disciples'
oratorical skill and their capacity for fine-spun argument
as to the unmistakable evidence that the power of God
to heal and to bless was at work amongst them. But they
preached as well as healed, and the present passage gives
a good summary of the kind of preaching in which they
engaged (30–32). One notices that it was not moralistic or
"intellectual" (although in time this kind of preaching

also would find its proper place). The apostolic preaching was a simple, straightforward proclamation of the fact that the power of God—the Holy Spirit—had become available to all men through the death, resurrection and ascension of Jesus Christ. In other passages where more extensive examples of preaching are given (as in Peter's sermon at Pentecost), we see that the apostles laid considerable emphasis upon the fact that God's work in Christ had been accomplished in fulfillment of the promises given in ancient times to the people of Israel.

We observe, then, that among the marks of the earliest Church were: a spirit of brotherliness, a consciousness of God's present and available power, and a deep conviction that both true brotherhood and spiritual power have their source in the kingly rule of Christ. But there is one other mark of the Church that must also be noticed—that of a willingness to suffer for the name of Christ. In the story of the Jerusalem church we can see foreshadowings of the coming of the age of the martyrs. In the passage we have just been looking at we read of the arrest, imprisonment and trial of the apostles (17–41). Although they were released on this occasion through the counsel of Gamaliel (34), a wise leader of the Pharisees and (according to Acts 22:3) the teacher of St. Paul, Acts goes on to tell of other imprisonments and of the execution of at least one of the original twelve (12:1–3). The honor of being the first martyr, however, goes not to one of the apostles, but to a humbler Jerusalem Christian, Stephen (Acts 6:8–15; 7:55–60), a member of a group within the Church called the Hellenists (KJV "Grecians"), probably meaning "Greek-speaking Jews" (see Acts 6:1–3). Because of their Greek background these men were more willing than the original apostles to see that the Christian Gospel involved a radical break with Judaism (6:14). Consequently they aroused far more violent antagonism in the Jewish community (7:54). Stephen, one of the leaders of this group, became the prototype of all the later company of martyrs who gave their lives for the Faith. Like them he died with a vision of the reigning Christ in his heart (7:55) and words of forgiveness on his lips (v. 60).

For various reasons the Jerusalem community did not long continue to hold a dominating position in the Christian world. As we shall see, the center of the Church's life shifted from Judea to the lands and cities of the Gentiles. But the lesson of brotherhood was not forgotten and it is pleasant to read that when the Christians ("the saints") at Jerusalem fell upon evil days, special arrangements were made in the Gentile churches to raise funds for the support of the now weakened and impoverished mother church (I Cor. 16:1–4).

XXIV. ST. PAUL—THE MISSIONARY

Isaiah 49:1–6; Acts 9:1–22; 13:1–3, 13–16, 38–48; II Corinthians 11:24–33; Acts 28:16–31

The ancient Covenant of Faith included the promise "in thee shall all the families of the earth be blessed" (Gen. 12:3). Throughout much of her history the old Israel had tended to forget this larger purpose of her calling and to act as if God had no real concern for other nations. But the greater vision never died among the prophets. From generation to generation they continued to affirm—usually to unreceptive ears—that God did not exist for Israel's glory, but Israel for God's. The time must yet come when the knowledge of God would cover the whole earth as the waters cover the sea (Isa. 11:9).

The most striking and fully-developed expression of this view is to be found in the writings of Second Isaiah, especially in the passages which speak of Israel as "the servant of the Lord." In Isaiah 49:1-6 the prophet warns his contemporaries in exile that the restoration of Israel alone is not a sufficient task for God's Servant. He must also become "a light to the Gentiles" and bring God's salvation "unto the end of the earth."

The original apostles and the church at Jerusalem, of which they were the heart, do not seem—at least at the beginning—to have made much effort to realize this larger vision of the prophets, which was also of course the vision of Jesus. Whatever the reason may have been, the Jerusalem church apparently was content to develop its own spiritual life and to recruit new members chiefly from its Jewish fellow citizens. It seems to have been only with the coming of Stephen and the Hellenists that the Church began consciously to extend her energies toward actively evangelizing the Gentile world.

The Hellenists were responsible, at least indirectly, for the most crucial event of the period, the conversion of St. Paul (Acts 9:1-22). Since we are explicitly told that Paul was in the crowd which stoned Stephen (7:58), we can hardly doubt that his conversion was due in part to impressions formed on that occasion. Although Paul had been one of the fiercest opponents of the new faith, he must have been touched by the remarkable combination of heroic devotion and a gentle spirit which Stephen showed. One can imagine the question "Why?" continually obtruding itself upon his consciousness, followed at last by another, "Could Stephen possibly have been right?" Some such psychological preparation seems necessary to explain the conversion which occurred so dramatically on the Damascus road and which brought all Paul's exuberant vitality into subjection to the rule of Christ.

When Paul was converted, he was converted all the way. He does not seem to have undergone the painful process of gradual readjustment to new ideas which the original apostles had found so difficult—or, if he did, there is no record of it, even in the long, hidden years before he began his active ministry. Perhaps because he was born in Tarsus, a pagan city, he knew the spiritual hunger of the Gentile world and was aware that their fields were white to the harvest. So, when he found the Jews antagonistic to his preaching, he turned without hesitation to the Gentiles and found there an immediate and enthusiastic response. The story of his experiences at Pisidian Antioch, as related in Acts 13:1-3, 13-16, 38-48 is typical of this phase of his career.

The rest of the book of Acts is taken up with the account of his missionary activities among the Gentiles, activities which carried him through most of the important cities of the Roman Empire, founding churches wherever he went. His own summary of the hardships of those days, in II Corinthians 11:24-33, is the best witness to the magnitude of his achievement and the price he was willing to pay. Few men in history have had more active or adventurous careers and certainly few have had more revolutionary effect upon the life of later times. Led by the Holy Spirit, Paul was chiefly responsible for the transformation of what might have seemed to many only a new Jewish sect into an overwhelmingly Gentile, and therefore universal, Church. Through him, more than any other human agent, light came to the Gentiles and blessing to all the families of earth.

All this was not accomplished without some struggle within the Church itself. Certain passages in Acts reveal that many in the apostolic Church thought that the Gentiles could not become Christians without undergoing circumcision and observing meticulously all requirements of the Jewish law. But Paul, who was as rigorous toward others as toward himself, fought this battle through and vindicated his Gentile mission as successfully on the theoretical front as he prosecuted it on the practical (the course of the controversy can be traced in Galatians 2 and Acts 15). By the end of his career the Church was Catholic in mentality as well as in actual fact.

The book of Acts ends (28:16–31) with St. Paul in prison at Rome. Nothing is known for certain about the outcome of his trial, or whether indeed it ever took place. So far as the Bible is concerned there was no reason to carry the story beyond this point. From the standpoint of history, a knowledge of Paul's ultimate personal fate is of little importance. What is important is the fact that his great battle for the universality of the Gospel had been won and the work of preaching to the nations would be carried on in his spirit by an innumerable host after him.

XXV. ST. PAUL—THE PASTOR

Ezekiel 33:1–11; Galatians 5; I Corinthians 8;
Philippians 1:1–21

St. Paul was first of all a missionary, concerned with establishing new churches wherever he could. But he was also a pastor—or, as he would have been called later, a bishop—watching carefully and affectionately over the welfare of the churches he had founded. The chief evidence of his activity in this direction is to be found in his numerous epistles, or letters, which have been preserved in the New Testament. Other New Testament epistles show that many great figures of the apostolic age were also, like Paul, engaged in active supervision of young churches.

Before looking at a few typical pastoral passages from Paul's letters, it will be of interest to turn to a remarkable chapter of the Old Testament in which, for the first time, the office and duties of a pastor are described (Ezek. 33:1–11). Before the time of Ezekiel, the prophets had thought of themselves chiefly as the mouthpieces of God, with the obligation of declaring His will whenever He chose to make it known. They do not seem to have had any great sense of continuing responsibility for the spiritual life of the community; their functioning was only sporadic and occasional. But Ezekiel felt that God had called him to a position of spiritual oversight of the people. He was to be a "watchman," constantly concerned for the welfare of his nation and of the individuals who composed it. While he could not be blamed if any member of the flock disregarded his advice, he would be held to account if he failed to give warning where warning was needed. If Ezekiel was not in actual fact the first pastor in the history of the Church, he was at least the first clearly to articulate a definition of the pastoral office.

Paul's relation to the churches he had founded was conceived along these lines. A passage from Galatians is a good example of the warnings he sometimes felt impelled to give. We have seen already that Paul had to fight for his conception of Christianity as a new way of life completely free from any observance of the Jewish ceremonial law. Galatians was written, during the height of this controversy, to a church in Asia Minor which he had founded, but which seems temporarily to have been won over by his adversaries. The Galatian church was insisting upon Gentiles being circumcised before they were admitted to church membership. Paul, it has been said, was "red-hot mad" when he wrote this letter. "O foolish Galatians," he says, "who hath bewitched you . . . ?" (3:1). In the present chapter (5) he presents the positive aspects of his argument. *Freedom* is the great sign of the Christian life (v. 1); faith and love, not circumcision, are its basic requirements (6); our obligations under the covenant of law are completely satisfied when we love our neighbors as ourselves (14); finally, a Christian is simply one who allows himself to be ruled entirely by the Holy Spirit (16–25). Where the Spirit is, there is no further need of the written Law (22f).

Another aspect of his pastoral ministry is illustrated by I Corinthians 8. Here Paul is not issuing warnings, but answering questions. The Corinthian Christians, only recently converted from paganism, were worried about meat, bought in the public market but previously offered as a sacrifice in the temple of an idol. Ought they to eat it or not? Paul's answer shows his immense common sense. He tells them first of all that no Christian need be concerned about this problem as a matter of principle since an idol cannot possibly affect the food one way or another (4–6). But as a matter of expediency and good judgment, he says, one needs to remember that some ignorant persons may think that a man who eats meat once offered to an idol is really approving the worship of idols. They might thus, by their misunderstanding, be led into idolatry. So, if one suspects that this might be the case, he had better not eat such food at all (9–13).

Finally, in the passage from Philippians (1:1–21), we see Paul simply as the affectionate friend of his people, anxious for their continued growth in Christian love and understanding. This letter was written while he was in prison at Rome and was addressed to a church (the first he had founded in Europe) which he seems always to have regarded with especial kindliness. The letter is a kind of thank-you note for their thoughtful remembrance of him in his troubles and for a generous gift they had sent him. He begins by telling them how much he loves them (vv. 3–8) and how he constantly prays for their spiritual advancement (9–11). Then he goes on to assure them about himself (12–21). Even his imprisonment, he says, has turned out for the best, since some have learned of the Gospel who would otherwise have had no opportunity (13); other Christians have been encouraged by his example to bear more convincing witness to the faith (14); and his own assurance that God in all things is working for good is stronger than ever.

In the pastoral ministry of Paul we see the pattern of Church life which would continue down through the centuries to come. From apostolic times to our own the Church and her ministry have provided the natural framework within which the devout life is nurtured and men grow in understanding and in love for God and other men.

XXVI. THE END OF THE STORY

Isaiah 25:1–9; 60:1–3, 14–20; Matthew 25:31–46;
I Corinthians 15:20–24; Revelation 21:1–4, 22–27; 22:1–5

In a sense we have already reached the end of the Bible story, for once the Church had been established the means of salvation had been brought within the reach of every man. God's great purpose of giving His blessing to "all the families of earth" had been, at least potentially, accomplished. The long history of man which follows the close of the New Testament period introduces no new factors into the situation; it tells us merely of the widening scope of the Church's life, her diffusion among many peoples and her deepening understanding of the Gospel with which she was entrusted.

But, in another sense, we cannot leave the Bible story at this point because the Bible itself does not do so. Neither to biblical man nor to common sense does it seem likely that the story of man's life upon earth will continue forever. Sometime, somehow, the curtain will fall upon the gorgeous pageant of human history; somewhere time must have a stop. But what will the end be? Some scientists have thought of it in terms of the cooling of the earth and the extinction of human life by the advancing icecaps. Others have thought of a final cosmic conflagration or an atomic explosion which would send the world up in flames.

To men of the Bible, however, the nature of the end was clearly determined by the presuppositions of their faith. Whatever might prove true from a purely scientific point of view about the fate of the physical universe, they had no doubt that on the spiritual level the end of history meant the final triumph of the Kingdom of God. Beyond the limits of secular history, with its ugly scars of sin and pride, they saw far off the coming rule of God. It was this vision which sustained them through the troubles of life in the present order of the world.

The readings suggested for this study are just a sample of great Bible passages which deal with the theme. One must not be disturbed by differences in the pictures they present, for they are trying to describe the indescribable. All are attempts to put into vividly conceptual, quasi-historical language truths which belong essentially to the spiritual and suprahistorical order.

The first (Isa. 25:1–9) is a brief passage from an apocalyptic work written very late in the Old Testament period (not by the prophet Isaiah). It pictures the final event as involving the destruction of human pride (vv. 2f), the rescue of the poor and distressed of earth (4), a feast which God will spread for the people of all nations (6), and the end of suffering and death (8).

The second passage (Isa. 60:1–3; 14–20) is from the oracles of Second (or Third) Isaiah and therefore somewhat earlier than the one we have just been examining. Originally it referred to the rebuilding of the city of Jerusalem after the Babylonian Exile, but the language is so extravagantly magnificent that it cannot be limited to any merely historical event. The author saw in the restoration of his people after the Exile a sign of God's coming restoration of mankind. Here, once again, we find the intermingled themes of the humiliation of human pride (v. 14), God's care for the afflicted (15), and the end of suffering (18). But the prophet also includes another theme—the glorious Presence of God in the midst of His people (19f).

In the third passage (Matt. 25:31–46) we find our Lord also dealing with the end of history, instructing his disciples as to the way in which they must enter "the kingdom . . . prepared from the foundation of the world." The scene is that of the final judgment (a frequent theme of the Old Testament also), with Jesus himself returned in regal dignity to act as Judge. Those who will be counted worthy to share in the glory of the Kingdom are the ones who willingly gave themselves to serve their fellow men. Since the abolition of human suffering is one of the goals of the Kingdom, those who would enter it must themselves have striven for this end; as he had said on another occasion, "Blessed are the merciful for they shall obtain mercy" (Matt. 5:7). The words of Jesus in this passage contain quite as much of warning as of comfort and, however we interpret them in detail, must be taken with the utmost seriousness.

The few verses from Paul (I Cor. 15:20–24) are included to show that he shared the common faith and especially how, in the coming triumph of God's Kingdom, he saw history coming full cycle, with Christ repairing the damage Adam once had done. So our last readings in the Bible story bring us back to the first.

The final passage (Rev. 21:1–4, 22–27; 22:1–5) is the most brilliant and rhapsodic of all pictures of the coming Kingdom. It is full of reminiscences of older prophecies, as one can see by comparing 21:4 with Isaiah 25:8, or 21:23 with Isaiah 60:19f (or 21:1 with Isa. 65:17). In 22:1–2 the writer of Revelation, like Paul, takes his readers back to the beginning of the Bible story and re-uses the images he finds there. Once again we find ourselves in the Garden of Eden, with its river (Gen. 2:10; cf. Ezek. 47:1 and Zech. 14:8) and the tree of life (Gen. 2:9; Ezek. 47:12). Poetically speaking, history began in the garden and there it will end. Once, by sin, man cut himself off from the garden and the tree (Gen. 3:24), but in the end God will bring him back to his proper home and he will find the tree of life freely offered for his use (Rev. 22:2). The leaves on the tree will be for healing the disorders of the scattered peoples of the earth, and God's servants will reign as kings (v. 5).

PART TWO: *DOCTRINE*

I. GOD THE CREATOR

Genesis 1:1–2:3; Psalm 104:1–9; Proverbs 8:22–34;
John 1:1–14

The Bible opens with a lengthy statement of the doctrine of creation. Like most doctrines in the Bible it is set forth in the vivid, dramatic language of poetry rather than in the cold, abstract language of philosophy.

The first chapter of Genesis is certainly not to be taken as a scientific description of the origin of the universe. It is merely the Hebrew version of a widespread myth of creation, but differs from pagan versions of the myth in at least two particulars. The first is that only one God is involved instead of many. Whereas the pagan stories leave one with a sense of disgust at the puerile behavior of many gods, this one conveys a feeling of awe at the lonely majesty of God, the sole Creator.

The other great difference lies in the thought of purpose and plan which runs through the Bible story. Creation was not the result of a momentary whim, but is the gradual unfolding of a plan which leads steadily to a final goal. Or, in more modern terms, the world is not the result of chance, not a shapeless confusion resulting from the accidental interaction of physical forces, but the beautiful and orderly expression of a single Divine Mind. "It is very good" (1:31).

One needs to emphasize again that this profound doctrine is expressed in poetic language. The Hebrews themselves could tell the story of creation in quite different language from that of Genesis. The opening verses of Psalm 104, for example, tell the tale in a much more obviously mythological form. Here God is pictured as an architect or engineer, building foundations, setting beams and covering all with the curtain of the sky. He is also a giant, shouting at the enemies, symbolized by the waters of the sea, who threaten to undo His work. Although the imagery of the myth is different, the doctrine it teaches is the same: the whole creation is the product of a single God whose power, intelligence and purpose underlie it all.

The idea of purposefulness runs even more clearly through the fine poetry of Prov. 8:22–34. The speaker in this passage is "Wisdom," a personification of the concept of order and purpose. The Hebrews of the late period in which this poem was written had come to feel that there is a rational order running through the world, a set of observable principles by which one must live if he would be a successful and happy person. One who lived this way they called a "wise" man; the body of principles they called "Wisdom." The point the poet is making is that the principles are not something which man has invented for himself, but are simply an expression of the divine order of creation which existed from the beginning. The truly wise man, therefore, is one who perceives the meaning and purpose which run through the universe and orders his life accordingly (v. 34).

The last selection, the familiar prologue to St. John's Gospel (1:1–14), brings the Old Testament doctrine of creation into direct relationship with the life and work of Jesus Christ. In the first chapter of Genesis we read that God created all things by means of His Word. ("And God *said* . . ." vv. 3, 6, 9, etc.). The author of the Fourth Gospel wants us to understand that the creative power by which God created the universe has now appeared upon earth in the person of our Lord. He was and is the divine Word which the Creator spoke.

But the chapter in John also reflects the thought of Proverbs 8, as a comparison of the language makes quite clear. The "Word" of God in John is the same as the "Wisdom" of God in Proverbs. The chief difference is that the former expression suggests the Creator's power to command whereas the latter suggests rather His plan and purpose. The author of John wishes to say that God's plan in creation is no longer hidden, but is evident in Christ. To know the mind of Christ is to know the mind of the Creator. "The Word was made flesh and dwelt among us" (v. 14). (Some readers may wish to look up other references to this set of ideas: I Cor. 1:24; 8:6; Col. 1:15–17; Heb. 1:1–3.)

The doctrine of creation was perhaps not a part of Old Testament religious faith in its earliest form. In early times the Hebrews were more concerned with God's work in history than with His work in creation. But with the passage of time and the growth of reflective thinking, it became clear that the doctrine of creation is the most basic doctrine of all. The God whom Israel had come to know in her historical experience *must be* the same God from whom the physical universe took its origin. So, in the Bible, as in the later creeds of the Church, this doctrine stands first of all, the foundation stone upon which all the rest are built.

Our understanding of the manner in which the world was created has changed greatly since the days of the ancient Hebrews, but our doctrine of creation is identical with theirs. Although we think of creation as taking place by a gradual evolutionary process occupying inconceivably long periods of geological and cosmological time rather than by a series of abrupt beginnings occurring within a single week, Christians continue to affirm the essential faith: that God stands at the beginning of the process and the whole is the unfolding of His plan.

This is not only the starting point for Christian thinking, but also a basic axiom for Christian living. We shall return to this later, but even now we can perceive the far-reaching practical importance of the belief that it was not Chance, but God, who created heaven and earth—and ourselves.

II. GOD THE ALL-POWERFUL

Exodus 19:10–18; Isaiah 40:21–31; 43:11; Psalm 115;
Mark 7:31–37; Hebrews 12:18–29

Long before the people of the Old Testament had developed a fully articulated doctrine of creation such as we find in Genesis 1 they had ample experience of the overwhelming power of the God whom they served. Indeed one of the commonest Hebrew words for God (*El*) seems to be derived from a verb which means simply "to be powerful." From the beginning of her religious history this thought of tremendous, terrifying power was a central element in Israel's consciousness of God.

This is very clear in the story of God's revelation of Himself to Moses when the Covenant of Law was established at Sinai (Exod. 19:10–18). As with so many of these Old Testament stories, one must of course understand that the passage is less a literal description of an historical event than a record of the profound impression which the event made upon those who experienced it. The deliverance from Egypt, and the covenant which followed it, were the two basic experiences upon which Israel's faith was built. Through both of them the nation had come to know a God whose power was infinitely greater than the insipid gods of the heathen and utterly beyond the comprehension of feeble man. Many stirring passages of the Old Testament bear witness to the continuing centrality of this sense of the power of God. In the theological language of later time one might speak of it as a "doctrine of divine *omnipotence*," but (perhaps fortunately) the men of the Bible had no such abstract terms to use. They used, instead, vivid concrete language drawn from the violent forces of nature. In the present passage the sense of God's power is expressed in terms taken from two of the most awe-inspiring phenomena of the physical world—a thunderstorm (v. 16) and a volcanic eruption (18). Although the poetry comes from a different thought-world than our own, it still has the capacity to arouse in men's minds a profound feeling for the majesty of the power of God.

In much later times the same thought would be expressed in less violent, though no less effective, terms. The Second Isaiah, who is often called the theologian of the Old Testament, was the first to give unambiguous expression to the thought of the absolute uniqueness—in being and power—of the God of Israel (see, for example, Isa. 43:11). It seemed clear to the prophet, surveying the long history of his people, that the God who had known, judged and saved them must be the only God who exists at all, the creator of all things and the sovereign possessor of all the powers of the universe. God reigns, he says, in tranquil majesty over His creation, fashioning and directing it (Isa. 40:21–31). Kings have no power except what God gives them (vv. 23–24). The stars, which the Babylonians thought to be gods themselves, are only servants of God, created to do His will (26). From this passage we get the impression that God's power is not primarily destructive, but creative and beneficent. Most encouraging of all, God gives His power to those who love and fear Him (27–31). Weak, helpless man is not so helpless after all. Those who "wait upon the Lord shall renew their strength . . . they shall run and not be weary, and they shall walk and not faint."

One of the hymns of ancient Israel (Ps. 115) expresses in the language of popular devotion this thought of the unique and absolute power of God, and the consequent sense of dependence and gratitude which should fill the hearts of His worshipers. Incidentally, the psalm comes as close as the Old Testament ever does to putting the doctrine of God's omnipotence in terms of a simple formula: ". . . our God is in the heavens; he hath done whatsoever he hath pleased" (v. 3).

When we turn to the New Testament we find there was little need by that time to dwell on the thought of God's power, since this had already been so firmly established in the Old Testament as part of the basic faith of Israel. But it is important to notice that one of the things which most impressed the contemporaries of Jesus was that he himself was able to manifest this divine power among human beings as no other had ever done. His deeds of healing were particularly striking, and men must often have said, as it is reported in Mark 7:31–37: "He hath done all things well; he maketh both the deaf to hear and the dumb to speak."

We shall not understand either the Old or the New Testament unless we see first of all how the consciousness

of God's power permeates them both. Without this primary
sense of power, God's other qualities, His love and mercy
and even His righteousness, are likely to seem merely
forms of weakness. The God of Israel, who is also the God
of our Lord and Saviour Jesus Christ, is worthy of our
worship because in the first place, He is the sole creator of
all that is and the absolute possessor of all power, whether
in the world of nature or human society.

A rather curious passage in the Epistle to the Hebrews
(12:18–29) compares Israel's experience of God at Sinai
with the Christian's experience of God in Christ. We are
perhaps inclined to think that they are utterly different,
but the author of the epistle sees them as similar and
parallel. The passage is worth reading if only to correct
the sometimes too-sentimental view of our relationship to
Christ. As in Exodus, the emphasis here is on the reverence
and awe with which man must always approach the Omnipotent God—at Bethlehem and Golgotha as well as on
Sinai.

III. GOD THE ALL-KNOWING

Genesis 11:1–5; I Samuel 16:1–13; Psalm 139:1–6;
Matthew 6:1–18; John 2:23–25; I John 3:20

If God is all-powerful, He must be all-knowing too.
Throughout most of biblical history men understood that
this was so. But we must remember that the full implications of God's self-revelation came only gradually and

the Bible still contains traces of an older point of view. Primitive man thought of the gods as having much more knowledge than men, but not as knowing everything. There are some passages in the Old Testament, part of the Hebrew inheritance from earlier times, which reflect this more limited conception of God's knowledge.

The first of the passages to be examined here illustrates this early theology (Gen. 11:1–5). The story is that of the building of the Tower of Babel. The people of Babylon are represented as trying to obtain security for themselves by building a tower to reach the sky. The oldest version of the tale no doubt pictured an attempted assault upon the dwelling place of the gods. In the Hebrew version, however, the purpose of the tower is never made clear and the story is told merely to illustrate the absurd presumption of a fallen race. It is taken for granted that there is only one God, but we cannot help noticing that God has to "come down" (v. 5) to discover what was going on. It is doubtful that the Hebrews in historic times ever thought of God as really having to acquire knowledge in this way. Such stories were told simply because they were old and picturesque and could be used to exemplify great truths, but the conception of God which they contain had long been outgrown.

The men of the Old Testament understood perfectly well that the omnipotent God who created heaven and earth also possessed all knowledge and did not need to be instructed by anybody. This is a frequent theme of the philosophical Wisdom Literature (Job, for example), but was also part of the theology of daily speech. One popular account of the manner in which God chose David to be king expresses the theme of divine omniscience in classic form (I Sam. 16:1–13). It was said that when the prophet Samuel came to visit the family of Jesse, believing that the future king of Israel would be found among them, he was first tempted to select Eliab because of his handsome appearance (v. 6). But it was revealed to him that the man whom Yahweh had chosen was the youngest and apparently least important member of the family. Samuel could judge men only by their superficial qualities, but ". . . the Lord seeth not as man seeth; for man looketh on the outward appearance, but the Lord looketh upon the heart" (7).

This was the aspect of God's omniscience which seemed most important to men of the Bible. It seemed wonderful that the Lord knows all the secrets of the universe; but it was even more wonderful that He could look into the human heart and know all man's hidden thoughts and impulses. This profound and sobering thought has never been put into finer words than those of the very late Psalm 139 (vv. 1–6): "Thou knowest my downsitting and mine uprising, thou understandest my thought afar off" (2). If we contrast the sublimity of these verses with the crudity of the idea of God in the Babel story, we shall have some real conception of the gradual refinement of the theology of Israel which took place during her long history.

The New Testament view of God is, of course, precisely the same. In the Sermon on the Mount the theme of God's secret and all-encompassing knowledge occurs repeatedly in our Lord's discussion of almsgiving, prayer and fasting (Matt. 6:1–18). The test of value to be applied in each case is not the opinion of men, whose imperfect understanding is based only on what they see, but the judgment of the heavenly "Father, which seeth in secret" (vv. 4, 6, 18). It is as imperative for men to be reminded of this principle today as it was for the contemporaries of Jesus. The thought of God's omniscience is not an academic theological principle, but a doctrine which has the deepest significance for man's moral and devotional life.

In the tradition represented by the Gospel of John, Jesus himself is represented, even in his life on earth, as sharing the unclouded vision of the Father: ". . . he knew all men, and needed not that any should testify of man: for he knew what was in man" (John 2:23–25). The Synoptic Gospels do not lay so much stress upon this, but we can hardly doubt that theologically the Fourth Gospel is right. The eternal Son of God who lives in us and we in him certainly knows the secrets of our hearts. To realize this, even momentarily, is to experience some of the purifying power of His presence. It is the best of antidotes for the poison of hypocrisy and pretense and the best cure for the anxiety and frustration to which they give rise.

At first glance, the thought of divine omniscience might seem merely terrifying. One whose mind is full of dark, uninhibited passions (and to a greater or less extent this means all of us) may find it intolerable that there is no corner of his being so remote as to be hidden from God's knowledge. Judgment for him will be an ever-present reality. But the Bible shows us the other side of the picture also. God is not only our judge. The All-knowing is All-loving too. He understands us better than our neighbors do and better than we understand ourselves. "If our heart condemn us, God is greater than our heart and knoweth all things" (I John 3:20).

IV. GOD THE INESCAPABLE

Jonah 1; Psalm 139:7-12; Jeremiah 23:23-24; Acts 17:22-28;
Matthew 18:20; Ephesians 1:15-23

It took men longer to realize that God is everywhere present than it did to understand that He is all-powerful and all-knowing. The psychological explanation of this is easy, for God's power and knowledge can be conceived in terms of human qualities raised to an infinite degree of magnitude; but there is no human analogy to the universal presence of God. Men, however powerful and wise they may be, are always limited to certain places and it is hard to think of God as not limited in the same way.

This was true even in ancient Israel. Since Yahweh had revealed Himself to the ancestors in particular places, what could be more natural than to suppose that these were the places in which He actually dwelt—Sinai, the Temple, or at best the land of Israel? It was not until a late period in the nation's history that even its great leaders became completely adjusted to the view that God—in His nature, as distinguished from the mere manifestation of Himself to men—must necessarily be equally present everywhere.

The Book of Jonah is the greatest milestone in the progress of Israel's thinking along this line. It is unfortunate that the book is still widely misunderstood so that ordinary discussion of it is usually confined to arguments about the physiological structure of whales. One must realize at the outset that the book is fiction of a common oriental type and is meant to be read as a parable, not as history. The wonders which it relates were introduced in order to make the story more interesting and memorable so that the reader would not easily forget the great truths about God's universal love and universal presence which it was designed to teach.

The first chapter tells of a man's failure to escape from God. Jonah is represented as being a rather stupid person who still held to the old view that the presence of God is confined to the soil of Palestine. When given a distasteful job to do, he tried to avoid it by fleeing on a ship to Tarshish at the far end of the Mediterranean, but to his dismay he discovered that God is just as truly present and just as powerful on the great sea as in the land of Israel. We are intended to see him as a foolish and laughable figure, whose God was too small to fit the realities of life. The unidentified author of the book must have known many whose doctrine of God was as inadequate as Jonah's and he wants us to feel how ridiculous this is.

The 139th Psalm, which contains in its opening verses so beautiful an expression of God's omniscience, goes on to picture in even more sublime language the thought of His divine omnipresence (vv. 7–12): "If I take the wings of the morning and dwell in the uttermost parts of the sea; even there shall thy hand lead me, and thy right hand shall hold me." It is worth noting again that the doctrines of the Bible are rarely expressed in doctrinal terms. In the Book of Jonah the vehicle of the doctrine is a parable; in the psalm it is a prayer. The psalmist is not interested in expressing an abstract idea in abstract language; the doctrine emerges almost unconsciously in the course of his devotions as a product of his life with God.

The third Old Testament passage to be considered

(Jer. 23:23f) is more doctrinal in form than the others, but even here the context is a practical one—a denunciation of false prophets—and the words are placed in the mouth of God Himself: "Can any hide himself in secret places that I shall not see him? saith the Lord. Do not I fill heaven and earth?" Although Jeremiah lived a century or so before the author of Jonah or Psalm 139, he had already arrived at a fully matured conception of the omnipresence of God.

By New Testament times the best even of pagan thinkers had come to think of God in the same terms, so when St. Paul came to speak before the philosophers of Athens he felt he could appeal to them, in this matter at least, on the basis of a common faith (Acts 17:22–28). Like the men of the Old Testament they had come to see that God cannot "be far from every one of us" and that "in him we live, and move, and have our being" (vv. 27f).

What is new in the New Testament, with respect to this doctrine, is the application of it to the person of Christ. What the Old Testament says of God the Father, the New Testament says of the Son also. We find it already clearly stated in the Synoptic Gospels. A familiar verse in Matthew (18:20) says that wherever the disciples of Christ are found, Christ himself will be "in the midst of them." By this time the reader will probably have noticed that when the Bible speaks of God's omnipresence it is almost always in terms of His relation to *persons*. The Bible writers were not concerned so much to assert that God is present in the farthest star or in every part of inanimate nature (although common sense tells us this must be true) as to show that He is always near to men that seek Him. The universal presence of Christ can be a meaningful reality only for those who love and obey him and who gather together "in his name."

The final passage (Eph. 1:15–23) is an exhortation to

enlarge our conception of the greatness and glory of Christ. In the Old Testament we learn of the inescapability of God; from the New Testament we must learn also of the inescapability of the cosmic Christ, whose Church is "the fulness of *him that filleth all in all.*"

V. GOD THE RIGHTEOUS JUDGE

Genesis 18:23–33; II Samuel 12:1–10; Isaiah 5:1–7; Matthew 23:23–28; Romans 2:1–11

In our study of the biblical doctrine of God we have as yet learned nothing of His moral character. Conceivably God might be all-powerful, all-knowing and everywhere present and yet neither good nor loving. Pagans have sometimes believed in gods like this. But the Bible leaves us in no doubt as to the morality of deity, for it is far more concerned with God's moral character than with what theologians call His "metaphysical" attributes.

The first of the moral attributes of God to be distinctively emphasized in Israel was His righteousness. God, as He is revealed in the Bible, can always be depended upon to do what is right. He does not act capriciously, doing one thing today and another tomorrow, nor does He apply different standards to different people. It is, of course, not possible always to understand why God behaves as He does, because, from our finite, mortal point of view, we have so few of the facts at our command, but we may be sure that what God does is always right and fair.

To put it another way, God will be *at least* as just as human beings would be in the same situation.

Our first reading (Gen. 18:23–33) makes exactly this point. The passage is not history, but a dramatic philosophical dialogue in which Abraham and God are represented as discussing the justice of God's intentions toward the city of Sodom. Should all the people of Sodom be destroyed because some—or even most—of them are guilty? The ancient author of the tale obviously believes it would be wrong. This is implicit in Abraham's argument: the enlightened human conscience does not approve of indiscriminate punishment and God cannot be less just than man. "Shall not the judge of all the earth do right?" (v. 25). The story intends to answer this question with an emphatic affirmative: the justice and righteousness of God are as certain as His knowledge and His power. As the psalmist puts it so impressively: "Thy righteousness standeth like the strong mountains; thy judgments are like the great deep" (Ps. 36:6).

Since God is righteous, He expects righteousness from His children. Because God is both all-knowing and all-just, no one can please Him who does not strive to be just and righteous himself. There are no short cuts to God's favor; over and over again the Bible—and especially the Old Testament—emphasizes that sacrifices, prayers and ritual acts have no value if they are not accompanied by righteousness of life. "What doth the Lord require of thee, but to do justly, and to love mercy, and to walk humbly with thy God" (Mic. 6:8)?

No one was exempt from this demand for justice, not even the king himself. II Sam. 12:1–10 tells the story of a courageous prophet who confronted the greatest of Israel's monarchs to denounce him for a cowardly crime and to tell him of God's anger and disgust.

This was also the typical message of the great "literary" prophets, as could be illustrated by innumerable passages. Just one (Isa. 5:1–7) will have to suffice. Here the prophet appears as a minstrel singing of the feelings of God toward His people, picturing Him as a farmer addressing his vineyard. The song starts softly, as if love were to be the theme; then suddenly, at the end of v. 2, the mood changes to satire. The farmer, says the prophet, looked for grapes and found only *wild* grapes. God "looked for justice, but behold oppression; for righteousness, but behold a cry." (7) The verse is far more effective in Hebrew than in English because it uses two striking puns, but even in English the point is unmistakable—Israel's divine Lover has become her righteous Judge.

It is sometimes thought that emphasis upon the justice and righteousness of God belongs exclusively to the Old Testament, but there are many passages in the New Testament which speak of it quite as forcibly. For example, the words of Matt. 23:23–28 are as uncompromising as anything in the prophets. We must be careful in reading them not to generalize too broadly about the Pharisees, for certainly many Pharisees were sensitive and upright people. But amongst them, as all too often among Christians of today, there were those who thought they could make of religion a cloak to cover their moral nakedness. Our Lord declares that though they may succeed in the sight of men, they cannot in the sight of God. God's righteousness is a fierce light which exposes man's secret sins; a fire which consumes hypocrisy.

In Romans 2:1–11, we find St. Paul, also, speaking of the righteousness of God, but in sober and measured terms quite unlike the emotional utterances of the prophets. The conviction that God is absolutely righteous was the first article of the Pauline creed, but also the source of Paul's greatest intellectual and spiritual problem. For God's perfect righteousness must require perfect righteousness from man; and how can man, with his corrupt and sinful nature, ever attain such righteousness? How can he ever hope to cross the gulf which separates him from the perfectly just and righteous God who is "of purer eyes than to behold evil" (Hab. 1:13). Later we shall consider Paul's answer to this question, for it is a problem which all thinking men must eventually face; for the moment it is enough that we thoroughly grasp the basic Pauline—and biblical —truth that God is perfect in His righteousness and demands that men be righteous also.

VI. THE GOD OF LOVE

Exodus 34:1–7; Jeremiah 31:1–9; Psalm 103; Luke 15:11–32; I John 4:7–12

God's righteousness and His love are not incompatible qualities. At different times men have tended to emphasize one of them to the exclusion of the other, but if we read the Bible carefully and as a whole we can see that God is always perfect in both His righteousness and His love. He is righteous precisely because He is a God of love; it is because He cares so much about men that He is concerned for justice and right dealing among them.

In much of the Old Testament the emphasis seems to be more on God's righteousness than upon His love, because this was the lesson the people of Israel needed most to learn. Throughout much of their history they were *too* sure of God's love and were inclined to misinterpret it in two directions. On the one hand they were inclined to think that God loved them alone among all the nations of the earth, and, on the other, to think of Him as a kind of unmoral, indulgent father who was indifferent to their conduct so long as they continued to honor Him with sacrifices and prayers. It was the special task of the prophets to disabuse them on both counts. The great prophets taught that God loved other nations just as He did Israel (e.g., Amos 9:7) and also, as we saw in our last set of readings, that one cannot please God by any expression of pretended religious feeling which is not accompanied by righteousness of life.

All the time Israel and her great prophetic teachers knew that God, above all else, is a God of love. The most frequent statement made about God in the Old Testament is the one we find embedded in the account of Yahweh's revelation to Moses upon Mt. Sinai (Exod. 34:1–7). God is "merciful and gracious, long-suffering, and abundant in goodness and truth, keeping mercy for thousands, forgiving iniquity and transgression and sin . . ." (vv. 6–7). While we cannot be sure in what particular age this formula arose, it is significant that the historians of Israel felt it to be so important that they associated its proclamation with the fundamental revelation upon which the very existence of Israel as a nation depended. In later literature it is quoted again and again (e.g., Neh. 9:17; Ps. 86:15; Jonah 4:2). The full sense of it is brought out even more clearly in the Revised Standard Version, in which the word translated above as "mercy" is rendered more accurately as "steadfast love." The modern reader will perhaps be offended by the words which follow and which speak of God punishing the guilty for several generations. Since we have no space here to explain the full meaning of this expression, the reader should either turn to a commentary for a fuller account or at least accept the assurance that it does not contradict the first part of the formula. It is intended to prevent those who recited it from supposing that God's love meant that He was indifferent to wrong-doing.

As we have previously seen, Hosea was the special prophet of God's love in ancient Israel. While in some ways Hosea was even more severe in his pronouncements of judgment than other prophets of his time, he was the first to speak habitually of God as Israel's Father and Husband, whose love had been violated by her unfaithfulness and who longed for her to return to Him in penitence. Once Hosea had introduced this kind of language, it became natural for others to use it, as we see in the passage, Jeremiah 31:1–9, which promises the restoration of Israel after the Exile. Notice especially v. 3 (which has sometimes been called the motto of the whole Bible story), and the concluding words of v. 9.

The most extended and impressive account of God's love in the Old Testament is that of the 103rd Psalm, a hymn composed in late times when men could look back upon the long history of the nation and see that, however hard the road may have been, it was God's love which had guided them all the way. In v. 8 the formula of Exodus 34:6f is quoted once again, but the author no longer feels the need to repeat the concluding words about the punishment of the guilty. He is content to say, "As a father pities his children, so the Lord pities those who fear him" (v. 13).

From these words we turn naturally to our Lord's parable of the Prodigal Son (Luke 15:11–32), where the meaning of God's Fatherhood is displayed more clearly than anywhere else in Scripture. The central figure of the story is, of course, not the prodigal, but the father who stands in the door of his home waiting in love for his foolish and errant son to return. In a sense this parable summarizes in brief the entire drama of the Bible: mankind is the prodigal son and God has always been waiting for the race to "come to itself" (v. 17) and find its way home.

Our final passage is the familiar one from I John (4:7-12) which states simply that God *is* love. This means that if we could attribute only one quality to God, it would have to be this. But the author goes on to say that God can be truly known only by men in whom the same quality predominates. God cannot be known by the mind alone; only those can know Him who in some profound respect are like Him. As God's righteousness demands righteousness in men, so His love requires that men be loving also. "Everyone that loveth is born of God and knoweth God" (v. 7).

VII. GOD AS OUR HELP

Genesis 24:1–27; Psalm 46; Isaiah 41:10–17; Matthew 6:25–33; Romans 8:31–39

Because God is a God of righteousness and love, He offers help to the righteous man who needs it. The whole Bible is filled with the conviction that men never ask for such help in vain. The God of whom the Bible speaks is not a distant sovereign, indifferent to the needs of His creatures, nor the impersonal Absolute of some philosophers, unable to sympathize with the needs of men and incapable of responding to their pleas for support. He is a Father to His creation, so intimately concerned with what happens on earth that He has numbered the hairs of our head and notes the fall of the sparrow (Matt. 10:29f).

In every period of biblical history, men were confident that one could turn to God for help and find it. The first reading suggested above, Genesis 24:1–27, takes us back to the early days of Hebrew religious experience. It tells how the patriarch Abraham sought a wife for his son Isaac. Abraham had long lived in the land of Canaan, but wished his son to marry a woman from his former home in distant Mesopotamia and so sent a trusted servant to find a suitable person for the purpose. The story describes the journey of the servant and how at length he found her; but for the modern reader, the most striking aspect of the passage is not the bare bones of the tale, but the sense of the reality of God's providence which pervades it. Abraham is sure that God will prosper the journey, for He had always guided and helped him in the past (v. 7); when the servant comes to the well, he turns to the God of Abraham for help (12); and finally, when he has accomplished his mission, he gives thanks for God's providential guidance (27). Whether these incidents ever occurred or not is relatively insignificant. What is important is that Israel believed in this kind of God; in the ancient times when the story was first told, men knew that God could be depended on whenever help was needed in any form.

The next passage, Psalm 46, puts this belief into the form of a hymn, "God is our hope and strength, a very present help in trouble"—a psalm which, incidentally, provided the inspiration for Luther's great hymn, "A Mighty Fortress Is Our God." The psalm pictures the final catastrophe which would come at the end of the world. Even among falling mountains and raging waters (vv. 2, 3), God's people will dwell secure in a city through whose midst the river of God flows in majesty and peace (4, 5; cf. Isa. 33:21). God can be depended on to frustrate their enemies (6) and bring wars to an end (8, 9). So, both collectively and individually, the people of Israel could always look to God for assistance, for "The Lord of Hosts is with us, the God of Jacob is our refuge" (7, 11).

The practical importance of the doctrine of God's providential care is brought out in the passage from II Isaiah (41:10–17). Israel was in exile in Babylon and many had lost heart, feeling that God had deserted His people. The prophet repeatedly protests that this cannot be true, for the God whom they and their fathers served is the only God, all-powerful and all-loving, who by His actions in time past has showed that He cares for them. What had been true in the past was still true; those who put their trust in Him would find an adequate supply of strength to carry them through their difficulties, even the apparent hopelessness of their life as exiles in a foreign land. The prophet's intense personal conviction gives to his words of encouragement an eloquence which is rarely equalled in the Bible, or elsewhere. The present passage (like 40:28–31, which we have previously studied) is typical of his message and style. The popular hymn "How Firm a Foundation" is a paraphrase of certain parts of it.

Beautiful as are these Old Testament expressions of trust in God's capacity and willingness to help, none of them are quite as impressive as the words of Jesus in the Sermon on the Mount (Matt. 6:25–33), where he draws the lesson that worry about material things has no place in the life of a Christian, since God knows men's physical needs (v. 32). But our Lord also adds to this thought a necessary warning: we cannot expect God's help unless we have really made "his kingdom and his righteousness" the chief aim of our lives (33). This point needs to be specially noticed in our own day, when some people and even some popular preachers seem to think that God is merely a convenient resource for achieving peace, prosperity and worldly success. God's help, we may be sure, never fails, but it is given in His way and on His conditions. We cannot *use* God; we can only permit Him to use us.

It is the thought of God's help and care for His people which inspired St. Paul, also, to bring the first part of his epistle to the Romans to such a rousing conclusion (Rom. 8:31–39). "If God be for us," he says, "who can be against us?" In his long and adventurous career, filled with sickness, danger and conflict, Paul had had sufficient opportunity to find the answer to this question. He knew that in all his trouble God had never failed him and that all men could become "more than conquerors through him that loved us."

VIII. MAN AS GOD'S CREATURE

Psalms 8; 139:13–16; 104:27–30; Jeremiah 18:1–6; Romans 9:20–21; Matthew 20:1–15

From the biblical doctrine of God we now turn our attention to the doctrine of man. The first great truth the Bible teaches is that man is a creature; he is not a self-made, autonomous being, but the creation of an all-powerful, all-loving and all-righteous God. This is the most basic fact about him and the wise man is the one who fully understands it and orders his life accordingly; sin and folly have their origin at the point where man denies his creaturehood and attempts to live as though it were not so.

We have already examined the two important passages which tell, in different ways, the story of man's creation (Gen. 1 and 2). The first of them speaks of man as having been made "in the image of God" (Gen. 1:26–27), which, whatever else it means, implies that at least man is like God in having a mind and a capacity for living by plan and purpose. Genesis also makes the point that men share with God the privilege of "dominion" over His creation (Gen. 1:28).

It is this thought which provides the theme for Psalm 8. The poet has been looking at the sky, in the clear splendor of an oriental night, and is overwhelmed by the idea of man's insignificance in comparison with it (1, 3, 4). "What is man, that thou art mindful of him? and the son of man, that thou visitest him?" Many a thinking person of our own time has been disturbed by the same question: in view of the vast size of the physical universe, grown incomparably greater since the days of the psalmist, how can we believe that the life of the tiny, fragile creature we call man has any value or meaning whatever? The psalmist raises the question only to answer it with a positive affirmation. Despite appearances, he declares, man is the crown of all creation, only a little lower than God Himself (the Revised Standard Version is right in reading "God" instead of "angels" in v. 5). Man alone, of all the creatures, shares in God's "dominion" over the world, a fact that is being constantly demonstrated anew as men gain greater and greater control over their physical environment.

So the Bible doctrine of man begins with a declaration of the glory and dignity of human existence. This is an aspect of the true character of man which must never be forgotten. But, unfortunately, man is even more inclined to pride than to despair, and needs continually to be reminded that, if he is the most glorious of God's creatures, he is nevertheless still a creature. Man's wonderful powers were never intended for his own aggrandizement, but for proclaiming God's glory and advancing His kingdom. So men must constantly be recalled to a sense of their dependence upon God and their helplessness without Him.

The next two passages, from the Psalter also, are intended to reinforce this feeling. The first, Psalm 139:13–16, describes in a surprisingly modern way the formation of the human embryo. This is God's work also. God did not somehow create the first man and then let the further development of the race take care of itself. It is still God's creative power alone which makes possible the conception and birth of every individual human being. Furthermore, throughout his whole existence, man is dependent upon God for everything he needs and could not exist a single instant without Him. Like all the rest of creation, man must "wait upon" God that He may give him food in due season. Death and life are entirely in God's hands (Ps. 104:27–30; cf. Ps. 145:15f).

The most rigorously logical expression of this thought is found in two passages, one in the Old Testament and one in the New, the latter of which is obviously dependent on the former. Jeremiah, watching a potter one day, was reminded that God stands in much the same relation to His creation as a potter to the products of his craft (Jer. 18:1–6). After all, one story of creation suggests poetically that God made man much as a potter molds his pots (Gen. 2:7). Surely the potter has a right to do what he wishes with the thing that he has made; even more certainly God has sovereign and absolute rights over His creatures.

For Jeremiah this image had primary reference to God's dealings with Israel, but St. Paul took over the image and applied it to individuals (Rom. 9:20–21). The individual man has no right to *demand* anything from God, for he is merely a creature and God can do with him exactly as he chooses. Paul does not mean to suggest that God actually deals with men in this arbitrary way, but only that in strict logic He has the right to do it if He wills. It is a disturbing and even frightening thought, but at some point in the thinking of each of us it is important to recognize that it is true. God is the Creator and we are merely His creatures; until we have faced up to this fact and accepted all its corollaries, we cannot hope to understand the nature of our existence or see clearly the path which we must follow.

While our Lord does not use the image of the potter in his rather difficult parable of the workers in the vineyard (Matt. 20:1–15), the point he makes is the same— God's absolute sovereignty over His creatures (v. 15). It is characteristic of Jesus, though, that he places the emphasis upon God's unpredictable generosity rather than upon the mere inscrutability of His will.

IX. MAN AS A SINFUL CREATURE

Genesis 6:11–13, 18–22; 8:13–9:1; Jeremiah 17:5–9;
Job 4:17–21; Psalm 51:1–5, 10–11; Romans 7:14–25;
Luke 18:9–14

Although man is the creature of God, made in his image and intended for a glorious destiny, the Bible never lets us forget that he is a *wayward* creature—a sinner—who prefers to follow his own will rather than God's. His natural tendency is to do wrong rather than right. This is what the Church means by the doctrine of "original sin." The term itself does not occur in the Bible, but the idea certainly does. All through the Bible there runs the thought that there is something essentially wrong with man, some corruption of his nature which makes it easier for him to sin than to be what he ought to be. In the Bible, sin is not just an occasional, unfortunate transgression of the Divine Law, but a dead weight which must be lifted, an enemy which must be conquered, a disease which must be healed.

The classic expression of this doctrine is, of course, the account of the "fall" of man (Gen. 3), which we have already examined as a part of the Bible story. The tale of Noah and the Flood in Genesis 6–8 is yet another attempt to put the doctrine of the universality of sin in vivid, narrative form (Gen. 6:11–13, 18–22; 8:13–9:1). It is said that after man was expelled from the Garden of Eden and began to spread over the earth, his wickedness became so great that God determined to destroy him utterly. "The earth was corrupt . . . and filled with violence" (Gen. 6:11). Only one man, Noah, was saved from the catastrophe, but God recognized that even this drastic purge would not solve the problem, for it was still true after the flood, as before, that "the imagination of man's heart is evil from his youth" (8:21).

This story is no more to be taken as literal history than the story of the Fall. It is rather a dramatic expression of ancient Israel's conviction that God loathes the sin which is lodged in the heart of man, and longs to destroy it. The story contains primitive elements and represents God as acting in ways which later generations would find incredible, but it would be difficult to think of a more forceful way of expressing the three basic ideas it is intended to teach: (1) that sin is a universal fact of human nature, (2) that God hates sin with all His Being, and (3) that He nevertheless loves our sinful race and seeks to bless it (8:21–9:1).

The preaching of the prophets of later times is filled with denunciations of the sinfulness and incorrigibility of man. Innumerable examples could be found, but the prophet who came closest to formulating his pessimistic view of human nature in doctrinal rather than merely hortatory terms was Jeremiah (17:5–9), who first of all warns his disciples against putting any trust in human nature (v. 5) and then states the principle that "the heart [of man] is deceitful above all things, and desperately wicked" (9). By the "heart" he does not mean merely our obviously fickle emotions, but the very deepest springs of our being. Jeremiah is no more a total pessimist than any other of the biblical writers, but he is sure that human nature can never be trusted to do what is right apart from the transforming grace of God.

The author of the Book of Job puts a similar thought on the lips of one of his characters (4:17–21, RSV is best). In God's eyes all men are sinners and untrustworthy. Viewed objectively, man is a pretty contemptible thing: small, insignificant, transitory and evil. This is, of course, not the whole story, but it is an important part of it, and one cannot expect to have a full understanding of the nature and destiny of man unless he sees that this proposition, as far as it goes, is essentially true.

Psalm 51 is the finest *devotional* expression of the doctrine of man's universal sinfulness (vv. 1–5, 10–11). The author of it is not so much concerned with particular sins he may have committed as with the sinfulness of his heart, and with his need for a new one which only God can create (v. 10). The familiar words of v. 5 are not to be understood as an indictment of the psalmist's mother. They merely express, in exaggerated language, his conviction that he had always been a sinner, even from the moment of his conception. Only God's Holy Spirit (11) can save him from himself.

Turning to the New Testament, we see in the epistle to the Romans how deeply Paul felt the sinfulness of his own nature. In chap. 7 (especially vv. 14–25) Paul shows that the doctrine of original sin was not an abstraction for him, but a reality by which he was constantly haunted. Much as he desired with his mind to do what is right, his unruly nature always drove him to do what is wrong. The kind of discouraging moral experience which Paul describes here so vividly has its counterpart in the life of every thoughtful Christian.

Finally we see how our Lord enforces the same lesson in his own gentle way in the story of the Pharisee and the Publican (Luke 18:9–14). The man who goes "down to his house justified" is not the proud church member, confident of his own rectitude, but the contemptible tax gatherer who at least knows that he is a sinner. For the Bible, our approach to God must always begin with an acknowledgement of both our creaturehood and our sinfulness, with the recognition that "there is no health in us" and that only God can restore the health which should be ours.

X. THE UNITY OF MAN'S NATURE

Genesis 2:7; Deuteronomy 28:1–6; Song of Solomon 2:8–13; Amos 9:13–15; Luke 7:33–34; 5:33; John 2:1–11; Romans 12:1; I Corinthians 6:19–20

The Bible regards man as a unity of soul *and* body. He is not, as some of the Greek philosophers taught, a soul somehow unhappily imprisoned within a body which is really no proper part of him. This latter view, found in certain oriental religions and some types of Puritanism, gives rise to an unhealthy kind of asceticism which seeks to degrade and even destroy the body so as to free the soul entirely from association with it. But whenever the Bible has been allowed to speak clearly, it has always been heard to reaffirm the dignity of the body and the physical world of which the body is a part. Man is not an immaterial soul burdened and trammeled by a material body, but a unified being composed of two inseparable parts created to live harmoniously together.

Since the Bible is not a philosophical treatise it never formulates this view in precisely chosen words. The nearest it ever comes to stating categorically that man is a psycho-physical unity is in the story of creation, Genesis 2:7, where we read that "the Lord God formed man of the dust of the ground and breathed into his nostrils the breath of life, and man became a living soul" (or, as the RSV more correctly says, "a living being"). The bare, disembodied "breath" was not the man. Man came into being only when the immaterial breath was united with the material body.

This is the assumption which underlies the whole biblical view of man and is implied in many passages which ostensibly deal with quite different matters. Everyone who reads the Old Testament is aware of the uninhibited way in which the Hebrews describe the rewards of righteousness in terms of physical blessings and the satisfaction of bodily needs. Deuteronomy 28 is a classical example, vv. 1–6 summarizing the thought of the whole chapter. Here it is promised that those who obey the Lord's commands will have many children, rich harvests and fruitful cattle, with no lack of good things to eat (4, 5). For the Hebrew, the productivity of the physical world and the adequate satisfaction of the body's healthy needs were a kind of sacramental token of God's favor. The Hebrews were not crude materialists, but men who saw in nature's harmonious care for their physical needs a symbol of the inner harmony of their bodies and souls with the will of their Creator.

In the little book called the Song of Solomon there is an appreciation of the physical world and the pleasures of the body which rises at times to high poetry, as in 2:8–13, a passage which rapturously celebrates the love of the sexes, the beauty of spring and flowers, the singing of birds, and the smell of new blossoms in the orchard. The language of this book is not typical of the Bible, but it is significant that it is found there at all.

Likewise, in their view of the future, men of the Old Testament could not conceive of a paradise either in heaven or on earth in which the body would not have its part. Some verses added by a late writer to the Book of Amos (9:13–15) describe the miraculous fertility of the land in days to come when "the mountains shall drop sweet wine" and God's people will have an abundance of food and drink. When the Hebrews came later to think of a future life, it had to be in terms of a resurrection of the *body* (see Isa. 26:19).

If in the Old Testament the emphasis perhaps is laid too exclusively on the body and its satisfactions, the balance is corrected in the New Testament in favor of the soul and its profounder needs, but this is merely a correction of stress, not a reversal in the point of view. Although the New Testament shows a deeper concern for the spirit of man, there is no rejection of the body or denial of its legitimate place in the totality of man's being. In the time of Jesus Judaism had already become partly infected by an unhealthy oriental asceticism, but Jesus would have none of it. He did not engage in extreme ascetic practices like John the Baptist and was accused of being a wine-bibber and a glutton (Luke 7:33f); his disciples evidently followed his example (Luke 5:33).

The story of the changing of the water into wine at the wedding feast in Cana (John 2:1–11), whether strictly historical or not, bears striking testimony to Jesus' reputation for being at home among the normal, healthy pleasures of his countrymen.

One must not, of course, go to the extreme of exalting the body above the spirit or of supposing that the Bible allows men to indulge their physical appetites without restraint. In the harmony of soul and body which is the nature of the ideal man, the soul must always be the ruling principle and there will always be need for *some* kind of asceticism (which means "exercise") to keep the body in its proper place.

The point is simply that the body must never be regarded as evil or unclean and the physical world treated as beneath contempt. The whole world is God's creation and is good (Gen. 1:31; Rom. 14:20); the body is an integral part of man and must be treated with respect. It has its important part to play in worship—eyes, tongue and posture. We receive God's grace through elements which normally minister only to the body's needs—water, bread and wine. The truly Christian attitude is not to despise the body, but to present it to God along with the soul as a "reasonable sacrifice" (Rom. 12:1); to treat it as a temple of the Holy Ghost and thus to glorify God with the *whole* of our being (I Cor. 6:19f).

XI. MAN'S CAPACITY FOR REDEMPTION

Psalm 146:1–4; Jeremiah 10:23; Romans 3:9–20;
Matthew 14:22–31; Psalm 146:5–10; Isaiah 61:1–3;
Luke 4:16–21

If man, though sinful, is the wonderful being the Bible describes, a marvelous harmony of soul and body, godlike in his abilities, created to walk in fellowship with his Maker, can he be allowed simply to persist in his tragic, fallen state? Is there not some way in which the tide of his affairs can be reversed, and the frustrations of his existence alleviated? In later Israel, whose outlook on the existing state of the world had become increasingly dark as a result of the disaster of the Babylonian Exile and the discouraging years which followed the Return, the question was raised chiefly in connection with the possibility of a material restoration of the nation. But the answer to the question was often given at a far deeper level than this (e.g., Jer. 31:31–34; Ezek. 11:17–20), and the frequency with which other nations were pictured as sharing in some way in Israel's restoration (e.g., Isa. 2:2–4; 25:6,7; Zech. 8:23; 14:16) shows that at least the greatest men of the Old Testament were aware the problem was not merely that of the redemption of Israel, but of the whole of mankind. Granted, however, that humanity stands in need of redemption, by what agency can it be accomplished?

The biblical answer has both a negative and a positive aspect. On the negative side, the men of Israel became increasingly certain that there was no help in man himself— that, as the Book of Common Prayer concisely states it, "we have no power of ourselves to help ourselves." Many passages express this thought, but we need note only a few typical examples. Psalm 146:1–4 puts it quite clearly, "put not your trust in princes, nor in any child of man; for there is no help in them (v. 3)." The voice is not that of some theoretical pessimist, but of a nation which had exhausted its human resources in the effort to find a satisfactory basis for living in a sinful world, and had finally been forced to the conclusion that human nature is too fragile and ephemeral to provide it (4).

A verse in Jeremiah (10:23) gives succinct expression to the same conviction: "It is not in man that walketh to direct his steps." Man's vision is too limited for him to make out the road by which he should travel.

It is in Paul, however, that this basic biblical certainty finds its classic expression, particularly in the great epistle to the Romans. In 3:9–20 Paul insists upon man's universal sinfulness and absolute helplessness. He begins by putting Jews and Gentiles upon the same plane; however different they may be in other respects, they are identical in their common sinful humanity (v. 9). He proves this by a series of quotations from the Old Testament (10–18) and then turns to consider the ordinary Jewish view that if a man by his own efforts could keep the Covenant of Law he would be saved. Paul declares this to be impossible; he says elsewhere that man is incapable of keeping the Law, but here asserts merely that the purpose of the Law was not to provide a means of salvation but to make men realize how sinful and helpless they are, "for by the law is the knowledge of sin" (20). So even the best and most well-intentioned of man's endeavors are unable to deliver him from the bondage of a sinful nature. If this seems like harsh doctrine, one can say only that the experience of every generation brings additional evidence that it is profoundly true.

The dramatic story of Peter's attempt to walk on the water (Matt. 14:22–31) may be taken as a parable of the human situation and a guide as to the source from which help must come. With the best of wills, Peter attempts to imitate Jesus in defying the storm and the waves, but his weak human nature is inadequate to the demands that he puts upon it and he soon finds himself beginning to sink. At this point, driven at last to realize his inadequacy, he calls for help and Jesus immediately puts out his hand and helps him.

This is exactly what St. Paul and the great men of the Old Testament were attempting to say. Although man cannot save himself, God is prepared to save him;

man's redemption has, indeed, always been a part of God's plan. If we turn back now to the 146th Psalm, we find the thought jubilantly expressed. No trust can be put in any "child of man," but "blessed is he that hath the God of Jacob for his help" (v. 5). The men of the Old Testament were confident that God was able and ready to help His people and would be their "King forevermore" (10).

The basic paradox of biblical faith could hardly be set forth more clearly than in this psalm—almost complete pessimism with regard to man, but unlimited optimism with respect to God. The Old Testament story is in many ways simply the account of Israel's increasing certainty about these two fundamental ideas. The later prophets and apocalyptic writers exhibit a growing disillusionment with the moral possibilities of human nature, but a rising tide of confidence in God's purpose to redeem mankind and establish His Kingdom.

We have already, in different contexts, read many passages in which the hope of redemption, running like a golden thread through the later parts of the Old Testament, is the principal theme. Just one more, from a postexilic section included in the Book of Isaiah, will be sufficient for another illustration—Isaiah 61:1-3. Undoubtedly the thought of Israel's deliverance from political oppression is in the forefront of the author's mind, but greater thoughts are there also and he wrote more deeply than he knew. The peculiar poignance of this passage, apart from its intrinsic excellence as religious poetry, arises from the fact that it is reported to have provided the text of our Lord's first sermon, when He arose in the synagogue at Nazareth and proclaimed that God's redemption was no longer merely a future hope, but was within men's grasp as a present reality (Luke 4:16-21).

XII. MAN'S NEED OF A REDEEMER

Numbers 24:15–19; Psalm 2; Psalm 72; Isaiah 42:1–4;
Micah 5:2; Daniel 7:9–14; Matthew 2:1–11

It is natural that men should hope not only for redemption, but for a Redeemer. The word redemption suggests an impersonal process, but man is a person and his personality is the most important quality he possesses, the thing which makes him closer to God than any other creature. So it seems only fitting that deliverance should come to him through the activity of a person rather than through some abstract arrangement such as a new set of laws. The conviction that God would send such a personal Redeemer at the proper time was one of the foundation stones of the fully developed faith of ancient Israel; the declaration that He *has* sent him is the first principle of the distinctive theology of the New Israel.

It is not certain just when faith in a future Redeemer arose in Israel, although it can hardly have been before the time of the Hebrew monarchy, since the Redeemer was ordinarily pictured as a *king*. Many passages in the Old Testament which originally referred in somewhat fulsome terms to a reigning monarch were later reinterpreted to refer to the future King. It is hard in some cases to distinguish these passages from those which are genuinely "messianic," but the distinction is really unimportant, since all such scripture eventually became a vehicle for expressing Israel's God-given faith in the coming of a personal Deliverer.

One of the oldest passages of this kind is contained in the Book of Numbers, 24:15–19. Almost certainly this passage, which is placed on the lips of the heathen prophet Baalam in the days just before Israel's conquest of Canaan, was intended as a flattering reference to King David and was written by one of his court poets, but with the eclipse of the Davidic Empire and the degradation of his dynasty the words were hopefully transferred to that figure of the future who would one day arise as "a star out of Jacob" (v. 17) and deliver Israel from bondage. It is known that this passage sustained the Jews during some of the darkest days of their later history.

Israel's hymns, also, naturally gave expression to the messianic faith, though here again we meet with the phenomenon of songs originally composed to glorify a contemporary, secular ruler being adapted in later days to celebrate the power and dignity of the future Redeemer. Psalm 2, one of the most frequently quoted of the so-called messianic psalms, is a good example of the way in which older materials were re-used in this way. Composed to celebrate the coronation of a new ruler by the promise of victory over all who attempted to oppose him, it was later used, somewhat incongruously, to prophesy the purely spiritual victories of the Messiah (as in Acts 13:33).

A more attractive picture, both of the reigning monarch and the future Deliverer, is found in Psalm 72, where the function of a king is said to be that of establishing peace and prosperity for his people and of bringing justice to the oppressed. It is strange that this pleasing portrait is nowhere quoted in the New Testament as a prophecy of the Christ.

In our previous study we have already examined most

of the original specifically messianic passages of the Old Testament (such as Isa. 11 and 33:17ff). We need add to our list here only Micah 5:2, which declares that the Redeemer will, like David, come from Bethlehem and will be a member of the age-old Davidic family.

The image of the king, however, is not the only one under which men conceived the figure of the future Redeemer. Two others are especially important, since they show how varied the portrait might be. One is that of the *suffering servant,* an entirely non-royal figure who, as we have already seen, is found in certain passages of Second Isaiah, such as 42:1–4. Here the Deliverer—perhaps originally merely the nation of Israel—is represented as a gentle, kindly and courageous prophet. (Isa. 52:13–53:12 is, of course, the classic passage dealing with the Servant.)

The third image is that found in a mysterious chapter of the Book of Daniel (7:9–14) which tells how, in the latter days, God will judge the earth (v. 9f) and destroy the kingdom of evil (11f). At the end, it is said, there will come "one like the *Son of Man*" (meaning "one like a human being") who will establish an eternal and indestructible kingdom of righteousness (13f). Whatever the author of this difficult passage may have had in mind (and the reader must be referred to the commentaries for more detailed discussion), his later readers took it to be another portrait of the coming Redeemer. This interpretation forms the background for understanding the frequent references to the "Son of Man" in the New Testament (e.g. Mark 14:62).

Finally, in Matthew 2:1–11, we read a story which, in dramatic language, pictures men of various nations as eagerly awaiting the coming of a personal Redeemer. The Gentiles are represented as watching for his sign in the heavens; the Jews, as searching their sacred books. This is an accurate picture of a large part of the world in the days of Jesus, when multitudes of both Jews and Gentiles were searching anxiously for some kind of personal saviour and for a religion which promised redemption from the futility of ordinary human existence. Men are still, though often unconsciously, seeking a redeemer of this kind—one of their own flesh and blood who can give them God's peace and restore meaning and value to their apparently purposeless lives. The Bible tells us that such hope is not vain and foolish—that God has promised a Redeemer and that, indeed, he has already come.

XIII. JESUS THE FULFILLMENT OF MAN'S NEED

Isaiah 35:3–10; Matthew 11:2–6; John 4:25–29, 39–42; Matthew 26:63–68; Acts 18:5; John 20:30–31; Ephesians 2:11–22; I John 5:1–5

Central to the developed faith of the Old Testament is the assurance that a Redeemer would come and the Kingdom of God be established among men; central to the New Testament faith is the certainty that the Redeemer has *already* come and the Kingdom of God has begun to take visible shape in his person and his works. In dealing with this theme we shall naturally be concerned chiefly with passages from the New Testament rather than the Old, but it will be well to begin by looking at one Old Testament passage, both because it will remind us

of the intensity of Israel's hope and because there is a
reflection of this particular passage in the first of our readings from the New Testament.

This passage (Isa. 35:3–10), probably from Second
Isaiah, is especially attractive because it lays less stress
upon the triumph of Israel as a nation than upon God's
care for the sick and unfortunate. Although there is no
specific mention of the Messiah, the picture is, in the
broad sense of the term, a sketch of the glories of the
Messianic age, when order will be restored to a disordered
world and its present miseries finally abolished. There
will be courage for the faint-hearted, joy for the discon-
solate and healing for those who are sick in mind or body.

For those who knew Jesus in his earthly ministry such
things provided the chief evidence that he was indeed the
expected Redeemer. So we read in Matthew 11:2–6 that
when John the Baptist, who preached the nearness of the
Kingdom of God, was imprisoned for castigating the morals
of the royal household, he sent two of his followers to see if
Jesus was really the Messiah or only another preacher
like himself. The answer was given in terms of the Old
Testament passage we have just been reading. They could
see for themselves that Jesus' main concern was with the
weak and helpless and that he had power both to bring
healing to the sick and good cheer to the discouraged. The
extent of this power was the surest proof that he was in
fact the one "that should come."

The story of the long conversation Jesus is related to
have had with the Samaritan woman is intended to typify
the way in which the Redeemer was desired and accepted
even outside the borders of Judaism. The Samaritans, of
course, shared the Messianic faith of ancient Israel, but
they were not Jews and could represent, in the mind of
the evangelist, the larger, non-Jewish, world, which was

also in need of redemption. It, too, was awaiting the arrival of him "that should come." The emphasis in the story is not upon the mighty works of Jesus, but upon his insight into the human heart and his ability to satisfy the deepest needs of man's spirit (John 4:25–29). The more intimately men came to know him the more certain they were that he was indeed the Saviour of the world (39–42).

For the most part Jesus was content to let men draw their own conclusions with regard to his character and mission, but when he was brought before the high priest and challenged directly to state his claims he at last spoke so unambiguously that his condemnation and death came as an immediate consequence (Matt. 26:63–68). It seemed for a moment as though the forces of chaos and evil had defeated God's plan, but the events of Easter and Ascension Day showed that ultimate victory belonged to the Messiah and his Kingdom.

The Christian Church was built upon the simplest of creeds: Jesus of Nazareth is the Christ, the long-expected Redeemer of mankind. This was the chief burden of early Christian missionary preaching, as we see from such a passage as Acts 18:5; this is also the theme of our present written Gospels, as is evident from the original conclusion to the Gospel of John (20:30f).

The Church was not content however, to live with this bare statement of the essence of its faith. Christian thinkers soon began to meditate upon the significance of the great new truth in which they believed and to draw out its implications. Centuries later Christians would start dividing all time into two great periods, B.C. and A.D., illustrating their belief that the birth of Jesus was the chief turning point in the history of the world. In New Testament times they had not yet begun to do this, but already St. Paul saw in Christ's coming the climactic point

of the human drama—"the fulness of the time" (Gal. 4:4)
—and either he or one of his disciples pictured in rhapsodic language how the advent of Christ had restored the
broken unity of the human race (Eph. 2:11–22) and introduced a new element into man's understanding of
history and time. *"In time past"* (v. 11) the Gentiles had
lived without hope, aliens and strangers (12), but *"now"*
(vv. 13, 19) in Christ their alienation was ended; the wall
of partition was taken down and the way of peace and
free approach to God was open to everyone alike (17f).

There were others, like the author of I John 5:1–5,
who were concerned not so much with picturing the vast,
majestic sweep of history rising to its climax in the coming of Christ as with showing the effect of his coming on
individual human lives. To have faith in Christ, as the
Son of God, he says, makes men also sons of God (v. 1) and
this sonship comes to full expression in a life filled with
love toward men (2) and God (3) and in giving its possessor
a sense of personal participation in Christ's triumph over
the evils of the world (4, 5).

XIV. CHRIST OUR BROTHER

*Isaiah 32:1–8; 50:4–9; Mark 2:15–17, 23–27; 6:30–44;
14:32–42; Hebrews 2:11–18; 4:14–16*

The Redeemer whom the Bible offers us is not only
God of God, but man of man. We must begin with his
manhood if we are truly to understand his deity. In the

early ages of the Church there were several heresies which denied the truth of this paradox and rejected the idea of Christ's perfect manhood, making him either wholly divine or a kind of demigod, halfway between God and man. But the Church has always rejected such views whenever they have appeared and insists that Christ is as perfect in his humanity as in his divinity. He is not only our Lord and God; he is also our Brother.

It is not certain that the first passage selected for reading is (Isa. 32:1–8) Messianic in the strict and literal sense. But in the broad sense it undoubtedly is so, since it describes the rule of a future king under whose strong and righteous government the noblest qualities of human nature will have a chance to become evident. Men will be able to make clear and accurate judgments (vv. 3f); hypocrisy will no longer be able to deceive (5); the wicked man and the fool will appear as what they really are and the noble man will be recognized at his true worth; ". . . a man shall be as a hiding place from the wind, and a covert from the tempest, as rivers of water in a dry place, as the shadow of a great rock in a weary land" (2). This emphasis on the essential *man*liness of the future king and his kingdom provides an important counterbalance to some of the supernatural and even fantastic features attributed to them elsewhere.

The second Old Testament passage (Isa. 50:4–9) is another of the so-called "Servant songs" of II Isaiah. In contrast to the usual portrait of the Messiah, who in the Old Testament is a royal figure, the portrait of the Servant always emphasizes his common humanity, his sympathy with other men and the physical weakness which he shares with them. He comes, not to overwhelm men with his power, but to "speak a word in season to him that is weary" (v. 4). Like any other prophet, he must expect his message to be received with hatred and contempt (6), though he is always sustained by the confidence that God will help him (7–9). From our prevous study we know how important these Servant songs are for understanding the New Testament doctrine of Christ. The person of whom Pilate said, "Behold the man!" (John 19:5) is precisely this intensely human and appealing figure of the Servant of the Lord.

Jesus frequently shocked the staid church people of his time because he acted as though human need was more important than ecclesiastical regulations. This did not mean that he was indifferent to the Law, but only that he felt an even greater obligation to minister to the necessities of his sinful and suffering brother men. The two incidents recorded in Mark 2:15–17, 23–27 are excellent illustrations. In the first he disregards the law of ritual purity in order to associate with men who were in need of spiritual help; in the second he permits his disciples to violate the Sabbath in order to satisfy their hunger.

Innumerable other stories in the gospels testify to the humanity of Jesus, none perhaps more attractively than that of the feeding of the multitude (Mark 6:30–44). It opens by telling again of Jesus' care for his disciples' physical needs. As a man himself, he understood that men cannot work indefinitely without rest and food and so led them to a lonely place where they could find quiet and refreshment (vv. 30–32). When the crowd followed him even there, he was "moved with compassion toward them" also (34) and began to make plans to feed them. The most moving thing about the story is not the divine power which made the miracle possible, but the divinely human compassion which made it necessary. As Jesus moves among the crowd we see in him, of course, the divine Redeemer who satisfies men's needs; but we see in him, first of all, the perfect man who *understands* those needs.

The next to the last scene in the life of Jesus is the one which best reveals his profound identification with our humanity. In the garden of Gethsemane (Mark 14:32–42), he felt the aversion to pain (v. 36), the loneliness (37) and the general weakness (38) which are such characteristic elements in ordinary human nature. The nature which endured Gethsemane and Calvary and rose on Easter was not that of a demigod, but that of our own humanity. We recognize ourselves in him and, because we know him in his frailty as our Brother, we are able to receive him in his strength as our Redeemer.

This is what the author of the letter to the Hebrews tells us in the sonorous words of our next two passages (Heb. 2:11–18; 4:14–16). It is remarkable that this epistle, which has so much to say about the dignity of Christ, is also the most insistent on his complete humanity. This fact should encourage those who are afraid to acknowledge the full humanity of Christ for fear of detracting from his deity. The divinity and humanity of Christ are not antithetical qualities; always, as in this epistle, they are complementary and inseparable. It is through *our* humanity that Christ approaches us, and it is through *his* humanity that we must first draw near to him. His humanity is the door through which we must come into the throne room of his deity. "Let us therefore come boldly . . ." (4:16).

XV. LIFE THROUGH HIS DEATH

Job 3:1–16; Psalm 22; John 3:14–17; 13:1; 15:12–13;
Romans 5:6–19; Hebrews 10:19–25

A considerable part of the reflective literature of the Old Testament is taken up with the problem of the suffering of the innocent. Why is it that so many apparently undeserving people have to bear what seem unreasonable burdens of disaster, disease and mental agony, often leading even to death? No sensitive person can be indifferent to this problem and no intelligent and honest person can simply pretend that it does not exist. It is the hardest of all the facts of life to reconcile with the existence of a good and loving God. Israel's later history was filled with examples of innocent suffering and undeserved death, especially in the lives of her prophets. It was not without reason that Jesus accused Jerusalem of being a city which habitually killed its prophets and stoned those who were sent to it (Matt. 23:37). Jeremiah was an outstanding instance of a suffering prophet, and his book is full of anguished questionings of God about this problem (e.g., 12:1; 20:14–18).

But the classic treatment of the subject is in the dramatic dialogues of the Book of Job, from which our first selection (3:1–16) is taken. This passage is one of the most moving laments in the literature of the world, the cry of desolation of a blameless man confronted by the mystery of pain in almost unendurable form. It is im-

possible here even to suggest the nature of the long debate which follows, beyond saying that in the end (42:1–6)
Job is reconciled to God, although his questions are
never answered. The very existence of this book and its
nobility as literature, show how profoundly the Hebrews
were concerned with the problem it discusses. In Christian discussion the sufferings of Job have often been taken
as dimly prefiguring the sufferings of Christ.

Our second selection (Ps. 22), a hymn composed to be
recited by one suffering from mortal illness, is especially
significant for Christians because it was used by Jesus as
an expression of his own final agony (Matt. 27:46). Although its anguish is as deep as Job's, the psalm raises
the solution of the problem to a higher level, since it ends
with a song of praise and triumph (vv. 22–31), thus sug-
gesting to the devout reader that suffering may not necessarily lead to defeat but may be the essential prelude to
victory.

The most profound of the Old Testament passages
dealing with the sufferings of the innocent is one we have
already studied—Isaiah 53. Since it is so important for
understanding the Christian view of the meaning of
Christ's death, it might be well for the reader to review
it once again. Whereas Psalm 22 more or less accidentally
suggests that suffering may lead to triumph, Isaiah 53
declares unmistakably that in one case at least this was
certainly so. The "Servant," whoever he may have been
in the mind of the author, accomplished his great redeeming work, not in spite of his sufferings, but precisely because of them (vv. 4, 5, 11, 12). He did not abolish the
evils of man's lot by waving them away with an imperious
and godlike hand, but by bearing them away on his own
shoulders, voluntarily bowed to suffering and death.

This is the Christian interpretation of the death of

Christ, an interpretation which sets the whole problem of innocent suffering in a new light. Christ's death was not a tragic accident; he did not die because he was weak and helpless, but because he was strong, strong in love such as no man had ever shown before. To save men, he became a man; to conquer suffering, he learned to suffer; to overcome death, he died as all his brethren must die. This is a theme which occurs repeatedly, especially in the Gospel of John: the death of Jesus was not evidence of his failure, but of his love and his will to save. Furthermore, his love was not the love of a pitiable and impractical prophet, but a manifestation in human terms of the very love of God Himself. All our quotations from John's Gospel (3:14–17; 13:1; 15:12–13) repeat this theme in some of its different aspects.

St. Paul in the Epistle to the Romans (5:6–19) also emphasizes that the death of Christ was a sacrifice of love (v. 8), the effectiveness of which depended upon his complete identification with sinful and suffering mankind. As the original and imperfect man brought disaster into the world by disobedience, a true and perfect man must, by obedience, even to suffering and death, remove it (12, 15, 17–19).

In all these things we are, of course, dealing with mysteries. *How* the suffering and death of Christ effect our redemption we can neither comprehend nor express in purely logical terms. But where the mystery of innocent suffering by itself is dark and frightening, the contemplation of *redemptive* suffering brings to men the light of hope and courage. Once we apprehend, even dimly, that the suffering and death of one man can bring life to many, we begin to see all suffering in a new perspective. We come to realize that God may use even our own sufferings for redemptive purposes.

Because redemption is necessarily a mystery, the nature of the process can best be expressed in poetic and imaginative language. Christ can be pictured (in Paul's terms) as the Last Man undoing the evil of the First Man; or as the Divine Hero defeating man's enemies in battle (Rev. 19:11); or by the best and most basic image of all, as the great High Priest offering the final sacrifice and opening the way into the Holy of Holies. This is the favorite image of the Epistle to the Hebrews. Much of the Pentateuch is occupied with the ritual of sacrifice; for Christians, and especially for the author of Hebrews, all this merely foreshadows the sacrifice of Christ. The meaning of the animal sacrifices of the Old Testament is to be found only as men see Christ offering on their behalf the perfect sacrifice—that of his own life (Heb. 10:19–25) —and as they endeavor themselves to follow him along this "new and living way."

XVI. VICTORY THROUGH HIS RESURRECTION

Ecclesiastes 9:1–6; Psalm 16; Acts 13:26–37;
I Corinthians 15:12–19; Philippians 3:7–21

For ordinary sinful man, death is the final defeat; for Christ it led to the ultimate victory. He shared our common nature and suffered our common mortality, but only to show that our true destiny is not death and corruption, but eternal life as the children of God. The resurrection of Christ is the central article of biblical faith and, once grasped, throws new light on the rest of the Bible, and on the total meaning of human life. For the old-fashioned paganism of the Greco-Roman world, the realities of life were essentially somber, and even for most men of the Old Testament the life of individuals had no ultimate meaning. The joyousness and sense of purpose which are characteristic of the Christian view of life are due entirely to the fact of Christ's resurrection.

The contrast between the Christian view and that of paganism or of Old Testament man at his unregenerate worst is well illustrated by the passage from Ecclesiastes (9:1–6) which is our first selection. This book is far from being typical of the Old Testament. Indeed it is so different from anything else in the Bible that readers frequently wonder why it is found there at all. But, whatever may have been the original reason for its inclusion, it has great value as showing what life is like without the resurrection faith. The author, a sophisticated Jew who lived at a late period in Israel's history and no longer shared the ancient hope of his people, can find no meaning whatever in life since death is the end of it all. His final, cynical and unheroic conclusion is that "a living dog is better than a dead lion" (v. 4).

Far more characteristic of the outlook of the Old Testament is Psalm 16, a hymn which, like Psalm 22, expresses the emotions of an invalid seeking deliverance from serious illness. He speaks of his absolute trust in God and his almost mystical feeling that a sense of God's nearness is the greatest blessing a man can have (vv. 2, 5, 11). He is sure that God's will for him is not death, but life, and that God will not permit his present sickness to end fatally (v. 10 should be translated "thou wilt not abandon me to Sheol [meaning, the realm of the dead]").

It is not likely that he hopes for personal immortality, but at least he is sustained at each stage of this earthly life by a serene confidence in the goodness and power of God.

As we noted above, the fact of Jesus' resurrection throws new light on the whole Bible story and when men of the New Testament read this psalm it seemed to them that the author (whom they assumed to be David) must not only have come near the resurrection faith, but must have actually anticipated it. So they understood the words of v. 10 to be a prophecy of Christ's rising from the dead. This is the way it is interpreted in Paul's sermon at Pisidian Antioch, part of which is recorded in Acts 13:26–37 (note especially 35–37). While a careful reading of the psalm shows that the author was speaking of his own deliverance from sickness rather than of the Messiah's resurrection, Paul's use of the passage is not entirely unjustified, because faith of such intensity as the author exhibits ultimately requires for its object a God who will deliver men (and therefore, above all, the Messiah) from death itself. As often happens, the psalmist spoke more largely than he knew.

The centrality of the resurrection faith in early Christian thought is illustrated by the passage from I Corinthians (15:12–19). St. Paul insists that neither his preaching nor his readers' faith has any meaning if Christ did not rise from the dead (vv. 14, 17). There were evidently some in the Corinthian congregation who, like some in the modern Church, felt one could be a good Christian without believing in the resurrection of the dead (12). For Paul the two things are inseparable—the resurrection of Christ and the resurrection of those who believe in him; the former is the assurance of the latter. If we believe in one we must also believe in the other. If we can believe in neither, then it would be better to have remained a pagan, without faith or hope, for our religion is an empty delusion and "we are of all men most miserable" (19).

The passage from Philippians (3:7–21) shows how profoundly the resurrection faith affected Paul's whole attitude toward life. This letter is the most attractive of all the Pauline writings, written late in his life, warm, mellow, nonargumentative, the ripe fruit of a life spent in Christ's service. He tells how his knowledge of Christ had come to seem the only possession worth having (vv. 7, 8). Dissatisfied with his old religion and its attempt to make men right with God through obedience to the Covenant of Law, he had found perfect harmony with God through faith in Christ (9). He had learned to be like Christ by sharing with him "the fellowship of his sufferings" and by this means had come also to know "the power of his resurrection" (10, 11). But Paul wants his readers to understand that his new-found strength has not caused him to be smugly satisfied with his achievements. He is in no danger of falling into a new kind of Christian Pharisaism. The resurrection faith is not a narcotic but a stimulant. The Christian, far from being content with what he is, must continually press forward toward a bright future in which he shall be more perfectly conformed to the image of the risen Christ (12–14, 20f).

XVII. THE KINGSHIP OF CHRIST

Judges 8:22–23; Psalm 98:5–9; Psalm 110; Acts 2:32–36;
John 18:33–37; I Corinthians 7:20–23

It is one of the great paradoxes of the Bible that he who is our Brother is also our King. This means that we are not only to admire Jesus as a man and love him as a friend, but to serve and obey him as our Lord and Master. In his earthly life, and still in his heavenly glory, he is one of us, but through his atoning death and victorious resurrection he has earned the right to reign as King over all God's creatures.

The search for the perfect king is one of the themes which runs through the Bible. Israel's adoption of ordinary monarchical government was inevitable, since this was the usual form of government in the ancient world, but there was always a party which opposed it and maintained that her perfect and only king was God. Such feelings naturally existed in later times when most of her kings had proved to be selfish and oppressive, but even in the days before the kingdom was established there seems to have been a strong anti-monarchical tradition.

Back in the obscure days between the Conquest of Canaan and the establishment of a central government under hereditary kings, Israel was ruled by a succession of military heroes—the Judges—who claimed to govern only by the direct authority of God. They obtained their power by achievement in battle, not by inherited right.

One of the greatest of these was Gideon, whose exploits in defending his people against Bedouin raiders from the desert are described in Judges 6–8. At the height of his power Gideon was offered the privilege of becoming hereditary king, but refused it because of his conviction that imperfect, human kings had no place in the constitution of Israel (Judg. 8:22–23). God alone should be Israel's King.

Even when Israel had lived for centuries under monarchical rule and was all too familiar with the failings of kings, it still seemed natural to use the language of kingship when speaking of God, as is shown by a psalm such as 98 (vv. 5–9). Disillusioned by the rule of sinful men, people longed for the perfect justice of the divine rule. "With righteousness shall he judge the world, and the peoples with equity" (9).

As we have already seen, there finally arose a conviction that someday God would send a human ruler, perfectly conformed to His will, who would establish on earth the Kingdom of God and exercise sovereignty on God's behalf. This ideal king of the future was called the Messiah or (in Greek) the Christ. Psalm 110, although not originally a Messianic psalm (it seems rather to refer to one of the reigning kings), was always understood in later times to be a prophecy of Messiah's rule. Some of it is difficult to understand, but the opening verses are clear enough. The king will sit at God's right hand, victoriously ruling (vv. 1, 2). This psalm was particularly appealing to New Testament readers because it combined two favorite symbols of the character of Christ: kingship and priesthood (4).

So Peter, in his sermon on Pentecost, uses part of this psalm to illustrate Jesus' new relationship to men (Acts 2:32–36). Just a short time before, he had been—to all appearances—only a wandering prophet, brought at last to a miserable death through misunderstanding and treachery. But now, by raising him from the dead, God had proclaimed him as the long-expected Messiah, the King who should reign at God's "right hand" as ruler of creation. "Therefore," Peter says, "let all the house of Israel know assuredly that God hath made that same Jesus whom ye have crucified both Lord and Christ" (v. 36). The search for the perfect king was ended. It is well to realize that the word "Lord," used so frequently of Jesus in the New Testament, had for Gentile ears much the same connotations as the term "Christ" had for Jews. The word Christ, or Messiah, being Jewish, was almost meaningless to Gentiles, but they understood perfectly the word Lord, which was a common title for gods and emperors and implied the right to command obedience. One might almost translate the phrase in Acts as "both Lord of the Gentiles and Messiah of the Jews," meaning "Jesus is now the king of all."

It is sometimes suggested that the kingship of Jesus is an invention of the Church and that our Lord Himself made no such claims. It is impossible here to discuss either the reasons for such an opinion or the arguments against it since the subject is a highly technical one, but there can be no doubt that the Gospels in their present form unanimously represent him as accepting, or at least as not rejecting, the title of Messianic King (Matt. 27:11; Mark 15:2; Luke 23:3). The claim is characteristically amplified and interpreted in the Fourth Gospel (John 18:33–37), where it is further made clear that Christ was seeking a moral and spiritual, not a grossly political, kind of kingship. His kingdom "is not of this world" (v. 36)— that is, it is not to be established by military force, but by the power of God and the loving obedience of men.

Our last selection (I Cor. 7:20–23) does not use the concept of kingship, but conveys the same thought by means of the metaphor of owner and slave. As Christ's disciples we are no longer free to do what we will. We are his possession, "bought with a price" (v. 23)—the price of his death on the cross. It is impossible for Christians to obey him with only half their hearts. He is not merely our teacher; he is the Master and we are his servants; he is the King and we must be his faithful subjects.

XVIII. THE DEITY OF CHRIST

Exodus 29:42–46; Ezekiel 43:1–9; John 8:54–59; 14:1–11;
Colossians 1:12–20; Revelation 1:12–18; John 20:28

Greater even than the paradox that Christ our brother is also our King, is the paradox that he who was perfectly man was also the perfect manifestation of God. That the prophet of Nazareth is "Very God of Very God" is the final and crowning affirmation the New Testament has to make about Jesus.

The roots of this doctrine are to be found in the Old Testament and its conception of the God of Israel as a God who desires to dwell in the midst of His people. The God of the Old Testament is often said to be a completely transcendent God, that is, one who is so high above the earth and so remote from men that He can have no contact with them. But this is only one side of the picture, for those parts of the Old Testament which are most insistent upon God's transcendence are the parts which also insist most strongly upon His desire to live in intimate fellowship with His children.

This concern with God's nearness took two different forms. First of all there was the priestly view which taught that God was already present in the temple in Jerusalem or in the tabernacle which was said to have been its prototype in the wilderness many generations before. This is the point of view of the first of our readings, Exodus 29:42–46, an excerpt from the rather tedious instructions given for the building of the tabernacle. The purpose of the building, and the ritual connected with it, is described as that of providing a suitable place where God might "dwell among the children of Israel and . . . be their God" (v. 45). This was exactly the function which the temple fulfilled in the life of the people of the Old Testament. It was the place where He could be found and His Presence be available to those who loved Him. Many of the psalms testify to the almost mystical rapture with which the devout worshiper approached the place of God's earthly dwelling (e.g., Ps. 84 and 42–43).

While the priestly writings speak of God's presence in the past and the present, the prophets, profoundly conscious of man's unworthiness, thought of the presence of God as being perfectly manifested only in the future. So Ezekiel (who tended to combine the priestly and prophetic points of view) sees the Glory of God, once driven from Jerusalem by the sins of its inhabitants, returning in the ideal future to take up its abode once more, and forever, in the midst of a purified people (Ezek. 43:1–9; 48:35).

Just as the Old Testament theme of the coming Messiah reaches its proper conclusion in the kingship of Christ, so the thought of the God who tabernacles among His people comes to fulfilment in the doctrine of the deity of Christ. This is one of the special emphases of the Fourth Gospel. The most explicit passage is part of a section we have studied in another connection—the prologue (John 1:1–14). It declares that the Word which was "with God" and "was God" (v. 1) "became flesh and dwelt among us" (14). The peculiar Greek word here translated "dwelt" was deliberately chosen by the author to suggest to his readers God's "dwelling" in the tabernacle in the wilderness. He wants them to understand that what was imperfectly foreshadowed in the ritual of ancient Israel has now been perfectly realized in the earthly life of Jesus.

Other passages in the gospel are quite as explicit in identifying the mind and presence of Christ with the mind and presence of God. One must of course remember that the discourses in this gospel are not always literal transcriptions of the words of Jesus, but in many cases represent devotional expansions of the actual words or, in some cases, simply the writer's meditations set down in dialogue form. We have no reason, however, for doubting the essential validity of the judgments they contain.

In John 8:54–59 we have Jesus represented as saying that he had existed before Abraham (vv. 56, 58), the words acquiring special force from his use of the phrase "I am," the very words with which God Himself addressed Moses in Exodus 3:14. Again in John 14:1–11 Jesus is pictured as claiming perfect unity, and even identity, with the Father. "He that hath seen me hath seen the Father" (v. 9). "I am in the Father and the Father in me" (11).

Using different language and imagery, Paul teaches the same doctrine in Colossians 1:12–20. This paragraph is an almost complete summary of the highest Christological teaching of the New Testament: Christ, who has achieved our redemption (vv. 13, 20) is the perfect man, the true image of God (15; cf. Gen. 1:26); he was God's chief agent in creation (16), is the ground and principle of all existence (17) and possesses the divine fullness (19; cf. Col. 2:9). Here is the solid New Testament basis for the tremendous affirmations of the Nicene Creed.

Finally, turning from the world of theology to that of poetry, we notice that the Book of Revelation (1:12–18) opens with a vision of the Heavenly Christ in which words and images used in the Old Testament only of God the Father are unhesitatingly applied to Jesus (compare, for example, v. 14 with Dan. 7:9 and 15 with Ezek. 43:2; also v. 17 with Isa. 44:6). Daniel's Son of Man, God's representative (Dan. 7:13), has now himself become the Ancient of Days (Dan. 7:9). To the titles Prophet, Priest and King, the Christian must now add the Solemn confession "My Lord and my God" (John 20:28).

XIX. SALVATION BY FAITH

Psalm 23; Isaiah 30:15–17; Habakkuk 2:1–4; Galatians 3:9–14; Romans 3:19–28; James 2:14–26; Luke 23:39–43

Once we understand that Christ, by his life, death and resurrection, has accomplished the redemption of the human race, the question naturally arises: How can individuals obtain the benefit of this redemption? Obviously, God is not going to force salvation on those who have no desire for it and make no effort to obtain it. Is there anything we can do to show that we wish it? Is there any price we can pay or any prescribed deeds we must perform?

The Bible answers unequivocally that there is only one thing to do and that is to commit our lives, by a continuing act of love, faith and trust, into God's hands and allow Him to use the merits of Christ to save us. This is what the Bible calls "justification by faith." "To be justified" means to be right with God and, in this sense, is really only another name for salvation. There is but one road by which we can arrive at the goal of salvation in Christ and that is the road of faith.

In our study of the Bible story we saw that faith is the basis of biblical religion, a fact which is symbolized by the narrative of the Covenant of Faith which God made with Abraham. "And he believed in the Lord," says Genesis 15:6, "and he counted it to him for righteousness." So, throughout the Old Testament, in spite of the later Covenant of Law, faith rather than obedience is the fundamental quality required of a man, not because obedience is unimportant, but because true faith always includes it. Obedience without faith is sterile; faith without obedience is impossible.

The three Old Testament passages we have included in our study are all expressions of this basic attitude. The first is one of the psalms (23)—typical of many others— in which the worshiper sings of his perfect trust in God. In vv. 1–4 he is the sheep and God the shepherd; in 5–6 he is the guest and God his generous host. The mood of the poem is one of unreserved submission to God, not merely because He is powerful, but because He is trustworthy and good.

In the second extract (Isa. 30:15–17) we find the prophet Isaiah contrasting those who put their trust in material weapons, which in the long run will certainly fail

(vv. 16f), with those who put their trust in the Holy One of Israel who can always be depended upon for victory and strength (15). It should be noted that the word "returning" means "repentance," so the attitude which the prophet demands is not one of pious relaxation but of concentrated moral effort. This is what was meant above when it was said that faith, in the biblical sense, always *includes* obedience.

The third Old Testament selection (Hab. 2:1–4) is one of the two crucial passages (Gen. 15:6 being the other) on which the New Testament doctrine of justification by faith is based. Habakkuk lived in the days when the New Babylonian (or Chaldean) Empire was ruthlessly extending its power by military conquest (see 1:6ff). The prophet who, like many others, found it difficult to understand how God could permit such things, tells us that God sent him a vision in which it was revealed that justice and truth would eventually prevail, however long the time might be (2:3), and that in the meantime the righteous man must live by his "faith," a word which in the Old Testament always includes the idea of "faithfulness."

Paul, in Galatians 3:9–14, makes this and the story of Abraham the great proof passages for his doctrine that man can "get right" with God only by exhibiting this kind of faith (note especially v. 11). The Pharisees of Paul's day maintained that justification was a reward for obeying the Law of Moses. Paul's argument against this, based upon the idea of the "curse," is difficult for us to follow and not really valid, but the true basis for his doctrine is a profound and unshakable conviction that men cannot really do anything to *earn* salvation. They can only accept, in faith, love and trust, the gift which God is willing to bestow.

The contrast between salvation by law and by faith

is made even more strongly in Romans 3:19–28, where it is stated explicitly that the function of the Mosaic Law was not to save, but only to make men realize that they are sinners who need to be saved (v. 20; note also 4:2f and Gal. 3:6).

Since there were some who misinterpreted Paul's doctrine to mean that it was no longer necessary for men to live righteously or do good deeds for others, the author of the little epistle of James (2:14–26) felt it important to insist again that true faith is not simply an attitude of mind, but must find its proper expression in obedience and in acts of love and mercy. The great men of faith such as Abraham, he points out, were also men of great deeds. "Show me thy faith without thy works, and I will show thee my faith by my works" (v. 18).

This, of course, is only relatively true, since good works, in this sense, are not always possible and, in any case, it is the underlying motive of faith, rather than the good works themselves, which obtain salvation. There is no better picture of the way in which justification by faith actually operates than in the story of the penitent thief in Luke 23:39–43. The man was no longer able to do good deeds of any kind; the only possible recourse for him was to effect quickly a basic change in his attitude toward life, to empty his heart of cynicism and self-will by offering it wholly to Christ and trusting in his goodness. But this was enough, for Jesus immediately responded, "Today thou shalt be with me in paradise."

XX. THE GIFT OF THE HOLY SPIRIT

Judges 14:1–6; Isaiah 63:10–14; Wisdom of Solomon 7:22–8:1;
John 14:16–17; 16:13; Romans 8:5–17; I Corinthians 12:7–11

The greatest blessing which comes to those who have been redeemed by Christ and are justified by faith in his redeeming power is the gift of the Holy Spirit. We have previously seen how men of the Old Testament came to realize that no one could achieve holiness without this gift (Ps. 51:10f); how they had come to believe that in the future God would make His Spirit available to everyone (Joel 2:28f); and how that hope was fulfilled on the day of Pentecost (Acts 2:1–4). The New Testament regards the age of the Spirit as already present and sees the Christian—the new man of the new age—as one who lives in the joyful consciousness of possessing the Spirit.

Unfortunately a good many Christians no longer have a clear understanding of what it means to have God's Spirit dwelling in them and no real comprehension of what the Spirit is. As with so many other concepts in our religion we need to go back to the Old Testament to see what the words originally meant. Our first selection (Judges 14:1–6) takes us to a book which at first glance seems to have very little theology in it and to a strange story which bears all the marks of an ancient folk tale. Its hero is Samson, a kind of Hebrew Hercules or Paul Bunyan, remembered more for his deeds of strength than for his acts of piety. This particular story tells how he became enamored

of a Philistine girl and went down from his hills to the plain
to win her for his wife. On the way, it is said, a young lion
met him and, when it roared, "the Spirit of the Lord came
mightily upon him, and he rent him as he would have
rent a kid" (v. 6). The story seems about as remote from
the thought-world of the New Testament as one could get
and yet it tells us the first, and most essential, thing about
the Holy Spirit, which is that He is *the giver of strength.*
Later on the Hebrews would come to understand that this
means moral and spiritual, rather than merely physical,
strength, but in the Samson story the doctrine appears in
its earliest form. Primitive as the story is, it shows that
when the Bible speaks of God's Spirit it means that power
from God which makes men able to do what they could
not do by their own unaided might.

In Isaiah 63:10–14 (some parts of which are difficult
to understand) at least two more things are evident. One
is that the Spirit gives not only strength but *guidance,* for
the whole passage is concerned with God's guidance of
His people through the desert at the time of the Exodus.
The other is that the Spirit is not simply an impersonal
force, like electricity, but is something like *a person,* since
it is said that men can grieve it (v. 10: KJV "vex"; cf.
Eph. 4:30).

The third passage (Wisdom 7:22–8:1) comes from
the Apocrypha, the link between the Old and New Testaments. Here we find the Old Testament conception of
Wisdom, which the New Testament sometimes connects
with the work of Christ, used as a synonym for the Holy
Spirit (as became common in later Christian theology).
Combining ancient Hebrew ideas with the language of
Greek philosophy, the author describes how Wisdom, or
the Spirit, which is the very image of God Himself (vv.
25f), pervades and sustains all things (22–24; 8:1) and "en-

tering into holy souls . . . maketh them friends of God
and prophets" (27).

According to the Fourth Gospel (John 14:16f), Jesus
promised his disciples that after his departure he would
send them "another Comforter," the Holy Spirit, who
would continually instruct and guide them (16:13). The
Spirit would no longer be the occasional possession of a
few choice souls, but would be freely given to all those
who live by faith in Christ.

St. Paul, of course, has more to say about the Christian
life as a Spirit-filled life than any other New Testament
writer. In Romans 8:5–17 he describes various aspects of
it. It is, first of all, a life in which men are ruled by God's
Spirit rather than by their gross physical passions (vv.
5–9). (When Paul speaks of "flesh" and "body" he does
mean to suggest that the material body is evil in itself; it
is evil, for him, only when it is allowed to usurp the place
which properly belongs to the Spirit.) In the second place,
life in the Spirit is a life in which immortality has already
begun (10f); heaven is a present fact (10), not simply a
future hope (11). And, finally, it is a life in which men
live in the full and joyful assurance that God is their Father (14–17).

In I Corinthians 12:7–11, Paul is not concerned so
much with the inner life of the Spirit-filled man as with
its outward manifestations. All Christians possess the
Spirit, he says, and all have some special gift which proves
it. Such gifts are to be used for the benefit of the Christian
community and not merely enjoyed privately and selfishly
(v. 7). The particular gifts he mentions—healing, the
power to perform miracles, the gift of tongues—are those
most characteristic of the church to which he is writing.
But there is an infinite variety of such gifts and all are
valuable. In a passage we shall read later (I Cor. 13), St.

Paul says that the greatest of all gifts is the power to love. The most important gifts of the Spirit are certainly the moral gifts, the capacity for faith, courage, goodness and love to a supernatural degree—that is, beyond the ability of ordinary unredeemed men. All Christians have, potentially, at least one of these gifts; our obligation is to *use* them—for the sake of Christ and the brethren.

XXI. THE HOLY TRINITY

Numbers 6:22–27; Ezekiel 1:1–5; 1:24–2:2; Matthew 3:13–17; II Corinthians 13:11–14; I Peter 1:1–12; I John 5:7 (KJV)

We have not been ready until now to finish our study of the biblical doctrine of God, because the Christian experience of the Holy Spirit, which we studied in the previous chapter, is such an important element in it. Looking back over the long history of biblical revelation we can see that the knowledge of God was not given all at once, but gradually, as men became increasingly able to receive it. As a rough rule we may say that the Old Testament reveals to us God the Father (that is the Creator and Law-giver); the Gospels reveal to us God the Son (the Redeemer); and the rest of the New Testament, God the Holy Spirit (the Strengthener and Sanctifier). This revelation did not come in the form of sudden, unprepared-for, flashes of new knowledge, but through the growing understanding of biblical men as they reflected on the meaning of God's activity among them.

When, finally, Christians received the full gift of the Holy Spirit, it became necessary to put into some intelligible form the whole biblical doctrine of God in order to answer such a question as this: "What is the true relationship of God the Father, as revealed in the Old Testament, to God the Son as revealed in the gospels and God the Holy Spirit as experienced in the life of Christians? Are there three Gods or only One?" The only possible answer was the one already given in the Old Testament: "Hear, O Israel, the Lord thy God is one . . ." (Deut. 6:4). In this way the doctrine of the Holy Trinity—the paradoxical belief that God is both three and one—arose as the final summation of the biblical revelation of God. Later theologians would spend much time and many words in defining the nature of the Trinity; the Bible itself states merely the basic fact—the One God is Father *and* Son *and* Holy Ghost.

Naturally we should not expect to find any specific mention of the Trinity in the Old Testament, although the ancient Hebrews certainly knew something about the Holy Spirit and had intimations of the coming of the tabernacling God. Some Christian interpreters have tried to find more definite statements of Trinitarian doctrine in passages such as the sonorous priestly blessing in Numbers 6:22–27 with its threefold repetition of God's name. But the most we can honestly claim for passages such as this (or Isa. 6:3) is that they show how natural it is to use the rhythm of three when speaking of God. They can, therefore, readily be used in Trinitarian Christian worship.

Much more important are the many Old Testament passages which emphasize the infinite mystery and complexity of the Godhead. None is perhaps more striking than the account of Ezekiel's call to be a prophet (Ezek. 1:1–5; 1:24–2:2). The God he met upon the vast plain of

Babylonia was One beyond all human comprehension. When the prophet speaks of God, he can find no adequate words to describe Him: he can only use such terms as "the appearance of the likeness of the glory" (v. 28). The God whom Ezekiel experienced was the Father—remote and mysterious—but also a spirit who entered into him (2:2). While Ezekiel had never heard of the doctrine of the Trinity, he would not have found it either strange or repugnant.

It is really only in the opening scene of our Lord's public life, the Baptism, that we catch our first clear glimpse of the triune God (Matt. 3:13–17). The voice of the Father claims the Son for His own (v. 17), and the Holy Spirit (16) provides the bond of unity between them. Even here there is no *doctrine* of the Trinity, but the threefold God is plainly present.

The nearest we come to an explicit Trinitarian formula in the New Testament is in the familiar blessing with which St. Paul concludes his second letter to the Corinthian church (II Cor. 13:14): "the grace of the Lord Jesus Christ, and the love of God and the communion of the Holy Ghost, be with you all." Christ and the Father and the Spirit are spoken of in one breath, on one level; and the blessing which the prayer asks for is sought equally from all of them.

More typical is the passage from I Peter (1:1–12) where the writer speaks quite easily of the work of the Father, Son and Spirit as different parts of an indivisible process of redemption. It was the Father who purposed our redemption; the Son who accomplished it by the shedding of His blood; and the Holy Spirit who sanctifies those who are faithful and obedient (v. 2). Our salvation is the gift of the Father's mercy and became effective through the resurrection of the Son (3). But the manner of the redeeming process had long been intimated by the Holy Spirit (10f; notice that He here is called the Spirit of Christ, as in the Nicene Creed which says that He "proceedeth from the Father *and* the Son"). And it is the Holy Spirit who still gives men grace to preach the Gospel (12). From passages such as this one sees how natural it was for New Testament writers to use Trinitarian language even though the doctrine of the Trinity is nowhere precisely formulated. To put the doctrine explicitly into words was the task of a later and more philosophical age.

The statement that the New Testament nowhere explicitly formulates a doctrine of the Trinity might seem to be contradicted by I John 5:7 in the King James Version. It has long been recognized, however, that this is a later addition to the book and so is omitted in all the Revised Versions. But, although we cannot treat it as a part of the Bible, we need have no hesitation in accepting it as an accurate statement of the biblical doctrine of God set forth in language provided by the later Church.

XXII. THE CHURCH

Genesis 13:14–18; Deuteronomy 7:6–11; Hosea 2:14–23; I Peter 2:1–10; Ephesians 2:19–22; Matthew 16:13–19

There is no place in biblical religion for selfish individualism. Redemption comes to men through their membership in a redeemed and redeeming society, not through some special arrangement made directly between

themselves and God. To say this is not to depreciate in any
way the importance of individual faith and personal righteousness, but only to assert that, in the Bible, faith always
leads men out of selfish isolation into the divine community and that righteousness always implies right relationships within a communal framework.

As we have already seen from our study of the Bible
story, God chose from the beginning to redeem men by
means of a family, a society, a nation—or, to use the language of later times, a Church. Looking back on the account of God's dealings with Abraham, we see God promis-
ing that he shall be the father of a vast family (Gen.
13:14–18) and elsewhere declaring that by means of it
"shall all the families (or nations) of the earth be blessed"
(Gen. 12:3, 22:18). Although the meaning of this statement is not quite so clear in Hebrew as in English, it is
certain that the greatest men of Israel, such as Second
Isaiah (and the unknown author of Isaiah 19:24f) understood it to mean that it was God's purpose to save mankind through the family of Abraham. Here we see one of
the fundamental patterns of the Bible: God working in
history to save men through the instrumentality of a special, chosen group.

At the next stage in the history of salvation, the group
is conceived of more in terms of a nation than a family.
Under the leadership of Moses, the loose association which
previously existed among the tribes claiming descent from
Abraham became an organized community living under
common laws and held together by a common faith and
common worship. This is the stage in the Church's history
represented by such passages as Deuteronomy 7:6–11:
"Thou art an holy people unto the Lord thy God." The
word "holy" here does not necessarily mean "morally
good"; it means rather "consecrated to God's service." The

next two verses (7f) emphasize that God's choice of Israel was not based upon any special merit on her part, but solely upon the inexplicable love and mercy of God. The concluding verses (9–11) warn that the continuance of God's favor is dependent upon her willingness to walk in His ways.

The next chapter in the story is that of Israel's final failure, in spite of her tremendous spiritual achievements, to finish the task for which God had chosen her. This was followed by God's promise to create in the future a trans-formed community to bring His work to perfection. Seeing her with somewhat kindlier eyes than those of the prophets, we shall probably feel that the passing of the old national Israel was a necessary stage on the way to the universal Israel of God, but the prophets could see her history only in terms of failure and judgment. Most of them, however, could also look beyond the evil present and see God's purpose ultimately being achieved by a renewed and purified people. This, for example, is the point of view in Hosea 2:14–23. God loves his people as a husband loves his wife and someday the affectionate relations of early days will be restored between them (vv. 14–20). To those who are no longer worthy to be called His people He will say again "Thou art my people," and to those from whom His justice was compelled to withhold mercy He will show mercy again.

I Peter 2:1–10 sees this promise at last fulfilled in the Christian Church (v. 10). Part of this passage (9) is also an echo of Exodus 19:5f, which we have read in another connection, and shows that the pattern of redemption through a redeemed and redeeming community is the same in the New Testament as in the Old. Although God's Church is no longer limited to those who are physically descended from Abraham, the spiritual descendants of Abraham—

those who have faith in Christ (Gal. 3:7)—still constitute "an elect race, a royal priesthood, a holy nation," whose purpose is to declare to the world "the praises of him who hath called you out of darkness into his own marvellous light."

The same writer, in vv. 4f, uses another image for the Church—that of the Temple. The individual Christian is only a single stone in a great spiritual structure erected for the worship of God. This thought is developed further in Ephesians 2:19–22. Verse 19 emphasizes the continuity between the old national Israel and the new Israel built upon faith. There are not two churches, but one. What happened through the work of Christ was that the community of the old Israel was expanded to include the Gentiles (to whom the letter is addressed) so that they are now "fellow-citizens . . . of the household of God." Jews and Gentiles, in so far as they both have faith in Christ, are part of a great temple which provides a fit habitation for God the Holy Spirit. The foundation stones of the temple are the prophets of the Old Israel and the Apostles of the New, and Jesus Christ himself is the cornerstone.

The mention of a cornerstone inevitably calls to mind the familiar passage about the founding of the Church in Matthew 16:13–19. While the interpretation of the passage is still a subject of much debate, it is at least clear to everyone that the stone upon which the Church—the new Israel—is to be built cannot be merely Peter the man, but Peter as the first to declare boldly his faith in Christ (v. 16). The true cornerstone of the Church is not Peter, but the faith which he expressed.

XXIII. THE MINISTRY

*Deuteronomy 33:8–11; Numbers 25:10–13; Malachi 2:1–9;
John 20:19–23; II Corinthians 3:1–6; 5:18–20; Titus 1:5–9*

Like any other society, the Church has its officers and ministers and both the Old and New Testaments testify that the ministry was not created by the human members of the society, but by God Himself. Although the form of the ministry, and to some extent its function, are different in the Old Israel and the New, the principle of its divine authority remains the same.

Our first selection is from one of the oldest poems of ancient Israel, called by tradition the Blessing of Moses. In the course of it each of the twelve tribes receives a blessing determined by its history and character. The one in which we are especially interested (Deut. 33:8–11) is that of Levi, the tribe which exercised the functions of the ministry in the Old Testament Church. Just as membership in Israel was a matter of birth rather than of choice, so the priesthood in the developed religion of Israel was a privilege conferred by birth on the members of a particular tribe. As a matter of fact the priesthood in the full sense (at least according to the so-called "priestly" document of the Pentateuch) could be exercised only by the members of one family within that tribe, the family of Aaron, while ordinary Levites were restricted to certain menial tasks.

The "blessing" begins, rather obscurely, with a refer-

ence to the mysterious Urim and Thummim, part of the
sacred equipment of the priest, probably used for divina-
tion, and then speaks of some unknown test to which the
tribe had been subjected in the past. Verse 9 says that
the priest is to serve God with complete dedication, not
allowing himself to be influenced by family ties. The most
important passage is v. 10, which speaks of the two great
functions of the priesthood: to teach the people God's will
and to lead in worship. These two functions remain constant throughout both the Testaments. The passage closes
with a blessing on the Levites' work (11).

In Numbers 25:10–13, the descendants of Aaron are
singled out for the priesthood and promised the gift of an
eternal covenant with God as a reward for their zeal in the
service of sound morals and true religion.

Since a priest, in spite of his authority, is only a man,
he is subject to the same temptations as other men; so it
is not surprising that individual ministers often proved
unworthy of their vocation and that at times the priesthood as a whole became corrupt. The prophets often speak
of this, but none more eloquently than Malachi (2:1–9),
whose denunciation of priestly sins gains added force from
his obvious sympathy with the basic principle of priesthood. He recalls the covenant which God made with the
ancestors of the tribe (vv. 4f) because of their goodness and
pastoral effectiveness (6), and emphasizes again the importance of the teaching function of the priest (7). But the
present generation has failed in its duty and must expect
God's curse rather than His blessing (1–3, 9).

The divine authority of the New Testament ministry
is stated in the strongest possible terms in John 20:19–23
which claims for the Christian minister a dignity parallel
to that of Christ himself ("As my father hath sent me, even
so send I you"), and gives him the right to make authorita-

tive decisions in cases of conscience which are brought before him (v. 23; cf. Matt. 18:18). To make it possible for him to carry such a heavy weight of responsibility, he is given a special endowment of the Holy Spirit (22). While no special mention is made here of the apostles' right to transmit their authority to others, the nature of the Church as a continuing institution made it necessary for them to do so. At least two New Testament passages refer to the ordination of younger men by the laying on of hands (I Tim. 4:14 and II Tim. 1:6).

The first seven chapters of II Corinthians, which are largely taken up with St. Paul's discussion of his own ministry, show the tremendous authority which the apostle —with the utmost personal humility—claimed for himself. After a moving reference to Paul's pastoral work in the Corinthian church, the first of the two passages selected here (3:1–6) tells of the grace which God gave him to bear the difficult responsibilities of his office as "minister of the new covenant" (vv. 4–6). In the second (5:18–20), Paul describes his work as a "ministry of reconciliation" between men and God, and calls himself and other ministers of the Church the "ambassadors" of Christ (20). The underlying conception, as in John 20:21, is that of one who is sent by a king or another powerful person to act in his name and on his behalf.

From Titus 1:5–9, we see that it was considered important that authorized ministers should be appointed in every church. But we also see, from the list of qualifications, that ministers of the New Covenant, like those of the Old, are weak, fallible human beings who are sometimes no better than they should be in spite of the dignity of their office. It would surely not have been necessary to give a list of such rather prosaic and self-evident requirements, if there had not been some who failed in precisely these ways. God can use even the most unpromising materials to do His work, but the Church, like the individual minister himself, must be constantly on guard to keep the material as fine and pure as is humanly possible. The Bible shows that the ministry is an office of great dignity and great danger—the dignity is from God, the danger from man.

XXIV. THE SACRAMENTS

Genesis 17:1-2, 9-14; Exodus 12:21-28; Matthew 28:16-20; Acts 8:35-38; Luke 22:14-20; I Corinthians 11:17-34

The Bible tells us that the Old Israel and the New both had definite ceremonial acts which served to bind the community together and continually remind it of its dependence on God's grace. In the later Christian Church these acts, believed to have been ordained by God himself, came to have the name of "sacraments." For both the Old and New Israel the most important of them were a *ceremony of initiation* and a regularly recurring *family meal.*

By the ceremony of initiation the new member was effectively incorporated into the life of the Israel of God just as a new branch can be effectively grafted into a tree. In the family meal the community did not merely *remember* that it had once been redeemed, but underwent again the experience of redemption and once more received the benefits of it. When the Passover was celebrated each year,

Israel passed once again through the waters of the Red Sea; and, when Christians celebrated the Lord's Supper, they stood again at the foot of the Cross and by partaking of Christ's Body and Blood received the benefits of his Death and Passion.

The first of our readings (Gen. 17:1–2, 9–14) contains the account of the institution of circumcision as the initiatory rite in ancient Israel. While, strictly speaking, one was made a member of the Israelite community by being born into an Israelite family rather than by being circumcized, yet one could not remain a member without receiving upon his body the sign of God's covenant (v. 14), so there is a real analogy if not a precise parallel between this rite and Christian baptism. It was evidence of a special relationship to God and a reminder of all the obligations which that special relationship imposed upon those who enjoyed it. Like all such marks of particular favor, it was easily abused and we learn from the New Testament that it often became an occasion for selfish pride rather than a stimulus to grateful humility. Because of this and because circumcision had so long been associated with a purely national religious community, it was abolished in the New Israel and a new initiatory rite took its place (Col. 2:11f).

Exodus 12:21–28 tells how, in the time of Moses, the religious life of Israel was strengthened by the establishment of a commemorative feast—the Passover—to remind the people that during the terrible events which preceded the Exodus God had spared ("passed over," v. 27) their homes, bringing them safely out of Egypt and settling them in the Promised Land. The first twenty verses of the chapter give explicit rules for celebrating the feast. The ceremony was divided into two principal stages: the slaying of the lamb, and the banquet which followed.

After the Crucifixion, which took place at the Passover season, Christians could hardly avoid connecting the death of Christ with the killing of the lamb and seeing in his sacrifice the fulfillment of all the Passover signified (I Cor. 5:7f).

It was firmly fixed in the tradition of the early Church that Jesus Himself instituted the sacrament of baptism and commanded his disciples to administer it to all who were receptive to their preaching (Matt. 28:16–20). Significantly, the initiatory rite of the New Covenant, by its use of water, suggests the need for moral cleansing and renewal and is not, like circumcision, merely a mark stamped on the body.

From Acts 8:35–38, we can see how closely baptism was connected with the preaching of the Gospel and how it was associated from the beginning, just as today, with a profession of faith in Christ and his redeeming work.

The great sacrament, which week by week binds together the members of the New Israel and unites them with Christ and his saving death, is the Lord's Supper. Luke 22:14–20 contains one of the stories of its institution. While there are small differences in the various accounts, they agree in telling how Jesus gave thanks, broke the bread, identified the bread and wine with his Body and Blood (that is, *himself*) and then distributed them to his disciples. Luke records also the command to "do this," that is, to repeat what he did, as an effective act of recollection and memorial (v. 19).

The most extensive account we have of a celebration of the Lord's Supper in the early Church is in I Corinthians 11:17–34. Since the purpose of Paul's letter was to correct certain abuses in the Corinthian Church, we find in it that curious mingling of the divine and human which has necessarily marked the life of the Church in every age. On the one hand, there is the wonder and solemnity of the sacrament, in which the mystery of Calvary is continually renewed (v. 26) and the Body and Blood of the Lord are truly received (27); on the other hand, the sinfulness and selfishness of men, which intrude even into the most sacred moments of the Church's life (18–22). For St. Paul—as for us—the Lord's Supper is not only an act of gratitude and a means of grace, but must be made also an occasion for self-examination and judgment (28–32).

XXV. LIFE AFTER DEATH

Job 10:20–22; 14:7–15; Daniel 12:1–3;
Wisdom of Solomon 3:1–8; Matthew 22:23–33;
I Corinthians 15:35–58

Strange as it may seem, the ancient Hebrews, until the very end of the Old Testament period, had no hope of a happy life after death. For early Old Testament man, death was no problem; it was merely the natural end of life. Man was born from the dust and to the dust he must return (Gen. 3:19; Eccl. 3:20). The Hebrew emphasis was upon the group rather than the individual and, so long as the group continued, the death of its individual members seemed of small importance. The only immortality the individual could hope for was the continuance of his family, and hence of his "name," after him.

But, although Old Testament man did not hope for a happy afterlife, he could not quite conceive of the complete extinction of conscious existence. In Hebrew thought the dead retained a faint, shadowy consciousness even in

Sheol, the dark underworld to which they all had gone. Under certain conditions they might even be restored temporarily to a state in which they could speak and be spoken to (like Samuel, in I Samuel 28:3–19). But life in Sheol was not immortality in our sense of the term; it was either a matter of indifference or an object of superstitious terror. One of the best descriptions of it is found in our first selection, Job 10:20–22.

Toward the end of the Old Testament period men became more reflective. They began to ask questions rather than simply accept the old primitive beliefs which had been handed down to them. Then death became a problem, particularly in view of the obvious inequities of life in the present world. They began to see that many of the insoluble questions which life presented would be answered if only God would use His sovereign power to give men a new life beyond the grave. This is the stage of thought represented by Job 14:7–15. The author points out that a tree, although cut down, can be expected to live again (vv. 7–9). This is not true of man (10–12), but what if it were! (13–15).

The author of Job never arrived at belief in eternal life (not even in 19:25f; see the commentaries). It was not until the time of the Maccabean persecutions, of which we read in the Apocryphal Books of Maccabees, when so many thousands of loyal Jews were slaughtered for their devotion to God and religion, that the thought of full, self-conscious existence after death came to seem the only possible way to reconcile belief in God's power and justice with the appalling injustices of life in the present, evil world. This is the stage represented by Daniel 12:1–3, written at this period, which promises resurrection of the righteous dead to "everlasting life" and the wicked dead to "everlasting punishment."

In the period between the Testaments this became a fixed article of belief for many Jews (particularly the Pharisees), as we see from Wisdom 3:1–8, probably the most exquisite passage ever written on the subject of human immortality.

But, though there were many Jews who accepted this belief, there were others who did not. The Sadducees of New Testament times categorically rejected it. In Matthew 22:23–33 we find them trying to trap Jesus by asking what seemed an unanswerable question about the conditions of life beyond the grave. Suppose a woman (in accordance with the law of Deut. 25:5ff) had seven successive husbands, who would be her husband in the future life? The question was a contemptuous one, intended to make Jesus look ridiculous, but he answered it seriously, pointing out that conditions in the other world, where there is no need to continue the species by procreation, must necessarily be quite different from the conditions of this world (vv. 29f). He then went on to give a new interpretation of an old text: If God said "I am the God of Abraham, and the God of Isaac, and the God of Jacob" must not this mean that Abraham, Isaac and Jacob are still alive? The method which Jesus used for interpreting the scriptures being one which the Sadducees themselves accepted, the question was a difficult one for them to answer.

However many Jews might accept the idea of life after death, it still remained only a pious conjecture, not a biblical doctrine, for it was not founded on any definite, historical, revealing act of God. It was still necessary for God, by His mighty act, to stamp the belief as true. This was—at least in part—the significance of the resurrection of Christ. Jesus showed the power of God to raise the dead and became himself the visible "first-fruits of them that slept" (I Cor. 15:20). It is important to notice that the emphasis in the Bible is not just on "immortality"—that is some natural privilege, inherent in *man*, but on "resurrection"—that is the power of *God*. He who created life in the beginning is able to re-create it and sustain it anew.

St. Paul, in I Corinthians 15:35–58, gives the classical statement of the biblical doctrine of the afterlife. The body must have its part in it, for the body is good, and an inseparable part of man. But it will not be the same body we know now, just as the plant which rises from the ground is not the same as the seed which was originally buried beneath it (vv. 36–38). The immortal body will be incorruptible, strong and controlled by the Spirit (42–44). The keynote of the chapter is "victory"—Christ's victory which is also ours (55–57). But it is not a victory which leads men merely to a self-satisfied assurance of their own immortality; rather it inspires in them a heroic determination to do God's work with all their power (58).

XXVI. THE GOAL—FELLOWSHIP WITH GOD

Job 38:1–7; 42:1–6; Psalm 27; John 15:1–11;
I John 3:1–3, 16–17, 23–24; 4:12

The Bible, as we have seen, teaches a doctrine of life after death, but it does not make everlasting life itself the goal of our earthly pilgrimage. The real goal is not the indefinite prolongation of human existence, but rather its transformation—already in this world—through the attainment of fellowship with God. Human life as most men live it is not worth being extended into eternity. Until men have learned to know God and live with Him in this world the idea of living with Him eternally in another can hardly have much meaning.

It is perhaps largely for this reason that the ancient Hebrews had no doctrine of eternal life until late in the Old Testament period. Israel had first of all to learn the full meaning of life with God in the present world. Then, when the time came, the idea of eternal life arose as a natural, and almost inevitable consequence. But even then the essential content of eternal life never became merely the survival of personal identity; for biblical man eternal life means a life lived in such firm fellowship with God that even death cannot destroy it.

The author of the Book of Job never arrived at the idea of eternal life beyond the grave, but he did discover that the greatest good in life is the assurance of God's nearness. Most of his great book is occupied by a long dialogue in which Job and his friends discuss the goodness and justice of God. All of them agree that God is all-powerful; but is He also all good? Job is pictured as a man who has lost everything that seems to make life worth living—property, family and physical health. He cannot understand why these things should have happened, for he had always been a good, devout man who had done nothing to make such a fate seem just. So he rails bitterly at God in language which stops barely short of blasphemy, and his friends are unable to comfort him.

The argument is too long to be summarized here, but toward the close of the book it is increasingly evident that Job is beginning to understand that his greatest disaster was not the loss of property and health, but the loss of a sense of companionship with God. In the closing chapters God suddenly appears in person (38:1–7) and Job's complaints and bitter questionings come promptly to an end (42:1–6). He realized that all his life he had known of God only by hearsay; now, for the first time, he knows Him in his own experience (v. 5). Although the book's final paragraph tells of the restoration of its hero's fortunes, this is really irrelevant, for Job has already learned that the highest good in human existence is not health or wealth, but the personal knowledge of God (the same thought appears also in Ps. 73:25–28).

While the Book of Job is the dramatic story of one man's discovery of God, Psalm 27 is the lyrical outpouring of another man who had been long accustomed to live in the daily consciousness of God's presence. His one desire was to have the vision of God his whole life through (v. 4); his basic attitude was to "wait for the Lord" (14)— to listen for His voice and to respond in love and obedience.

For Christians the goal of living in fellowship with God is much easier than for the men of the Old Testament. Christ has broken the power of sin and evil, the things which separate men from God, and has made it possible for all men to appropriate the fruits of his victory for themselves. And Christ himself, as both God and man, provides the natural meeting place for God and man. So, in John 15:1–11, he is described as the vine through which the divine life flows to his disciples, who are the branches. The chapter repeatedly makes use of the word "abide," for the relationship between Christ and his followers must be a permanent one, not just to be felt in rare mystical experiences but the profound reality underlying every thought and deed on every common occasion. It is not a relation based on feeling alone, but on a love which finds its natural expression in obedience (v. 10). And the end of it is a fulness of joy which cannot be known in any other way (11).

The partial experience of God's presence which one may have now is only the first step in an expanding life with Him (I John 3:1-3). We can know Him now as a child knows its father, but the future contains the promise of a relationship so close that no human words can describe it (v. 2). "We shall see him as he is." It is important to notice that, in biblical thought, the goal is not to be attained merely by some kind of formal mystical exercises, however valuable they may be; soundness of the moral life is even more important. Men must struggle constantly to purify themselves from evil, for God Himself is pure and will not walk in fellowship with those who are impure (3). Mysticism without morality is abhorrent to the biblical mind.

Finally, we notice that the biblical idea of fellowship with God is not a selfish one. Unlike some of the ancient religions of the orient, the religion of the Bible does not picture the goal of life as living *in solitude* with God. We shall return to this theme later, but it would be improper to conclude our present study without at least taking note of the fact, so strongly emphasized in I John 3:16f, 23f and 4:12, that fellowship with God can be found only by those who walk in fellowship with other men. God's love for us demands love for each other; our only assurance that God "abides" in us is the fact of our own sincere and abiding love for the brethren (4:12).

PART THREE: *LIFE*

I. LIFE UNDER JUDGMENT

Amos 7:7–9; Psalm 50; Matthew 25:14–30; Romans 14:10–12

As we turn from a study of biblical doctrine to the way of life which the Bible teaches, we need to observe first of all that there are certain broad conceptions which determine and control it. Three phrases will help us to grasp them: "life under judgment," "newness of life," and "life in Christ."

The thought of divine judgment dominates the whole Bible and the passages selected for our present study are only a sample of an immense number which deal with the same theme. For the biblical writers, man himself is never the "measure of things." Man in the Bible is not an autonomous being, determining what is right by some principle of human expediency, responsible only to his own educated conscience. What is right is determined by the will of God, and man is directly responsible to God, who will someday pass judgment upon him for what he is and does. This solemn consciousness of judgment pervades the whole biblical view of life and conduct.

The first of our passages (Amos 7:7–9) expresses the idea of judgment—which is especially strong in the Old Testament prophets—through a picturesque and unforgettable image. The prophet, in a vision, sees the Lord standing beside the wall of a building with a plumb line in His hand. If a wall is to be strong it must be vertically straight, and it is the task of the master architect to see that the wall built by his workmen conforms to this basic specification. It is possible, indeed probable, that Amos was inspired to use this picture by actually seeing a building under construction and observing the superintendent testing a wall in just this fashion. The wall of the prophet's vision, of course, is the life of the people of Israel and the plumb line is for the purpose of determining the measure of their conformity to God's will. In the prophet's view, Israel has clearly failed the test and must now expect the punishment of its sins. The Lord, whose very nature is righteousness and justice, has passed final judgment upon them.

The prophet, in this passage, leaves the precise nature of Israel's sins unspecified, though elsewhere he makes it clear that he is chiefly concerned with man's unkindness to his fellow man. The author of Psalm 50, however, has quite specific charges to bring. At the beginning of his poem (vv. 1–6) he pictures the scene, the Divine Judge appearing in beauty and power with heaven and earth as His assessors (4). Then follows the indictment (7–21). The charge against the people of Israel is not that they have failed to obey the ritual. They have been meticulous in offering sacrifice (8), but this is only an outward thing. In his anger, the psalmist speaks of animal sacrifice with almost sacrilegious contempt: God has no need for the offering of animals, for He owns "every beast of the forest . . . and the cattle upon a thousand hills" (10–13). What God is concerned about is the moral failure of His people and in particular the sins to which the "devout" are especially prone: cowardice in the face of public wickedness (18) and a propensity to indulge secretly in the sin of slander (20).

Our Lord, in typical fashion, discusses the theme of judgment in the form of a parable (Matt. 25:14–30). He compares God to a wealthy landowner who has gone into

a distant country and left his property, in varying large
amounts, in the hands of retainers, expecting them to use
their trust to his advantage. Two of them do so and, when
the master returns, he judges and rewards them accordingly. But the third, a shiftless and irresponsible servant,
had merely hid his sum in the ground and tried to explain his conduct as due to fear of his lord's hardhearted-
ness (vv. 24f). The lord refused to be fooled by so feeble
and transparent an excuse and ordered him to be punished
with pitiless severity (30). Jesus does not, of course, wish
us to think that God is hardhearted like the master in the
parable, but only to realize that He deserves at least the
same measure of devotion that an intelligent slave would
feel compelled to give to a rigorous, unfeeling earthly lord.
It is typical of the large-mindedness of Jesus that the sins
to which the parable refers are not particular infractions
of the moral code, but the sins which arise from men's
lazy refusal to use their God-given capacities to the utmost
of their personal ability.

St. Paul, writing to the Christians at Rome (Rom.
14:10–12), draws from the idea of judgment an important
conclusion: if men are to be judged by God it follows that
they should not be so presumptuous as to judge each other.
From a slightly different point of view, it is the same
principle stated by our Lord in the Sermon on the Mount:
"Judge not that ye be not judged" (Matt. 7:1f). One might
suppose that the conviction that all men are facing God's
judgment would make for a certain harshness of character. But, for Jesus and Paul, the thought of the in-
evitability of judgment does not inspire severity toward
others, but rather a greater sense of sympathy and understanding. We, too, must face the Judge and are well aware
of our inadequacy to meet Him. A Christian knows that
he could never hope to pass the test except as he is justi-

fied by the mercy of God in Christ. While the thought that he is living under God's judgment leads the Christian to view his own life with deepest misgiving, the thought of God's kindness and mercy toward himself ought to make him more generous than most men in his judgment of others.

II. NEWNESS OF LIFE

Leviticus 19:1–4; 20:22–26; Ezekiel 36:24–28;
II Corinthians 6:14–18; 5:17; Colossians 2:6–13; 3:1–14

Throughout the Bible it is repeatedly emphasized that the way of life of the people of God is qualitatively different from the life of ordinary men. In a passage we have already examined in a different connection Paul makes use of the memorable phrase "newness of life" to characterize the distinctive behavior expected of Christians (Rom. 6:4). They are not to be content with a standard of conduct a little better than that of the secular world, but must strive for a quality of life which is totally new. Natural goodness is not enough; only a special and *super-natural* goodness will suffice.

Already in the Old Testament the same point had been made. Since Israel was chosen of God and dedicated in a special way to His service, all her members had an obligation to conform to a new and higher standard of life. The principle is clearly set forth in the two passages from Leviticus (19:1–4; 20:22–26) which make up our first selection. "Ye shall be holy; for I the Lord your God am holy" (19:2; 20:26). All the provisions of the "Mosaic" Law—many of them purely arbitrary—with which the Book of Leviticus is concerned, were designed to create in the minds of the people a sense of separateness (i.e. "holiness") from other nations and of their duty to live by the higher moral law which God had given them. Brief examples of these laws are included in our reading (19:3–4; 20:25).

This strange mixture of purely ceremonial commands with high moral precepts will not appeal to the modern reader, and was, indeed, abolished by the Gospel. But we must not forget that the mixture served its purpose well for the time in which it was compiled and that the people of Israel, with all their defects, succeeded in manifesting a quality of moral life without any parallel among the nations of the ancient world—a fact which modern scientific study of the culture of the Ancient Near East is making us realize ever more clearly.

Israel's great prophets were the voice of her conscience, constantly calling her to higher levels of life than she ever actually attained. For them, the primary fact about Israel was her failure to be the "separate" and "holy" nation which God intended her to be, and the greatest of them began to look forward to the coming of a new and transforming power which would affect the innermost springs of her people's conduct. This is what Ezekiel was looking for when he predicted that in time to come God would sprinkle His people with clean water and give them a *new* heart and a *new* spirit (Ezek. 36:24–28). The Law had given to Israel a new and higher external standard of life; what the prophet desired was the bestowal of an inward grace which would effectively transform men's characters and give them a new quality of inner life as well (see also Ps. 51:10).

Although this hope was fulfilled by the gift of the Holy Spirit, it was still necessary for New Testament writers to exhort Christians to *use* their new-found power to achieve the "holiness" (separateness) to which God summoned them (I Pet. 1:15f). Paul, in II Corinthians 6:14–18, urges his people to recognize the absolute distinction between the way of life of God's people and that of ordinary men of the world. Christians live by new standards and a new inner principle and cannot compromise with the standards of the world. The Christian is not merely a better kind of worldly man; if he is truly a Christian, he is "a new creature" (5:17).

The visible symbol of the Christian's new character is the act of baptism with which his life begins. At the very moment of its inception his Christian life is stamped with a sign which marks it as new and qualitatively different. As a Christian he has been "sprinkled with clean water" and given "a new heart" and "a new spirit" (Ezek. 36:25f).

Paul develops this theme beautifully and at length in the passage from Romans (6:4–13) previously discussed and in the passages from Colossians (2:6–13; 3:1–14) selected for reading in the present connection. Like men of the Old Israel, Christians, he says, are circumcised—though with a purely spiritual circumcision—to mark them off from other men. Mystically buried with Christ by submersion in the waters of baptism, the Christian has died to his old way of life and risen with Christ to a new life which is potentially of altogether different quality (2:11–13).

Unhappily, most Christians, in Paul's day as in ours, failed to achieve fully the kind of life to which they were called and for which they were now prepared, so Paul appeals to them in moving language to stretch their moral muscles and take advantage of the privilege which is theirs (Col. 3:1–14). In the paradoxical words of a modern writer he asks them "to *become* what they are." The implications of the opening clause "If ye then be risen with Christ . . ." are as disturbing today as when it was first written. Even the poorest of Christians will occasionally show some of the qualities of Christian life, but few of them even begin to realize the amazing possibilities of the "newness of life" to which they are called and of which they are capable.

The precise form of that life will emerge from our later studies, but some of its marks are specifically mentioned in the passage before us: truthfulness (v. 9), indifference to distinctions of race and nation (11), a forgiving spirit (13) and love, the most basic quality of all (14).

III. LIFE IN CHRIST

Exodus 33:12–16; Psalm 42; Galatians 2:14–20;
Colossians 1:21–29; Ephesians 4:11–16; Romans 12:1–5;
Ephesians 3:14–19

A third characteristic of the way of life taught in the Bible is that it is a life lived "in Christ." This is the most essential characteristic of all, though in the nature of things it is defined only in the New Testament.

What is found in the Old Testament, by way of anticipation and preparation, is a certain stress upon the possibility of close fellowship with God and a sense that without such intimacy life would be very hard indeed. In

the first of the passages suggested for reading in this connection (Exod. 33:12–16), Moses is represented as saying
that the long journey from Egypt to the Promised Land
would be impossible unless the people were accompanied
by the presence of God. It was not enough for them to
be sure of His approval and help; they needed also the
consciousness that He was traveling in the midst of them.
Much of the elaborate priestly ceremonial of the Old Testament was designed to give Israel this assurance that God
was among them, and the daily encouragement which
comes from that knowledge.

If the sense of God's presence was necessary for the
life of the nation, it was equally necessary for the life of
devout individuals, as we see from the deeply felt words
of Psalm 42. Since, in Israelite theology, the presence of
God was sacramentally connected with the temple at Jerusalem, an individual who was prevented from attending
its services for a long period would naturally feel cut
off by this from the fulness of God's presence, just as a
Christian might feel if he were unable for some time to
receive Holy Communion. The author of the psalm lived
in the far north of Palestine, near Mt. Hermon (v. 6) and
was prevented, probably because of physical illness (10),
from making his customary pilgrimage to the temple (4).
His desire for the sense of God's nearness, he says, is like
the thirst of the wild deer for springs of refreshing water
(1). Nevertheless, he knows that his feeling of depression
is wrong and that God will soon restore to him the assurance of His presence (5, 11; cf. also Psalm 43, which is
really part of the same psalm).

This Old Testament sense of longing for companionship with God is fully satisfied by the New Testament
view of the life of believers as life "in" Christ. The Christian conception is that the believer lives in Christ as the

very atmosphere which he breathes; he lives in Christ as a cell lives in the body to which it belongs. The classical account of this relationship is to be found in John 15:1-7, which we have read in a different connection, but the idea occurs in many other passages, of which only a few have been selected here.

In Galatians 2:14-20 St. Paul is combating the belief of some Church leaders of his day that Christians were still obliged to keep the Jewish Law. Paul insists that believers are made right with God ("justified") solely by their faith in Christ, not by the Mosaic Law, which was valid in its day, but is now abolished (vv. 16-19). By reason of his faith, the Christian has died with Christ and been raised to a totally new form of life (a process symbolized, as we have seen, by baptism). The basic truth about his new life is that it is not actually his, but Christ's. His intimacy with Christ is so close that it is possible for him to say ". . . I live; yet not I, but Christ liveth in me" (20).

In Colossians 1:21-29 the same doctrine is taught in nonpolemical terms. Paul speaks of Christ's redemptive work and its effect upon men's relationship to God (vv. 21f), of his own preaching of the Gospel and his sufferings on its behalf (23-25), and, finally, sums up the whole content of the Gospel in the striking phrase "Christ in you, the hope of glory" (26f). In the course of these remarks, Paul refers to a significant aspect of life in Christ when he speaks of his *body* "which is the Church" (24). Life in Christ is not simply a mystical relationship between Christ and the individual believer, but is objectively based upon the individual's membership in the Church, which is the visible Body of Christ.

Ephesians 4:11-16 develops this same theme in a more elaborate way. All the gifts which Christians have received (11) are intended for strengthening the life of the whole Body of Christ (12) so that every member may achieve that fulness of life in Christ to which he is called (13–15). The passage ends with a complex picture of the harmonious interrelationship between the Body, its members and the life of Christ which is its animating principle (16).

In Romans 12:1–5 Paul appeals to his readers to exhibit the ethical fruits of their Christian profession by their transformed characters (the "newness of life" of which we have previously spoken; v. 2) and their humility of spirit (3). His ethical concern in this passage leads Paul to stress another profoundly significant aspect of life "in Christ." If we are members of Christ by being parts of his Body, then it follows necessarily that we are also members of each other (5); fellowship with Christ has as its inescapable corollary fellowship with other Christians. The implications of this doctrine for the moral life of individuals and the social life of the Christian community hardly need to be underlined.

This set of readings comes to a fitting conclusion with the magnificent peroration in Ephesians 3:14–19 in which the writer prays for Christ's continued dwelling in the hearts of his disciples (v. 17) and their growth in the understanding of all that this involves (18f).

As Baptism is the sacrament of "newness of life," so Holy Communion is the sacrament of "life in Christ." But to this we must return later.

IV. WORSHIP

Deuteronomy 16:16–17; II Chronicles 29:20–30; Psalm 95;
Mark 11:15–18; John 4:20–24; I Timothy 2:1–8;
Revelation 5:8–14

We have observed that religion, throughout the Bible, is not primarily individual but corporate. One cannot be a religious man, in the full biblical sense of the term, unless he is a member of the divinely established community—the Old Israel of the Mosaic Covenant, the New Israel of the Gospel. The idea of corporateness is even more strongly developed in the New Testament than in the Old because of the doctrine that life in the community is actually "life in Christ," since the Church is Christ's Body.

One of the first things to be noticed about the community of believers is that it is a worshiping community. From the earliest times it had been recognized that it is a fundamental obligation for all the members to assemble together on regular occasions to offer common worship to God. The law of Israel specified three such occasions during the year, as we see from our first selection, Deuteronomy 16:16f. In the developed theology of Israel it was believed that proper worship could be offered only in Jerusalem, so more frequent assemblies of the whole worshiping nation could hardly be required.

Nevertheless, worship was offered daily in the temple on behalf of the community, and devout persons came as often as they could. On great occasions there would be special services, such as that described in II Chronicles 29:20–30. The Books of Chronicles are especially valuable for the insight they give into the liturgical life of ancient Israel. The essence of Israel's worship, as one can see from this passage, was sacrifice and praise—offering to God the best gifts they had (vv. 21–24) and praising Him with joyful hearts (25–28).

Psalm 95 is the greatest of the Old Testament calls to worship and for that reason has always been a part of the regular morning service, in the tradition of the liturgical churches. The psalm does not mention sacrifice, the priest's activity in worship, but concentrates rather on the attitude of the worshipers. The first part of the psalm summons them to *adoration* of God (for what He is) and to *thanksgiving* (for what He has done). The second part, beginning with the challenging cry "Today!" (v. 7), suddenly strikes the new note of *penitence* and the need for being awake to God's moral demands, this being the most distinctive emphasis in biblical as opposed to pagan worship.

Jesus took very seriously the obligation of worship which was incumbent upon him as a member of the Old Israel. On the sabbath he was accustomed to attend the synagogue, where Jews of his day met for the study of the Law (Luke 4:16). And his last journey to Jerusalem was made so as to observe the Passover in accordance with the rule of Deuteronomy 16:16f. There he became so indignant at seeing the place of worship profaned by buying and selling that he drove the hucksters out (Mark 11:15–18). Though he knew the days of the temple were almost over (Mark 13:1f), he had only contempt for those who dared to violate its sanctity for private profit. The conditions of worship in the New Israel would be very different from those in the Old, but Christ himself continued to show the deepest respect for the worship of his people.

One of the most significant changes made by the Gospel was the abrogation of the command to worship God in only a single place. It was this which made possible the weekly worship enjoined on Christians. Like so many other commands of the Covenant of Law, the limitation of worship—in the fullest sense—to the temple at Jerusalem had its definite value at a certain stage in the religious development of the people of God, but it would have been a great hindrance to the spread of the Church under the New Covenant of Grace, when the Gospel was to be offered to all the nations of the world. John 4:20–24 is the classical passage. Valid worship can now be offered to God anywhere (v. 21). The passage does not mean, as many suppose, that formal, corporate worship is no longer necessary—that worship is to be "spiritual" in the sense of nonmaterial or nonexternal. What it means is that the worship of the New Israel will be blessed by the actual presence of God's Holy Spirit ("in spirit") and will therefore be more real and satisfying ("in truth").

There are numerous brief passages in the New Testament which give us pictures of the early Church at worship. Some of these we have already noted and to others we shall return in a different connection. I Timothy 2:1–8 is interesting because of its mention of prayer and intercession as another essential ingredient of worship, prayer not only for the Church and its members but for all men everywhere. The kings who are mentioned in v. 2 are of course the heathen rulers of the Roman Empire. It is interesting in v. 8 to notice the mention of the physical attitude of prayer practiced in the early Church—standing with upraised hands. There are still many Eastern Christians who pray in this fashion.

Finally, in Revelation 5:8–14 we have a picture of the ideal worship of the Church in heaven as an early Christian poet and seer imagined it. The formality and splendor of the worship are specially striking. While the worship of the New Testament Church was probably simple and austere, the later Church tended more and more to copy the pattern of heavenly worship even in matters of external detail, as, for example, in the use of incense (v. 8). But whether the worship in any particular congregation be simple or elaborate, it is still true that whenever the Church meets on earth to worship God it is joining its songs of praise to the unceasing worship of heaven in which every created thing has its part (13).

V. HEARING THE WORD

Deuteronomy 4:1–10; Micah 6:1–8; Psalm 119:97–105; Luke 8:4–15; 10:38–42; 11:27f; I Thessalonians 2:10–13

Along with occasions for adoration, thanksgiving, penitence, and intercession, one of the great functions of worship, as described in the Bible, is to provide an opportunity for hearing the Word of God. From the beginning this has been a distinctive emphasis of biblical religion. Whereas pagan religions tend on the whole to stress the *seeing* of God as the primary religious experience, the religion of the Bible tends to emphasize the *hearing* of His voice. This does not mean, of course, that the two experiences are in any sense mutually exclusive.

In Deuteronomy 4:1–10, we have what purports to be an extract from Moses' farewell address, delivered to his people just before he left them on the borders of the Promised Land. Since one can hardly suppose that a stenographer was on hand to take down his actual words on this occasion, it is perhaps better to think of this speech, like so many other speeches in ancient literature, as the creation of a later generation which felt that this is the sort of thing Moses would probably have said. Certainly this was the kind of address which was given year after year at the great festival assemblies of the people of Israel. On each such occasion the congregation would be warned that its very life depended on holding to God's Word (v. 1) and keeping it free from mere human interpretation (2). They would be reminded of the disastrous effect of disobedience in the past (3), of the rewards which came to those who heard and obeyed (4), and of the sense of God's nearness which came from the continual proclamation of His Word in their midst (7). Finally, they were instructed not only to hear the Word themselves, but to teach it to their children (9f). This has been called the original charter of religious education.

While the Word of God was regularly and formally proclaimed by the priests at Israel's public assemblies for worship, it was also announced spontaneously and informally by the prophets. The Word of God contained in the traditional priestly Law was fixed and unchanging, so the prophet had the special function of declaring God's will in relation to new occasions as they arose. The priestly Word emphasized the eternal changelessness of God's demands; the prophetic Word made clear their contemporary relevance. Almost any passage chosen at random from the prophetic books would illustrate the nature of the prophetic proclamation, but no finer could be found than Micah 6:1–8, which defines the character of true worship in reply to some who insisted that God was seeking more costly sacrifices (vv. 6f), perhaps even the sacrifice of men's first-born sons ("the fruit of my body," v. 7).

Although the Word of God as proclaimed in the Old Testament seems, more often than not, to be a word of stern warning rather than comfort, Psalm 119:97–105 reminds us that, in all its forms, the Word or Law of God was always a source of joy and assurance to the devout in ancient Israel.

Our Lord's great parable of the Sower (Luke 8:4–15) shows how important a place the idea of disseminating the Word of God occupied in his mind. He, his apostles and the ministers of his Church are those who sow the seed of the Word. Often their work seems pointless because the Word falls on unresponsive ears (vv. 5–7, 12–14), but the stress of the parable is rather on the Word's amazing productivity when it finally reaches a mind attuned to receive it (8, 15). In addition to the primary emphasis on the objective power of the Word, the parable also contains an implicit invitation to the hearer to examine himself with regard to his own subjective capacity to receive it when it comes.

Two other passages from St. Luke's Gospel (10:38–42; 11:27f) give further illustration of the importance which Jesus attached to the idea of listening for God's Word and obeying it. In the first of them he certainly does not mean to condemn Martha for being active in good works, but he does intend to suggest the importance of allowing, even in busy lives, sufficient opportunity for quietly listening to the Word of God. The second passage says that however desirable it may be to have a proper reverence for holy things and holy persons, it is even more important to have a mind which is receptive to God's Word and a will which is eager to obey it.

In our last selection (I Thess. 2:10–13) St. Paul reminds the members of one of the earliest congregations he had founded in Europe that his work among them had not consisted in teaching them some new and profound philosophy of his own devising, but in proclaiming what he believed to be the very Word of God. And, like all the great biblical teachers, he insists that this Word of God, once received, "effectually worketh" in the heart of the believer (13). God's Word is not merely an "inspiring thought" or a "good idea." It is a power which transforms the lives of those who accept it (cf. Isa. 55:10f; Jer. 23:29; Heb. 4:12).

The Word can, of course, come to men through various channels. It comes through the reading of the Bible—in private and in public—through preaching, through the prayers and liturgical acts of the Church, and to individuals in their private devotions. It must be sought in all these ways; the important thing is to seek it. The human ear is being constantly assaulted by the words of men; the man who lives by the Bible makes sure that he has regular and adequate opportunity to listen to the Word of God and to discover its meaning for his own situation.

VI. COMMUNION

Exodus 16:2–15, 35; John 6:30–35, 47–58;
I Corinthians 10:1–4, 15–17; Psalm 84

For Christians, worship involves not only the hearing of God's Word, but the regular receiving of Holy Communion. This is the sacrament of "life in Christ" as Baptism is the sacrament of "newness of life." As the Christian participates regularly in the sacred meal of his religion, he both reminds himself of his dependence on the life of Christ and actually receives that life through an effective means instituted by Jesus himself.

Christian commentators have always seen a dim foreshadowing of the act of communion in the Old Testament story of the manna in the wilderness (Exod. 16:2–15, 35), which is our first selection. The setting of the story is the desert into which the people of Israel came after their escape from Egypt under the leadership of Moses. In typical human fashion, they began to complain discontentedly of their meager diet and to think with longing of the rich, abundant food they had enjoyed in the land of Egypt (v. 3). So God, who can take care of His people in the most barren of regions, provided them with "bread from heaven" (4), "angels' food" as it is called in one of the Psalms (78:25). The Hebrews themselves called it "manna" from a phrase supposedly meaning "What is it?" The story comes to us from Israel's ancient traditions, handed down for many generations by word of mouth, and it is impossible to tell precisely what historical actualities underlie it. But, whatever the facts of history may be, the story was impressed upon the minds of later ages as a vivid symbol of God's ability to care for His people and to feed them, if necessary, with supernatural food.

The story of the manna in the wilderness is the text for the great Eucharistic discourse recorded in John 6:30–35, 47–58. The people are said to have asked Jesus for a miracle like the one which Moses performed in obtaining heavenly food for the children of Israel (vv. 30f). The answer was that a far greater miracle had already taken place. The manna was perishable bread which took care only of men's physical needs; Jesus himself was the eternal bread which satisfies the hunger and thirst of men's souls

(32–35, 47–50). The thread of the argument is a subtle one which moves almost imperceptibly from a general discussion of Christ as the bread of life to a more specific account of the sacrament of Holy Communion as the means by which that bread is received. Down through v. 50 the thought is plainly that of the Incarnation of the Son of God as an act which occurred in the past and continues in the present; suddenly, in the latter part of v. 51, the tense of the verb shifts to the future and Jesus is represented as speaking of the bread which he *will* give one day and which will be identical with his flesh offered upon the cross for the life of the world. The reference to Holy Communion becomes unmistakable in vv. 53–56 which speak not only of his flesh, which is the bread, but also of his blood, which is obviously the Eucharistic wine. If one looks again at any of the accounts of the Last Supper, such as Mark 14:22–24, the meaning of the words becomes plain. V. 56 says more explicitly than any other passage in the New Testament that Holy Communion is the primary means by which a Christian maintains and renews his life in Christ.

In a different connection we have already examined one of St. Paul's two important Eucharistic passages (I Cor. 11:20–34). The other is I Corinthians 10:1–4, 15–17 in which, interestingly enough, Paul also makes use of the Old Testament story of the manna in the wilderness. To the thought of the manna as the bread of communion he adds the thought of the water from the rock (Exod. 17:6) as the drink of communion (v. 4). The specific application to the Eucharist is made in vv. 16f and the important conclusion drawn that through receiving the sacrament Christians are not only brought into communion with Christ but with each other. It is of interest to notice that in vv. 5–14—omitted here for the sake of clarity—

Paul introduces the note of moral obedience as an essential ingredient of the sacramental life, just as he does in 11:27–32. The receiving of Holy Communion is not merely an occasion for mystical enjoyment, but for penitence and moral renewal.

Finally, we turn back in the Old Testament to one of the psalms which is traditionally used as a preparatory devotion for Holy Communion and which expresses better than any other the emotions which Christians feel as they approach the Table of the Lord. We have seen previously how the pious Jew regarded the Temple as the actual dwelling place of God on earth, so that a visit there had much the same value for him as the receiving of Holy Communion has for the Christian. The author of Psalm 84 was a devout Jew who lived in some distant part of the country and could visit the temple only after a pilgrimage through difficult and dangerous territory (v. 6). He wishes that, like the birds (3) or some of the priestly attendants (4), he could spend his life in the temple courts. This was, of course, impossible for him, but even his periodic visits there were sufficient to give him a sense of increasing strength (7) and a more certain knowledge that the Lord is a "sun and shield" (11). True to the biblical point of view, he knows that the joys of communion with God in His temple will be given only to those who "walk uprightly" (11)—to those who are prepared to obey God's law and seek His will as well as enjoy the comforting sense of His Presence.

VII. WORKING FOR GOD

Esther 4:13–17; Matthew 4:18–22; Acts 16:6–10;
Nehemiah 4:6, 15–23; Romans 12:6–13

Activism is one of the marked traits of Western civilization. When this takes the form of an exclusive concentration on external activity to the detriment of thought and feeling, or when it leads men to depreciate the value of contemplation and prayer, it deserves to be criticized severely. The trait itself, however, is in large measure due to the influence of the religion of the Bible, which always sees genuine faith as issuing in some kind of activity on behalf of God and God's people. Biblical religion comes to full fruition only when faith expresses itself in appropriate action.

The call to act is a constantly recurring motif in the Bible story: Abraham is called to leave his home and kindred (Gen. 12:1); Moses is called to deliver his people from slavery in Egypt (Exod. 3:10); Gideon, to preserve the nation from the ravages of the Midianites (Judges 6:14). The classic example is the call of Isaiah, which we have studied in another connection (Isa. 6:1–8), beginning as it does with a vision of God's glory (vv. 1–4) and ending with the divine query "Whom shall I send and who will go for us?" climaxed by Isaiah's quick response "Here am I; send me" (8).

Our selections include three further instances of such calls to action. The first is from the Book of Esther (4:13–

17). Because of her position as consort of the Persian king, Esther alone had the opportunity to intercede for her people and save them from annihilation by an unscrupulous enemy. At first she is reluctant to do this because of the personal danger involved, but her cousin Mordecai explains that her present privileged position had been given her as part of God's plan (". . . Who knoweth whether thou art come to the kingdom for such a time as this?" v. 14). If she fails to act, she will not, of course, defeat the divine purpose, but she and her family will have to face the judgment which comes inevitably upon those who hear God's call and deliberately ignore it. She accepts the call and the rest of the book tells of the success of her effort.

The other two passages—from the New Testament—tell, in familiar language, of two calls to serve Christ and his Church and of the immediate response which each evoked. In the first (Matt. 4:18–22) it is Jesus himself who summons his first disciples to leave their secular callings and serve him in a special way as "fishers of men." The second (Acts 16:6–10) tells how an already dedicated servant of God, St. Paul, was summoned to give up his carefully laid plans for missionary work and move in a different direction from the one he intended. It was thus that the evangelization of Europe began. These passages illustrate two different kinds of call: the one to a complete change of life, the other to allow God's plans for His work to prevail over one's own. Both illustrate the sensitivity of spirit and flexibility of mind which the biblical kind of life requires.

All of these accounts contain calls to special, individual and heroic action. But since the religion of the Bible is corporate rather than individual, it may be assumed that most people are called to do relatively unspectacular work within the larger framework of a community project. The two remaining passages give illustrations of this.

In the first (Neh. 4:6, 15–23) we read the story of how the entire citizenry of Jerusalem responded to Nehemiah's urgent request for help in rebuilding the city walls after the Babylonian exile. Nehemiah's own call, as related in chapters 1–2 of this book, is a fine example of individual response to the divine summons. But even more inspiring is the picture given here of the response of a whole people, who "had a mind to work" (v. 6), each of them taking his place as a mason, a carrier or a bearer of arms to protect his fellows. The story reminds one of the way in which the medieval cathedrals were built, with every citizen assisting in the task. The work of the particular individual in such circumstances may be very small, but the total achievement is enormous.

This is the kind of work to which the average Christian has been called by virtue of his baptism and this is the kind of work to which Paul, in Romans 12:6–13, urges the concentrated devotion of his readers. Each member of the congregation has a call to work for God and has received the grace which makes it possible for him to perform it. Some are called to the ministry, some others to help in the work of teaching, some to positions of responsibility in the administration of the parish, others merely to contribute to the needs of the Church or to do occasional acts of mercy (vv. 7, 8, 13). The scope of the work is not important. What is important is that it is done in response to God's call and with the wholehearted consecration which God's work requires—with cheerfulness, humility, fervor, prayerfulness and infinite patience (8–12).

VIII. THE MORAL STRUGGLE

Deuteronomy 30:15–20; Judges 7:15–25; Isaiah 59:15–19;
Ephesians 6:10–20; Luke 11:14–23; II Timothy 2:3–4

The hymn "Onward, Christian Soldiers" expresses a view of the Christian life which is deeply rooted in the biblical tradition. The Bible is not primarily concerned with teaching a system of philosophy or even with communicating a body of doctrine. It is chiefly concerned with the direction and motivation of human life, though not in the sense of inculcating merely minimum standards of social decency or giving additional force to conventional moral sanctions. The overruling passion of the biblical authors—and the Bible is nothing if not a passionate book—is to win men to total and militant commitment to God as He has revealed Himself in the history of His people, and to the kind of life which He has commanded.

Throughout the Bible there runs the view that the world is a battlefield between two opposing camps: God and His enemies, the Kingdom of God and the kingdoms of evil. It is not enough for men to lead "good lives"; they must deliberately choose to *fight* either on the one side or on the other—for the God of Israel or the gods of Canaan, for Yahweh or for Baal, for Christ or for the devil. As in wars between nations, neutrality is impossible and in many instances equivalent to treachery. At some point every man must make the choice, for *decision* is the first step toward moral maturity as the Bible understands it.

The Christian is assumed to have elected for God at his baptism, where he was enrolled to serve as "Christ's faithful soldier and servant unto his life's end."

The passage from Deuteronomy (30:15–20) sets forth in classical language the imperative character of this choice: ". . . I have set before you life and death, the blessing and the curse . . ." (v. 19). It inevitably reminds us of the language of Jesus himself when he presented the choice in terms of "the two ways," the broad way which leads to destruction and the narrow way which leads to life (Matt. 7:13f). Neither passage makes allowance for any deferred choice or for ambiguity of purpose once the choice has been made. In Deuteronomy the thrice-repeated phrase "this day" (15, 18, 19) underlines the urgency of the call to decision (cf. Ps. 95:7).

Having made the choice, men must then prepare to engage in the struggle. The soldier is a common image for the character of the Christian in the New Testament. In part, at least, this goes back to the original Old Testament conception of the people of God as a nation, in which, as in every other nation, the citizens had the duty of defending their country against foreign enemies. In Israel's later history this duty was largely delegated, as with us, to a professional or semiprofessional standing army, but in the Book of Judges we see the idea in its original purity. In that far-off day every Hebrew male was a member of a militia and personally responsible for the defense of the community. The story in Judges 7:15–25 is a typical instance of the way in which this operated. Notice how even here the religious implications of the struggle are conveyed by the battle-cry "For *the Lord* and for Gideon" (v. 18 RSV).

In every period the God of Israel Himself was conceived as a warrior, sometimes with a vividness somewhat shocking to our refined modern sensibilities. In Isaiah 59:15–19 the prophet sees God putting on His armor in preparation for a battle (v. 17) . . . "righteousness" as a "breastplate," "salvation" as a "helmet," "vengeance" for "clothing" and "zeal as a cloak." While undoubtedly there still remains here something of the old idea of Yahweh as the national champion of Israel, yet it is important to note that the background of the passage is the sinfulness and unworthiness of the nation (cf. vv. 1–15), and God's purpose is said to be that of establishing "justice" (15, RSV) and extending His righteous rule throughout the earth (19). (The reader may be interested to see how the same image is used in the Book of Wisdom, in the Apocrypha, 5:17–20).

In Ephesians 6:10–20 the Christian warrior is summoned to join in the same battle, taking God's armor upon himself—"the breastplate of righteousness" (v. 14), the girdle of "truth" (14), and "the sword of the Spirit" (17). At the beginning of the passage it is made clear that the conflict is no sudden or temporary emergency, but an unceasing warfare which must be constantly waged against the unseen powers of darkness (vv. 11f). The terms in which the author speaks belong to the peculiar world view of his own time which thought of the present age as being under the domination of evil spirits, but the realities with which he deals are the permanent facts of human existence. We cannot afford to take evil lightly; it is like a tireless invading army which can be defeated only by ceaseless vigilance and struggle.

Jesus, in Luke 11:14–23, speaks in terms of the same world view. He also sees the world as a battleground between two kingdoms—the Kingdom of Beelzebub and the Kingdom of God. It is by "the finger of God" (v. 20) that he defeats the power of Satan, and his wonderful works of healing (14) are evidence of the growing strength of the Kingdom of God amongst men (20). In the warfare which is being waged no one can be neutral—"He that is not with me is against me" (23). So we are brought back again to the theme of the choice which every man must make— the way of life or the way of death, service in the army of God or in that of His enemy.

The final selection (II Tim. 2:3f) may be taken as a personal appeal to every man to do daily battle against the spiritual enemy who attacks from within, and when occasion requires, to stand manfully against the evil forces at work in society without. "Rise up, O men of God!" "Fight the good fight." "Endure hardness, as a good soldier of Jesus Christ."

IX. STUDY

Hosea 4:1–6; Deuteronomy 6:4–9, 20–24; Psalm 119:17–24;
Luke 2:41–52; Acts 17:10–11; II Timothy 3:14–17

Religion is frequently defined in the Bible as "the knowledge of God." It is true, of course, that knowledge in this sense means not mere intellectual understanding but personal acquaintance with a Person. This cannot be emphasized too strongly. But it is also true that "the knowledge of God" *includes* what we call intellectual knowledge. While men must know God from direct personal experience, they must also endeavor to learn *about* Him—to gain some understanding of His nature and His ways. Such knowledge can be acquired only by serious effort and intellectual discipline. Biblical religion is not antiintellectual; since the mind is the gift of God which above all distinguishes man from the lower animals, it must above all other faculties be dedicated to God's service. "Thou shalt love the Lord thy God with all thy heart, and with all thy soul, and with all thy *mind*" (Matt. 22:37).

The chief complaint which the prophet Hosea (4:1–6) had to make about the people of his day was that they had no knowledge of God (vv. 1, 6). While he certainly meant by this that they had no personal sense of God's nearness and power, he also meant quite simply that they did not know God's laws, which forbade "swearing, and lying, and stealing, and committing adultery (2)." Because the priests and prophets had failed in their primary responsibility to instruct the people, they are singled out for special condemnation (4–6), but the punishment is to fall alike on every member of a nation which had become intellectually obtuse and spiritually ignorant (3).

The Book of Deuteronomy is commonly believed to be the product of a great movement for religious education and moral revival which took form in Israel in the 7th century B.C. Its basic principles were the unity of God (6:4) and His demand for total allegiance (v. 5). It is with Deuteronomy that the idea of "the Bible"—that is, of a book which bears authoritative witness to God's laws and mighty acts—really begins. So it is not surprising to find that the idea of reading and studying God's Law runs through it as a constant theme (6:6–9) and that the religious instruction of children is treated as a basic obligation (20–24). Verses 21–24 contain a kind of fundamental creed of ancient Hebrew religion which was to be memorized and expounded.

The whole of Psalm 119, which comes from a much later period than Deuteronomy, is concerned with the study of the written Law of God and the profit which it brings. Verses 17–24 are typical of the rest. The words "Open thou mine eyes, that I may behold wondrous things out of thy law" (18) can still serve as an excellent introductory prayer for the study of the Scriptures or any related subject. Verse 24 gives evidence that, for the devout Jew, the study of the Law was not a burden, but a source of pleasure and satisfaction (cf. vv. 97, 103). Undoubtedly the affinity which the modern Jew exhibits for intellectual pursuits, even in the secular field, owes a great deal to the emphasis upon the study of God's Word which was so important an element in the biblical and rabbinical tradition.

When we turn to the New Testament we see how our Lord conformed to this pattern from the beginning. There is no more charming picture in the Gospels than the one of the boy Jesus in the Temple (Luke 2:41–52) seeking out the learned men of his people "both hearing them and asking them questions" (v. 46). His own marvelous facility in the use of Scripture during his later ministry is —humanly speaking—not so much evidence of the perfection of his divine nature as of the devotion which he paid, in his human nature, to the regular study of God's Word and the unfolding of its deepest meaning. Notable examples of his command of Scripture are given in the traditional tales of the Temptation (Luke 4:4, 8, 12), of his first sermon at Nazareth (vv. 17–22), the Sermon on the Mount (Matt. 5:17, 21, 27, 33, etc.) and the story of the walk to Emmaus (Luke 24:27).

The intellectual traditions of ancient Israel were continued in the early Christian Church, though of course with a certain shift of emphasis. The modern Christian often has difficulty in following the closely knit arguments of the New Testament epistles because the authors were writing to congregations whom they could presume to be familiar with even the more recondite passages of the Old Testament and who were able to appreciate involved interpretations and novel combinations of texts. It is evident from Acts 17:10f that Christians were sometimes drawn from the most studious groups in Israel and brought their habits of study with them to enrich the life of the Church.

In II Timothy 3:14–17 the recipient of the letter is reminded of the fortunate circumstance that from a child he had received instruction in the Scriptures "which are able to make thee wise" and how necessary it was for him to continue on the path which he had then begun. Verse 16 is the classical New Testament passage on the authority of the Bible and the permanent, practical value of studying it. "The man of God" who wishes to be "complete, equipped for every good work" (v. 17 RSV) must not only subjugate his will and discipline his emotions, but must also learn to make full use of his mind to learn, through study of the Scripture (and also, of course, such related subjects as church history and doctrine) the things which belong to his peace.

X. PRAYER

I Kings 8:22–30; Psalm 141:1–4; Daniel 6:4–17; Luke 11:1–13; I Thessalonians 5:16–18; James 5:13–16

That prayer is one of the basic activities of the religious man is a proposition which hardly needs to be proved. Jesus, in the Sermon on the Mount, takes it for granted that—along with almsgiving (Matt. 6:2) and fast-ing (v. 16)—prayer (5) will always be one of the chief ways in which his disciples express their faith. This had been true in the Old Israel and would continue to be so in the New. What is novel in Christianity is not prayer itself, but the new spirit which animates it and the new convic-tion which sustains it.

Prayer may be defined very simply as "speaking with God." It may take many forms, but none of them is essen-tial. Whenever the human heart turns consciously to God —in petition, confession, thanksgiving, adoration, ques-tioning, or any other mood—that is prayer. Seen in this fashion, prayer is a privilege rather than a duty. Only the half-convinced will think of it as a burdensome obliga-tion; for those who take their religion seriously, faith can offer no greater comfort than the assurance that God is not deaf but always receptive to the prayers of His chil-dren, and is, indeed, "always more ready to hear than [they] to pray."

Among the great prayers of the Bible few are more im-pressive than the one attributed to Solomon at the dedica-tion of the temple (I Kings 8:22–53). It is not, of course, a literal transcript of Solomon's words, but rather a com-position of much later time placed by the author upon the king's lips as appropriate for so solemn an occasion. This in no way detracts from its value, since it still remains a fine illustration of the Old Testament ideal of prayer. The opening section (vv. 22–30), with which alone we are concerned here, is a petition for the security of the nation and the Davidic dynasty (24–26). It begins, like all great prayers, with an impressive characterization of the God addressed (23), includes a meditation on His attributes (27), and intercession for others (30). The paragraph con-cludes (30) with the simple word "forgive," illustrating the principle that the purpose of all true prayer is not so much to obtain a gift as to establish a right and harmonious relationship with God.

Psalm 141:1–4 is an Old Testament example of a more personal and informal type of prayer. Vv. 5–10 are corrupt and difficult, but show that the author was in danger from enemies and was anxious to be delivered from a trap which they had set. Nevertheless, he was also aware of his own frailties and asks for God's help to rise above them (3f). Particularly striking is his comparison of his own ascending prayers to the incense which rose to God from the altar of the temple (2), a comparison which is echoed in Revelation 5:8.

The story of Daniel (Dan. 6:4–17) illustrates the importance of regularity in prayer ("three times a day," v. 10) and the courage which its practice sometimes demands. His heroic fidelity, typical of the Maccabean martyrs, stands in striking contrast to the lethargic devotional spirit so common in normal times.

Luke 11:1–13 contains two of Jesus' instructions on the nature and rationale of prayer. There is first the model prayer which he taught his disciples (vv. 1–4), here given in more original form (see RSV) than in Matthew 6:9–13. It falls into three well-defined parts: prayer for the coming of God's kingdom (2), for men's physical needs (3) and for their spiritual well-being (4). By way of comment it may be noted that the "hallowing of God's name" and the "doing of His will on earth" are simply different expressions for the coming of His kingdom; that the prayer for daily bread is based upon a similar petition in Proverbs 30:8; and that the prayer for forgiveness is given a characteristically Christian emphasis by making it conditional on the forgiving spirit of the petitioner.

The second part of this discourse (5–13) urges upon

the Christian disciple the need for persistence in prayer.
God is not, of course, like the surly householder of vv. 5–8
except in the sense that, with Him also, perseverance in the
face of discouragement ultimately brings results. God's
real counterpart on earth is not the somewhat humorous
figure of the ill-natured friend, but rather the typical
human father, who hears the requests of his children and
gives them what they need (11–13). This is especially true
when they are wise enough to ask for the help and guidance of the Holy Spirit (13).

St. Paul, in I Thessalonians 5:16–18, speaks of the
necessity of being always in a prayerful state of mind. One
cannot *say* prayers "without ceasing," but he can learn to
have his mind habitually turned in God's direction.

The last selection (Jas. 5:13–16) shows the importance
of both individual and group prayer in the life of the
early Church, especially in the ministry to the sick. It
gives an attractive picture of a Christian congregation
united in mutual support by the prayers of all its members.

In the opening paragraph we said that Christian prayer
is characterized by a new spirit and sustained by a new
conviction. The new spirit is one of simple trust in the
accessibility of God; the new conviction, of which the new
spirit is the fruit, is that Jesus Christ has opened "a new
and living way" into the presence of God. Indeed, he is
himself the way. As the Christian comes to God the Father only *by* Christ and lives his life *in* Christ, so his prayer
must always be addressed to God "*through* Jesus Christ
our Lord" (John 14:6).

XI. FAITH

Genesis 45:1–11; Isaiah 26:1–4; Psalm 31:1–8; Luke 23:44–46;
Jude 3, 20–21; Hebrews 10:35–11:1

St. Paul, in a famous passage (I Cor. 13:13), says
that there are three abiding qualities which mark the life
of Christians: faith, hope and love. They are not, of course,
qualities of *New* Testament men alone, but characterize
the life of biblical man throughout the whole of the
Scriptures. In the light of God's perfect revelation in
Christ each of the words takes on a new depth of meaning,
but the essential pattern of life which they describe is the
same in all parts of the Bible.

The most basic of these qualities is that of faith, for
where there is no faith there can be no hope and, without
faith, love can be little more than emotional attraction or
a desperate clinging together like children lost in the
dark. In other connections we have already examined the
passages on faith which are of primary theological importance (Gen. 15:6; Hab. 2:4; Rom. 3:28; parts of Heb. 11).
Here we are not concerned so much with faith in relation
to biblical doctrine as with its significance as an indispensable ingredient in the character of biblical man. It is
the quality which, above all others, distinguishes the life of
the great men of the Bible from that of their pagan contemporaries or their only half-committed fellow-religionists.

It should be said at the outset that faith, in the Bible,
always has two aspects: it means, on the one hand, *faith*

in God, and, on the other, *faithfulness to duty.* The "faith-ful" man is one who believes whole-heartedly in the love and overruling purposes of God; but he is also one who can be trusted to discharge faithfully the tasks which are given him. Although these two aspects of faith can be distinguished logically, they are really inseparable, the second being an outgrowth of the first. In so far as faith-fulness is not mere native stubbornness, men are faithful because they have faith in the ultimate meaningfulness of the things they are doing.

In Hebrews 11:22 Joseph is singled out as one of the great heroes of faith (although the instance cited there may seem rather trivial). In actual fact, his whole history, as related in Genesis 37–50, is a saga of triumphant faith. We use the word "saga" advisedly since the story, as it now stands, is probably more a construction of the creative imagination than literal history. That is not really impor-tant, for the story was composed, like the parables of Jesus and many other excellent tales, to illustrate the *kind* of life which God wishes men to live. In spite of the ill-treatment Joseph received from his brothers and his fall from wealth into slavery, he is represented as never doubt-ing that God meant it all for good. And because he showed himself faithful, even in the service of an unbelieving master, he was finally able to save the lives of his entire family including the brothers who had abused him. Man's sense of the absolute trustworthiness of God has nowhere been more simply and adequately expressed than in Gen-esis 45:1–11 (note esp. v. 7).

The passage from the Book of Isaiah (26:1–4) brings out another of the qualities which mark the life of faith: its serenity. Perfect trust brings "perfect peace" (v. 3).

The prayers of Israel, like her other literature, breathe this sense of trust. Psalm 31 (vv. 1–8) is a typical example.

The poet was evidently in serious trouble because of the malicious plotting of his enemies (4). But he remained courageous and serene because he had faith in God. His prayer "Into thy hands I commend my spirit" (5) was to become a vehicle for expressing the faith of many generations of devout but troubled believers after him.

Our Lord's own devotional life was set firmly within the pattern established by the Old Testament Scriptures, as is shown by his constant use of them. The most impressive instance was on the cross itself where two verses from the Psalms (22:1; 31:5) are reported to have come naturally to his lips. From the standpoint of his human consciousness the most striking characteristic of Jesus' mind was the strong sense that his destiny was in God's hand and that he could safely leave it there, even though the pursuit of it might lead finally to defeat and death. The last victory of his faith was won in Gethsemane (Luke 22:42) and the most perfect expression of it was the ancient prayer which he prayed as death drew near (Luke 23:44–46).

Since faith—in the biblical sense—is not merely a kind of natural emotional optimism but is based upon profound convictions about God and His work which can be put into words and communicated to others, we can speak not only of "faith" but of *the* faith": meaning, by that, the intellectual formulation of the content of faith in doctrines, creeds and confessions. Because "faith" must be grounded in *the* faith it is not hard to understanding the insistence of the little Epistle of Jude upon the necessity of committing ourselves to the latter and "contending earnestly" for it (Jude 3, 20–21). Without solid intellectual foundations, faith can quickly degenerate into wishful thinking or cheerful sentimentality.

This discussion comes to a proper climax in the reading of the stirring appeal in Hebrews 10:35–11:1 which ends with the classic definition of faith as a readiness to order one's life by reference to the realities of the unseen world (11:1).

XII. HOPE

Genesis 17:1–8, 15–17, 19; Romans 4:14–25; Jeremiah 32:6–15; I Thessalonians 5:2–10; Psalm 130

As used in ordinary speech the word hope is tinged with wistfulness. It suggests a yearning for the unobtainable or, at best, an expectation which may all too easily be disappointed. But in the Bible and in Christian theology hope never has this wistful quality. It is one of the sturdiest and most virile of the Christian virtues, based not upon dreams and wishful thinking but upon faith in God. Hope, in the biblical sense, is simply the extended vision which is given by faith. Faith in the God of the Bible brings with it an understanding of His ways in the past and therefore an acceptance of His promises for the future.

The man of the world, who does not share the biblical faith, necessarily lives in a narrow room, with no horizons beyond the limits of his daily experience. The most he can hope for is that tomorrow will come and be at least no worse than today. But the man of faith knows that God rules the world in accordance with an eternal plan and that his own life has a place within that plan. So, when he lifts his eyes to the future, he sees, not the next day only, but the *last* day, when God's purpose will be fulfilled and His kingdom established. To live in the light of this far-extended vision is what the Bible means by living in hope. Since the Christian also believes that "in *everything* God works for good with those who love him" (Rom. 8:28 RSV), it follows that hope colors his view of the passing present as well as the distant future.

The two passages with which we begin present the biblical idea of hope dramatically through the experience of one of the great religious figures of the Bible, the patriarch Abraham. We have already seen how the piety of ancient Israel and the early Christian Church made Abraham a symbol of the man of perfect faith. Since faith and hope are inseparable qualities he emerges also as the man of perfect hope. The particular incident used to illustrate this quality is that of his belief in the promise which God gave him (Gen. 17:1–8, 15–17, 19) that in spite of his great age and that of his wife, he would become "a father of many nations" (v. 5), and that the covenant which was to bring blessing to "all the families of the earth" would be established with Isaac, a son who was yet to be born (19).

The point which St. Paul makes in Romans 4:14–25 is that Abraham's subsequent history shows that he accepted God's word with implicit faith and ordered his life hopefully in accordance with the pledge which God had given him. In this instance Abraham's hopefulness was based upon a specific promise which God had made; in two other famous stories told of him—his migration from the home of his ancestors (Gen. 12:1ff) and the story of the sacrifice of Isaac (Gen. 22:2ff)—Abraham received no precise assurance as to what the outcome would be. His hope had to be based upon a general trust in the goodness and power of God. Both kinds of hope have their normal place in Christian character: on the one hand, a confident anticipation that God's specific promises will be fulfilled, and, on the other, a hopeful attitude toward life in general, rooted in the assurance that God has prepared for those who love Him "such good things as pass man's understanding."

The next selection (Jer. 32:6–15) is another good illustration of how hope operates in the life of a man of God—this time in the career of the prophet Jeremiah, who was not merely a symbolic figure such as Abraham may have been, but a flesh-and-blood personage like ourselves. The incident described took place during the final siege of Jerusalem in 587 B.C., when the city was about to fall. For nearly forty years the people had complacently rejected the prophet's repeated warnings that ruin for Israel was on its way. Now that the doom was actually at hand and even the blindest could not ignore it, they went to the opposite extreme and professed to see no sign of hope for the future. Since the true prophet is always one who runs counter to the main currents of his time, it was only natural that Jeremiah, who had spent his life announcing the approach of God's judgment, should then dramatically proclaim his faith in God's purpose of restoration. He purchased a piece of land, and by doing so gave public witness to the hope that was in him: "Houses and fields and vineyards *shall be possessed again* in this land" (v. 15). The whole career of Jeremiah makes it clear that his hope was not the result of any natural, temperamental optimism, but was based on certain profound convictions with regard to the nature of God and His ultimate intention to redeem His people.

The pagan, ancient or modern, can of course in no way share this hope. The "gloom of paganism" arises from its inescapable view of every human life as a day which is moving relentlessly toward the sunset as its final goal. I Thessalonians 5:2–10 expresses the sharply contrasting Christian view that sees our life as a journey toward the sun*rise,* even though, at times, the surrounding night may seem very dark indeed (see also Prov. 4:18). Moreover, the night is one in which the believer has Christ the Lord as a constant companion (v. 10).

Psalm 130 sets forth the same biblical hope, in the language of personal devotion. This hope, the psalmist says, is founded upon a knowledge of God's true nature, which is to be merciful (v. 4; where, it should be noted, "feared" means "had in reverence"). It leads the devout child of God to look toward the future—the future which a merciful God is even now creating—as expectantly as a tired watchman, after a long night's turn of duty, looks for the coming of the day (5f).

XIII. LOVE

Deuteronomy 6:4–5; Leviticus 19:9–18, 33–34; Luke 10:25–37; I Corinthians 13; I John 4:15–21

Of all the qualities which mark the Christian life, love is the most distinctive. The Old Testament has prepared the way by making love for God and man one of the essential demands of true religion; it remained for the Gospel to exalt love into the one "royal law" (Jas. 2:8) which sums up all the others and gives to the ideal of Christian character its peculiar color and fragrance.

The idea that love is a basic duty which man owes to *God* seems to have won its place in Israel through the great reforming movement associated with the Book of Deuteronomy. The thought occurs over and over again in that book and in the literature associated with it. The greatest passage is Deuteronomy 6:4f, which we have considered previously but is so important that we need to examine it again. These words became the fundamental creed of Judaism and are as important in the Jewish liturgy as the Apostles' Creed in the liturgy of Christians. From the proclamation of the unity of God it draws the corollary that He demands the undivided loyalty of His worshipers. What is distinctive of Deuteronomy as compared with some other parts of the Old Testament is that this loyalty must express itself, not in terms merely of fear, enthusiasm or even obedience, but of whole-hearted love.

The law of love toward *men* comes from a surprising place: from the Book of Leviticus (19:9–18, 33f), which one might otherwise be tempted to consider the most unrewarding of Old Testament books. This serves as a warning against too great haste in discarding or disregarding any part of the Bible. The whole passage has to do with being generous and kindly towards one's fellow men and concludes with the remarkable statement that a man must not hate another person even in his heart (v. 17) but must love him as sincerely and devotedly as he loves himself—not merely out of humanitarian good-will but because it is the command of the eternal God ("I am the Lord"—18). If it be objected that the command has to do only with *Jewish* neighbors, the answer is to be found in vv. 33f which provides that the same rule is to be observed toward foreigners who are living in the land of Israel and have asked for the protection of Israel's God.

The central importance of these two commands had

already been noted by Jewish scholars before the Christian era, but it remained for Jesus to take them out of their original context and erect them into the two basic laws of the New Israel—two laws which are really one, since the command *to love* is the heart of both of them. How he did this is told by the gospels in several different ways. In Matthew (22:34–40) Jesus declares that the meaning of the entire Old Testament ("all the law and the prophets") is summarized in the law of love. But the most striking version is found in Luke 10:25–37, which tells how our Lord first of all elicited a statement of the general principle from one of his questioners (v. 27) and then went on to show that the obligation of love towards one's neighbor cannot logically be limited to members of any racial, national or religious group (29–37). Neighborly love is required wherever there is neighborly need; and neighborly love is not mere affection and kind words but such *acts* of love as the situation demands.

It was St. Paul who sang most passionately the praises of Christian love (I Cor. 13). As we have already seen, faith and hope are two of the foundation stones of Christian character. The third, he says, is love, which, in its Christian form, cannot be dissociated from them. Christian love is not geniality or natural kindliness; it is a supernatural quality which flows from faith and hope. It is not a product of healthy glands and a sense of personal well-being; it is a reflection of the love which God has for His creatures (see I John 4:19) and which includes the unlovable and sinful individual as surely as the man of personal charm or sanctity. It is because Christian love has this special quality that the King James Version translates the Greek word in this chapter by the somewhat colorless word "charity." Because of its present-day connotations this is not a satisfactory translation, but it at least serves to remind the reader that the "love" of which the apostle is speaking is something different from the sentimental love which is the subject of so many popular songs and stories.

While the story of the Good Samaritan makes it evident that love which does not express itself in action is no love at all, St. Paul makes it equally clear that objective good deeds which are not motivated by subjective love are cold and worthless in the sight of God (vv. 1–3). In vv. 4–7 Paul describes the various ways in which love manifests itself. The rest of the chapter shows how faith, hope and love—but especially love—point beyond the reach of man's daily, imperfect existence to his eternal destiny, which is to know perfectly the perfect love of God.

The part of the New Testament where love is most consistently the dominant theme is the so-called Johannine literature—the Gospel and the three epistles "of John." The passage selected from I John (4:15–21) is typical. Here God's nature is defined as love, so to live a life filled with love is in some real sense to be filled with God (v. 16). The author assures us also that love is the secret of courageous living, since love and fear cannot exist together (18). Finally, he insists that the two great commandments are inseparable, since one *cannot* love God unless he also loves his fellow man (20f).

XIV. PENITENCE

Psalm 32:1–7; Joel 2:12–18; Leviticus 16:1–5, 20–22, 29–34;
Matthew 3:1–12; 4:12–17; Revelation 3:14–19

Since man is a fallen creature, penitence is the attitude which best becomes him. No note is struck more persistently by the biblical writers than this. A proud heart and impenitent spirit are the most formidable barriers in the way of man's approach to God and until they are broken down reconciliation between man and God is impossible. Penitence is the door one must open if he wishes to reach God's audience chamber. As is said so incisively in the 51st psalm, ". . . thou desirest no sacrifice, else would I give it thee," but "a broken and contrite heart, O God, shalt thou not despise" (vv. 16f).

The profundity of the biblical conception of penitence can be realized only when we see that it involves a total and constant reorientation of life and not merely an occasional act of repentance for specific instances of wrongdoing. In the biblical view man is not just a creature who commits sins, but a *sinful creature*—that is, one whose very nature is somehow estranged from God. For this reason penitence must be an ingrained habit of mind, an habitual consciousness, even when things are going well, that "the burden of our sins is intolerable." This is why the Church includes a prayer of confession in all her principal acts of worship and why no private prayer is complete without an act of penitence also.

The 32nd psalm is one of the classical biblical expressions of the meaning and importance of penitence. It begins (vv. 1f) with a statement that happiness is the fruit of forgiveness. Throughout the Bible the word "blessed," as applied to man, means simply "happy" and might best be so translated. There can be no happiness in any profound sense where men are conscious of alienation from God. The psalmist tells us that he had personal experience of this fact, induced apparently by physical illness (3f), and found relief from his misery only when he made sincere confession of his sins (5). It was the pilgrimage of his soul through alienation, penitence, and finally the knowledge of God's forgiveness, which led him to the sense of peace and assurance so gratefully proclaimed in vv. 6f.

The second passage (Joel 2:12–18) is a reminder that both sin and penitence can be corporate as well as individual. We are not only sinners as individual human beings, but we live in a social environment where every relationship has been to some extent corrupted by sin; as the prophet Isaiah says, "I am a man of unclean lips and I live in the midst of a people of unclean lips" (6:5). Every community and nation—not excepting our own— is sinful and deserves the judgment of God. The passage from Joel arises out of a great national emergency—in this case a plague of locusts—when the prophet called his people to an act of public supplication and penance. Notice that he declares the outward demonstration to be useless unless accompanied by a sincerely penitent spirit within, and that the motive which he feels should lead men to turn toward God is not the fear of His wrath but rather confidence in His love and mercy (vv. 12f.). It is primarily this sense of corporate sin which is expressed in the liturgical general confessions of the Church.

The Old Testament observance which underlined most sharply the importance of penitence and confession was the strange ceremony of the Day of Atonement, described in Leviticus 16:1–5, 20–22, 29–34, in which the high priest confessed the sins of the whole nation for the previous year over the head of a goat which was then supposed to be able, by the gracious providence of God, to carry them out into the desert (v. 22). The solemnity of this mysterious, primitive rite on the most important holy day of the year prevented the people of later Israel from ever forgetting the fact of sin and the need for repentance, confession and amendment. The work of the high priest on this occasion was seen by one of the New Testament writers as a foreshadowing of the priestly work of Christ (Heb. 9:6–14).

The proclamation of the Gospel, also, opens with the call to repent, both in the preaching of John the Baptist (Matt. 3:1–12) and of Jesus (4:12–17). Repentance was the sole content of John's message. When John was arrested and Jesus took up his work, the message he announced was, in the beginning, the same. Although ultimately our Lord's teaching went far beyond any point that John did or could have reached, his first reported words are identical with John's: "Repent: for the kingdom of heaven is at hand" (4:17).

The last book in the Bible contains a scathing little letter addressed to a Christian Church in Asia Minor which was conscious of no need for penitence (Rev. 3:14–19). The deep-seated, festering corruption of merely "respectable" Christians who have no sense of sin has never been more devastatingly pictured than here. The words apply directly and obviously to many in the modern world who, having made their peace with the world, imagine that they have made their peace with God. Throughout the history of the Church—both in the Old Testament and in the New—the call to repent has always been directed even more toward those who think they are righteous and need no repentance than toward those who are admittedly sinful, even in their own eyes. The prophets were concerned with those "that are at ease in Zion" (Amos 6:1); our Lord was offended at the Pharisee who thought he was not as other men are (Luke 18:11); the author of Revelation pours his scorn upon those benighted persons who do not even *know* that they are "poor and blind and naked" (v. 17).

XV. THANKFULNESS

Deuteronomy 8:1–10; Isaiah 51:1–3; Psalm 107:1–32;
Luke 17:11–19; I Timothy 4:1–5; Colossians 3:12–17

If penitence is one of the basic qualities of the Christian life, thankfulness is possibly even more so. G. K. Chesterton once said that the principal difference between a Christian and an infidel is that the infidel takes everything in his life for granted, whereas the Christian receives even the most commonplace blessings with wonder and gratitude. It may well be argued that the foundation stone of all high religion is not, as is sometimes said, a sense of numinous awe in the presence of the unknown, but rather a feeling of gratitude toward the Author of life for His "goodness and loving-kindness." Man's religion is less mature when he worships God through fear of what

God *might* do than when he gratefully adores Him for what He has already done.

Thankfulness is, of course, a quality which marks the lives of *individuals* in the Bible, but it is even more important to note that it is a distinctive mark of the Church's *corporate*, liturgical life, in both the Old Testament and the New. Our first selection is a reminder of that fact (Deut. 8:1–10). In form, this passage purports to be part of Moses' address to the people of Israel just before they entered the Promised Land. In reality, as we have seen, it is a typical sermon for one of the great feasts of the liturgical year and its chief interest lies in the insight it gives into the character of ancient Hebrew worship. The dominant note was joyful recollection of the things God had done for His people throughout their history—how He had led them out of Egypt and through the desert (vv. 2–5), punishing them sometimes but always with a kindly purpose, teaching them their complete dependence upon Him (3), leading them at last into a good land, well-provided with everything they needed (7–10).

In the selection from Second Isaiah (Isa. 51:1–3), the great prophet of the Babylonian Exile first turns his gaze to the past and invites his readers to recall how God had once blessed Abraham, the father of them all (vv. 1f); then he directs their attention to the future and to the glories of Israel's coming restoration (3). That age is to be marked with "joy and gladness . . . thanksgiving and the voice of melody." So the idea of thankfulness came to be associated with Israel's thought of the future as much as it had been with her recollection of the past. The later men of Israel could appropriately have used the General Thanksgiving in the Book of Common Prayer, which says "We bless thee for . . . the means of grace and for the hope of glory."

Within the context of Israel's corporate thanksgivings there was also abundant opportunity for the individual to give thanks for his particular blessings. Psalm 107 (vv. 1–32) is a good example of a liturgical prayer in which various groups in the congregation gave public thanks to God for special evidences of His grace and mercy: 1–9 are for travelers who have safely crossed the desert (note vv. 4f); 10–16 for prisoners who have been set free; 17–22 for sick persons who have been healed; 23–32 for travelers by sea, come to safe haven after a dangerous voyage.

The familiar story in Luke 17:11–19 illustrates the carelessness about saying thanks which is so typical of the average human being. It still is true that even Christian books of devotion usually allot far more space to prayers of petition and intercession than to thanksgiving. On the occasion described by Luke, ten men were healed of leprosy, yet only one was thoughtful enough to return to Jesus and thank him for what he had done. It was particularly humiliating to pious Jews that the one thankful man was not a well-instructed member of the Jewish community, but a despised Samaritan. The story was undoubtedly preserved by the early Christian Church to remind its members of the importance of thankfulness and the constant danger that even "good Christians" may forget it.

I Timothy 4:1–5 is a warning against a certain type of heresy—not unknown in our own day—which declares that the body and all its material satisfactions are essentially evil. The author warns his readers that this is not Christian doctrine. Christians, who have a sacramental view of the material universe, see the whole world as God's creation and everything in it as capable of being consecrated to God's service. The author tells his readers that the principal means by which this is done is to use things in a spirit of thankfulness. "Nothing," he says, "is to be rejected if it be received with thanksgiving" (v. 4).

The Greek word (*eucharistia*) which is here translated "thanksgiving" is the same one which underlies the liturgical word "Eucharist." This fact is important because of the clue which it provides to the meaning of the service of Holy Communion. The basic mood of this central service of our religion is not one of gloom or morbid abasement, but of glad and grateful recollection of God's infinite mercies, especially for those which are associated with our redemption—Christ's "blessed passion and precious death, his mighty resurrection and glorious ascension" and "the innumerable benefits procured unto us by the same."

Colossians 3:12–17 is an example of the summaries of the Christian virtues which occur frequently in the Pauline letters. It is instructive to see how, in a series which includes love, humility, a spirit of forgiveness, and peace, thanksgiving actually occupies the climactic place (vv. 15–17), and to note that just as the prayer of petition must be offered to God "through Jesus Christ our Lord" so also must the prayer of thanksgiving. Christians do not dare even to give thanks "to God and the Father" except "*by him*" (17).

XVI. HUMILITY

Numbers 12:1–8; Isaiah 2:10–17; Zephaniah 3:9–12;
Psalms 131; 37:11; Matthew 5:1–5; 23:1–12; Romans 12:3, 16;
III John 9–11

Moses is said to have been "very meek, above all
the men which were upon the face of the earth" (Num.
12:1–8, v. 3). It is a strange statement, since no one, merely
reading the account of Moses' career, would be likely to
apply this particular adjective to him. Whatever words
one might use to describe his character, "meek" seems
curiously inappropriate for one who is credited with having boldly faced the wrath of Pharaoh, rolled back the
waters of the sea, and braved the lightning and thunder
of Mt. Sinai. The meekness of Moses was obviously not the
cringing servility which we often associate with that word.
The fact is that the meekness of Moses—and the quality
of humility which is praised throughout the Bible—is not
primarily a characteristic of man's relationship to his
fellow men, but rather of his relationship to God. The
nature of Moses' meekness is disclosed in vv. 7f which tell
of his *receptiveness* to God's word. The humility, or meekness, of which the Bible speaks is, in essence, this reverent
willingness on the part of men to listen to God's voice
rather than insist that God listen to theirs.

In systems of Christian moral theology pride is always
listed as the first of the seven "deadly" sins. This is an
accurate reflection of the biblical point of view which sees

pride as the one great and insurmountable barrier between man and God. Pride was the beginning of sin, for
man was not content to be God's creature; he wanted to
be like God Himself (Gen. 3:5). Since pride was—and is—
the cause of man's alienation from God, the humbling of
pride and the destruction of its monuments must be the
decisive act in the establishing of God's Kingdom. This
event is nowhere described more impressively than in
Isaiah 2:10–17, a fragment of a great eschatological hymn.
"The cedars of Lebanon" and "the oaks of Bashan" in
verse 13, "the high mountains" and "the hills" of 14 are
the arrogant rulers of the earth; the "high tower," the
"fortified wall," the mighty ships which go to distant
Tarshish, and the "beautiful craft" (15f RSV) are the
material objects which pride has created.

The great teachers of the Bible had no doubt that the
future belongs not to the haughty, but to the humble.
Zephaniah 3:9–12 presents another picture of the judgment to come, but adds to Isaiah's exclusive interest in
the destruction of pride the positive promise that the
humble and meek will be left in possession of the land.
God says, "I will remove from your midst your proudly
exultant ones" but "will leave in the midst of you a people humble and lowly" (vv. 11f RSV).

The quiet, receptive attitude of mind which marks
the humble man is set forth in the simplest possible
language in Psalm 131. Jesus would one day say that a
person cannot enter the Kingdom of Heaven unless he
humbles himself and becomes as a little child (Matt.
18:3f). Possibly he had this very psalm in mind, for the
point it makes is the same, although it uses the language
of prayer rather than of exhortation. One should remember in reading it, that, as with many other hymns
and prayers, the poet is not so much boasting about a state

of mind already attained as he is describing an ideal in which he believes and to which he aspires.

Psalm 37:11 gives unqualified expression to the thought that the ultimate destiny of mankind is in the hand of people such as this, for "the meek shall inherit the earth." This verse, significantly, became on the lips of Jesus the third of the "beatitudes" (Matt. 5:5). The two preceding beatitudes (vv. 3f) have essentially the same content and are addressed to the same group, for the terms used in them must be understood as primarily religious rather than social or secular. It was among devout groups of people who specially cultivated the virtues of poverty of spirit, penitence, meekness, gentleness, quietness, and receptivity to the divine word, that the message of Jesus found most ready response.

The condemnations found in Matthew 23:1–12 are directed particularly against the conventional religious leaders of Israel, who, as often happens in similar circumstances, were sometimes more impressed with their own dignity than with their opportunity to be channels of God's love and mercy toward those placed under their charge. While humility in the biblical sense is, as we have seen, basically a matter of man's relationship to God, it should have its natural reflex in a gentle and large-minded courtesy in dealings with men also.

St. Paul, in Romans 12:3, 16, shows from another perspective that humility has nothing to do with egregious servility. It is simply honesty in self-evaluation. It is seeing ourselves as we really are—not as gods, but men; not as supermen, but sinful men who stand in desperate need of the grace of God.

III John 9–11 is uncomfortable evidence that even in the earliest Christian churches there were occasional leaders who, like some of the Pharisees, "loved to have the preeminence" (v. 9) and by their arrogance showed that they were neither "of God" nor had ever "seen" him (11). It provides a useful warning that long membership in the Church or even the holding of a responsible position of Christian leadership does not exempt men from the necessity of self-examination and the intensive cultivation of basic Christian virtues.

XVII. WISDOM

I Kings 3:4–13; Proverbs 9:1–6; 10:19–21; 14:29–30;
15:1, 13, 15; 25:6–7; Luke 14:7–11; 16:1–12;
II Thessalonians 3:6–12; Job 28:20–28; Colossians 2:1–3

It has been necessary previously to emphasize the supernatural origin of many of the characteristics of the Christian life, for the life of biblical man is intended to be truly a new kind of life and not merely the ordinary good life raised to a somewhat higher degree. But, important as this distinction is, it must not be pressed too far, since it is obvious that the good Christian will in many respects be like the good pagan or like the good man who makes no profession of religion at all. There are certain qualities of character which have been admired and cultivated generally by men of every race and every form of belief. The Bible teaches emphatically that the follower of the true God must, and will, possess these qualities in at least as high a degree as his nonbiblical neighbor.

Collectively, these qualities are described by the Bible

as "wisdom," although from another point of view wisdom might be regarded as merely the first and greatest of them. In classical theology these have been summarized as the four "cardinal" virtues: prudence (or wisdom), justice (or a sense of honesty and fair play), temperance (or modesty and self-control), and fortitude (or courage). If we think of wisdom as being not only the first of the cardinal virtues, but as a comprehensive name for all of them in the aggregate, we may define wisdom as the ability to manage one's life in accordance with intelligence and understanding rather than by emotion and prejudice. The man of the Bible yields to none in his admiration for this kind of life. Christianity does not negate the good life of the natural man, but rather enhances and enlarges it.

Our first selection (I Kings 3:4–13) contains a popular tale told in ancient Israel about King Solomon, who—however little he may have deserved it—had the reputation of being the wisest of all her kings. It was said that at the time of his accession to the throne God gave him the choice of the gift he would most desire and he then chose wisdom rather than wealth or victory over his enemies. Little as the story may tell us about the actual historical Solomon, it shows unmistakably the high value the Hebrews placed on intelligence and the practical ability to handle difficult situations with diplomacy and skill. The story which occupies the rest of the chapter is intended to illustrate through a typical situation what the men of ancient Israel understood wisdom to consist in.

So important is the conception of wisdom in the Old Testament that a whole group of books—Proverbs, Ecclesiastes, and Job—is simply called "the wisdom literature," though probably only the first of these deserves the name in the strictest sense of the word. The Book of Proverbs is a collection of essays and aphorisms composed by Israel's teachers of wisdom, a special class of men who had charge of the instruction of the young and who sought to present in as appealing a fashion as possible the attractions of the quiet, thoughtful, well-ordered life. In Proverbs 9:1–6 "Wisdom" is personified as a gracious hostess inviting all men, but especially the young ("the simple" of v. 4), to partake of the feast which she has prepared in her spacious home (the "seven pillars" of v. 1 are simply indications of its size and magnificence). The other selections show some of the particular emphases of the wisdom teachers: 10:19–21, the need for strict control over the tongue; 14:29f and 15:1, the importance of having a serene spirit; 15:13 and 15, the value of cheerfulness; and 25:6f, the desirability of modesty in deportment.

To some it may seem surprising that Jesus played the role of wisdom teacher as well as that of prophet, since the cautious, prudential approach of the typical "wise man" seems so foreign to his mentality. Yet, whatever the explanation, there can be no doubt that he did so. Two episodes from Luke's Gospel illustrate the fact. In 14:7–11 He takes the very passage we have just been reading (Prov. 25:6f) and makes it the basis of one of his discourses. It is an excellent example of the full humanity of Jesus and evidence that nothing which concerns man's welfare was alien to his spirit.

In the second selection (Luke 16:1–12) he chides his disciples for not being as intelligent and forethoughted about the affairs of God and his Kingdom as ordinary men are about the material affairs of life (v. 8). One can hardly suppose that Jesus approved the morality of the steward's conduct; what he did applaud was his quickness of wit and his promptness to take action when action was needed.

The pastoral ministry of Paul constantly exhibits his remarkable capacity for dealing with difficult human situations in a wise and practical way. When, for example, some good but foolishly visionary members of the church at Thessalonica decided to stop working at their regular jobs in anticipation of the imminent return of Christ, Paul did not react by writing them a theological essay, but by laying down the blunt rule "If any will not work, neither let him eat" (II Thess. 3:6–12). There is nothing specifically Christian about handling the problem in this way, but it is in complete accord with "sanctified common sense" and the universal judgment of the old teachers of wisdom, for whom idleness was one of the most vexatious forms of folly (see, e.g., Prov. 6:6–11; 19:15).

Yet, however closely biblical wisdom may sometimes resemble worldly prudence, it is necessarily a deeper thing because the Bible sees it as derived from God alone (Job 28:20–28) and perfectly manifested only in Jesus Christ (Col. 2:1–3). Consequently, the profoundest wisdom is accessible only to those who know and wholeheartedly accept the finished revelation of God as it is found in the Gospel.

XVIII. JUSTICE

Psalm 15; Nehemiah 5:1–13; Exodus 2:11–15; Luke 12:41–48; I Corinthians 6:1–11; Philemon

The sense of justice seems to be a normal part of human nature. Whether men perfectly exemplify the ideal or not, most of them respond instinctively to appeals made to the need for honesty, fair play or just dealing. Christians can claim no monopoly on this kind of virtue and many an honest pagan can put the merely nominal Christian to shame. But what the Christian can rightly claim is that the biblical faith puts the idea of justice on a much firmer foundation since it treats it not merely as a socially valuable instinct of the natural man, but as an expression of the character of God Himself. In the Old Testament, justice is the imperious demand of a just and righteous God; in the New Testament it is a manifestation of the new relationship which has been created among men by the saving work of Jesus Christ.

While the basic law of Israel, as found in the Pentateuch, attempted to enforce just dealing in human relationships, and the prophets continually appealed to the nation's leaders to establish justice among the classes, it is perhaps even more significant that the public liturgy set forth ethical righteousness as a formal prerequisite for the worship of Israel's God. Psalm 15 is the classic expression of this requirement. The psalm has the form of a catechism, in which the first verse asks "Who is permitted to enter the temple and take part in its worship?" and the rest answers the question and describes the character the worshiper must exhibit. He must be truthful (2), not given to evil-minded gossip (3), must associate with men of integrity, keep his pledged word at whatever cost (4), not take interest on a loan, and not be receptive to a bribe (5).

The prohibition of interest should especially be noted, since this was one of the fundamental laws of Israel (Exod. 22:25; Lev. 25:35–37). The reason was that in a simple, noncommercial society such as ancient Israel's, only extreme necessity would prompt a man to ask for a loan, and a just man would naturally respond to human need by a generous gift, freely offered; he would not expect to make a profit from another man's misfortune. The selection from Nehemiah (5:1–13) shows that there were times, even in Israel, when this principle could be forgotten; but so great was the force of Israel's traditional sense of justice that the influence of a single strong and dedicated personality such as Nehemiah's was enough to arouse men's consciences and make them restore their unjust gains.

The passion of the later Hebrews for justice may well have its historical source in the example and teaching of Moses. It is true, at least, that the first two incidents which tradition relates about him as a mature man (Exod. 2:11–15) show him intervening violently in the interests of fair play, once between an Egyptian and a Hebrew and a second time between two of his own people. His flight to the desert was a direct consequence of his concern for right dealing among men (v. 15).

While the parable in Luke 12:41–48 was not told primarily to teach the lesson of God's concern for justice (it was rather a warning to be prepared for the Lord's coming), it does reveal incidentally the profound sympathy Jesus had for the underprivileged and his dislike for those who exploit them. The portrait of the brutal supervisor who takes advantage of his employer's absence to indulge himself and mistreat his inferiors (v. 45) is calculated to awaken disgust in the mind of the readers. The ideal servant—the "faithful and wise"—is the one who deals out fairly to each his "portion of meat in due season" (42). The Lord, when He comes, will judge justly, and—as justice requires—will deal more severely with those who have been honored by great responsibilities than with those who have but few (48).

As there were men in ancient Israel who failed to measure up to Old Testament ideals of justice, so there were those in the early Church who failed also in this basic human obligation. Paul, in I Corinthians 6:1–11, denounces a church which permitted its members to engage in lawsuits with each other. Surely in the Church of Christ, of all places, men should be able to live together in an atmosphere of fair dealing and a mutual, brotherly concern for justice! What a scandal it was in the eyes of pagans that such outrageous behavior as that mentioned in v. 8 should be found amongst Christians—those who professed to have been "washed," "sanctified" and "justified in the name of the Lord Jesus" (11). The church at Corinth was, of course, not typical of early Christian congregations, nor is such conduct very common in churches today, but the passage is a good, if somewhat unsavory, reminder that Christians are at all times expected to be more, not less, sensitive to the demands of ordinary human justice than their unbelieving neighbors.

St. Paul's little letter to Philemon is as eloquent, though subtle, an appeal to a man's sense of fair play as has ever been written. Onesimus, a slave owned by Philemon, had run away and finally become Paul's servant in prison. Paul sent him back and wrote this note to beg his master not to treat him rigorously, as the law allowed, but for love's sake (vv. 7–9) and Paul's sake (13, 17–20), to receive him kindly and as a brother. Although, admittedly, Onesimus had done what was wrong, he had redeemed himself by his subsequent conduct (11) and was entitled not merely to cold human justice but to the higher justice which Philemon had learned in Christ (4–6).

XIX. TEMPERANCE

Proverbs 15:16–17; 25:28; 30:7–9; Ecclesiastes 5:10–12;
7:16–17; Ecclesiasticus 31:12–22; Luke 12:13–34;
Philippians 4:10–14; II Peter 1:2–7

Most pagan moralists were inclined to believe that the greatest of virtues is temperance or self-control, which is also the principal source of another important group of virtues: patience, contentment and calmness of spirit. The man the pagans most admired was the one so completely master of his passions that he remained imperturbable whatever the circumstances of his life might be. The Bible, in the nature of things, cannot attribute so central an importance to temperateness and the other qualities associated with it, since the biblical ideal of human character is that of passionate devotion to God and His righteous rule. Without passion the great men of the Bible would be nothing, as is evident from the briefest consideration of the lives of the Old Testament prophets or of our Lord and his disciples.

But, granted that the passion for God is the basic element in the character of biblical man, it is also true that self-control, temperance, patience and contentment have their place. Even though there must be no attempt to limit the scope of man's dedication to God, there still remain large areas of life in which men must have a real concern with purely secular things—their physical needs, for example, and those of their families—and in these areas the

Bible calls for the same kind of temperance and self-mastery as did the great moral thinkers of the pagan world. On this level the Christian ideal of virtue is different from the pagan only in that it provides it with a securer basis. The pagan commends these virtues only on the basis of self-regarding wisdom; the men of the Bible see them as also rooted in the will of God and His generous concern for the welfare of His children.

It is naturally in the wisdom literature rather than in the prophets that we find these things emphasized. Our reading includes several brief selections from Proverbs, all of which praise the life of moderation and self-control. The first (15:16f) speaks of how much better it is to live simply, with reverence for God ("the fear of the Lord") in one's heart, and love as the bond of one's family life, than to strive for wealth and luxurious living ("a stalled ox"), which so often bring only trouble and hatred. The next passage (25:28) pictures the man of uncontrolled impulses—the angry, greedy or fretful man—as being like a city whose walls are already breached and open to the enemy. The last (30:7–9) is an appealing little prayer that life's necessities may be supplied only as required, and in moderate measure. We have previously noted that one of the petitions of the Lord's Prayer ("give us this day our daily bread") is based upon v. 8.

Ecclesiastes is the one book of the Old Testament which approaches closely the pagan idea of moderation without improving upon it. Nevertheless it contains some good common sense, as one can see from 5:10–12, which points out how foolish it is to be anxious for wealth, since this is a desire which feeds upon itself and is never satisfied. Furthermore, wealth brings vexatious responsibilities and cannot increase one's ability to enjoy the simple pleasures of life (12). The strangest passage in this strange book is

one which advises moderation even in piety (7:16f)! There
is perhaps, even here, a useful reminder that genuine religious zeal can become perverted into the vice of bigotry
or fanaticism and this has no true place in the character of
a man of biblical faith.

The selection from Ecclesiasticus (in the Apocrypha)
is a good example of the skill with which the wise men of
the Bible used humor to re-enforce their lessons. The implied portrait of the glutton, stuffing himself with free food
and then afterwards "breathing hard upon his bed" is
amusing—but also disgusting (31:12–22).

When we turn from the wisdom literature to the teaching of Jesus (Luke 12:13–34) we find ourselves moving
upon a noticeably higher plane. In the incident of the two
brothers quarreling over their inheritance (vv. 13f) and
in the parable of the rich man who felt that his wealth was
adequate insurance against all the ills of life (16–20) we
have unforgettable pictures of the ordinary unconverted
man whose life is dominated by an uninhibited passion
for possessions and financial security. But our Lord's
warning to his disciples is really not so much against greed
and immoderate love of material things as it is against the
kind of restless anxiety about the future which so often
afflicts even the regenerate. Intemperate worry of any kind
is wrong for the Christian, since the man of faith should
know that God is always doing more for us "than either
we can desire or deserve." The Christian's journey through
the world should be a calm one, untroubled by violent
winds of covetousness (15) or fretful discontent (22).

This was the lesson which Paul had learned so well
and expresses so beautifully in Philippians 4:10–14. He is
writing to thank his friends in Philippi for a gift which
had been sent to him while in prison. He is grateful for
their help and for the thought which prompted them to

send it as soon as the opportunity came (v. 10); but at the same time he does not want his benefactors to feel that his previous lack of comforts and necessities had made him discontented or impatient (11–13). Moved at all times by a restless zeal for Christ, he nevertheless knew the secret of self-control and could meet the crises of his private life calmly, temperately and in a spirit of deep content.

II Peter 1:2–7 contains a list of virtues such as is found in many of the New Testament epistles. The reader will notice the prominent place given to those with which we have been concerned in this discussion (v. 6).

XX. FORTITUDE

Proverbs 28:1; Jeremiah 15:15–21; II Kings 6:8–17; **Psalm 91;**
John 11:1–16; Acts 21:7–14; Hebrews 11:32–12:2

The fourth of the virtues which men of biblical faith admire in common with good men of every other creed is that of fortitude, or courage. As with the other natural virtues, the Bible simply adds to it a more solid foundation, because it makes fortitude an expression of faith in God rather than evidence merely of personal strength of character. Fortitude means primarily the capacity to persevere in one's appointed task in spite of opposition and discouragement. It may take different forms: on the one hand there is the spectacular courage which is called forth by a sudden emergency such as a hand-to-hand battle with an enemy; on the other, there is an undramatic kind of fortitude which makes it possible

for a person regularly to peform duties which are dis-
agreeable, burdensome or even worse. In many respects
the latter type is the more difficult and therefore the more
to be desired and cultivated.

The Book of Proverbs (28:1) furnishes a good motto
for this discussion: "The wicked flee when no man pur-
sueth; but the righteous are as bold as a lion." To the
writer of this verse there was no doubt that evil is essentially cowardly. The wicked man is self-centered; he has no
great causes to which he can give himself and for which
he is willing to die; his courage cannot rise above the level
of petty self-interest. There is probably some over-sim-
plification in this view, but it contains enough of truth to
make it worth saying. While history knows of some in-
trepid criminals whose courage seems their one redeeming
quality, the criminal type is, on the whole, a cowardly
type—as any daily newspaper will demonstrate.

Courage, on the other hand, is one of the characteristic marks of the righteous man. He speaks up for the
truth in the face of every temptation to be silent; he does
not hesitate to take the unpopular side of an argument if
he knows it to be right; he persists over long periods of
time in unpleasant tasks if convinced that duty leads him
in that direction. The prophet Jeremiah is an excellent
example of this type of person. A man of natural timidity,
he became strong through God's grace, and for nearly forty
years carried out a distasteful mission to announce the
imminence of judgment and the necessity for repentance
to a prosperous and self-satisfied people who, most of the
time, merely laughed in his face. Jeremiah 15:15–21 is one
of a series of remarkable passages in this book in which
the prophet discloses his secret doubts and his appeals to
God for help. Vv. 15–18 contain his prayer, a pathetic complaint which shows how discouraged even the boldest saint

may become. Vv. 19–21 are the reassurance which came to him, in answer to prayer, that if he was faithful to God, God would be faithful to him, and make him "a fortified wall of bronze" (RSV).

The second passage (II Kings 6:8–17) is not, perhaps, to be understood as strictly historical, but it is at least an admirable parable of the convictions which make the righteous man "as bold as a lion." Elisha's servant was fearful because he knew the insufficiency of the city's human defenses (v. 15). But the prophet saw with the eyes of faith and was able to show him that as long as the two of them were on God's side the forces "that be with us are more than they that be with them" (16f). The courage of the man of biblical faith is always larger than that of the merely natural man because it rests upon a more accurate assessment of the resources at his disposal.

Psalm 91 is an expression, in classic devotional form, of this same conviction. The righteous man, who has committed his life to God, is sustained by invisible forces. One must, of course, beware of interpreting the poetic language too literally, for the real protection God offers is not so much against physical mishap or even major disaster as it is against permanent loss and ultimate defeat.

The story told in John 11:1–16 is a fine illustration of the simple, imitable courage which was so important an element in the human nature of Jesus. The point of vv. 9f (with which 9:4 should be compared) is that his life was too short to permit the luxury of cowardice. What was to be done was to be done *immediately,* without fear for the threats of enemies (v. 8). The concluding verse (16) shows how our Lord's courageous attitude inspired an immediate and corresponding courage in his disciples.

Acts 21:7–14 records a similar display of courage on the part of the greatest of the followers of Jesus. When

Paul arrived in Caesarea, at the end of his last "missionary journey," he was warned that he should not go up to Jerusalem because he would probably be arrested when he got there (v. 11). But neither his personal sense of danger nor the tears of his friends could stop him from making a pilgrimage which he was sure would be for the glory of Jesus' name (13).

The most stirring statement about the fortitude of the men of God is that found in Hebrews 11:32–12:2. The passage is an almost poetically rapturous catalogue of the bold deeds of the great men and women of the past, and particularly instructive because of its insistence that *faith* was the source of their courage (v. 33). It concludes with an appeal to the readers to exhibit the same kind of boldness in running whatever course God may call them to run and to keep always in mind the courage and fidelity of Jesus, "who for the joy that was set before him endured the cross, despising the shame" (12:2).

XXI. MARRIAGE

Genesis 1:27–28; 2:18–25; Deuteronomy 24:1–4; Isaiah 62:1–5; Mark 10:2–12; Ephesians 5:22–33

If the Bible has many things to say about the life of individual man, it also has much to say about various areas of his collective or social life, such as marriage, the family, the state, and relations among nations. It is to these matters we must now turn our attention.

The first and most basic of all social relationships is that between the sexes. While all other human relationships might conceivably disappear, this one—together with that of the family, which flows from it—could not be lost without involving the destruction of man himself. Since religion is concerned with the whole sweep of human life, it must necessarily have a special concern with this primary relationship—the reasons for it, the spirit and the laws which should govern it, and the obligations which it should impose.

The passages which are fundamental to all the thought of the Bible on this subject are Genesis 1:27f and 2:18–25, both of them belonging to the ancient Hebrew account of the creation of man. The details of the stories (there seem to be two) belong to the realm of folklore rather than of science, but the view of marriage which inspires them is unexpectedly profound and of universal validity. The first point to be noticed is that the Bible sees nothing shameful in the sexual relationship since God is responsible for it and commanded that it be continued (2:24); shame is the unhappy product of man's first sin (cf. 2:25 with 3:7). The purpose of marriage, according to the Genesis accounts, is twofold. The more austere "priestly" story, which stands first in the Bible, says that it is intended for the continual propagation of the human race ("be fruitful and multiply," 1:28).

From a purely logical and scientific point of view, this is plainly so, and must be seriously considered in any discussion of the nature of matrimony, but it is pleasant to note that the older story, now found in Gen. 2:18ff, saw in the institution of marriage also a kindly provision of God for alleviating the loneliness of man's lot ("it is not good for man to be alone," 2:18). It is almost startling to realize that this story, which originated in a polygamous society, unmistakably contemplates monogamous marriage as the ideal. It tells us that God's purpose was that *one* man and *one* woman should become *one* flesh, presumably forever.

The second passage (Deut. 24:1–4) is an extract from the civil code of Israel (attributed at that time to Moses) which deals with the institution of marriage in an altogether different spirit. Although the ideal of Genesis no doubt held the allegiance of many high-minded people, the prevailing law dealt with marriage in a more practical way, allowing the tie to be broken, in accordance with the common law of the ancient Near East, at the will of the husband—with the one proviso that the woman's rights must be safeguarded by providing her with legal proof of her freedom (the "bill of divorcement" of v. 1).

That marriage, in spite of this somewhat pragmatic and brutal way of regulating it, was still held in highest honor in ancient Israel is shown by such a passage as Isaiah 62:1–5, in which God's relation to his people is pictured in terms of husband and wife. During the days of the Babylonian Exile Israel had seemed like a forsaken wife, but the time would come, the prophet says, when she would be called "My delight is in her" ("Hephzibah") and her land called Married ("Beulah") (v. 4). (In verse 5 the words "thy sons" are probably a mistake and should be read "thy Builder.") The idea of God as the husband of Israel, which is also found in several other places in the Old Testament, seems to have originated with the prophet Hosea as the strange and almost miraculous outgrowth of his domestic misfortunes. It is worth noting that the inclusion of the Song of Solomon in the canon of the Old Testament was apparently due to its having been reinterpreted as celebrating in poetic form the marriage between Yahweh and Israel.

When Jesus was asked about the permissibility of divorce (Mark 10:2–12), he replied that the law in Deuteronomy was merely a temporary concession to human weakness, the true divine law of marriage being found in Genesis ("from the beginning," v. 6). Now that the Kingdom of God was drawing near in his own person, Jesus implies, men must already begin to live by its laws. What had been regarded in the Old Israel as a fine ideal must in the New Israel be translated into actual fact. The unity created by marriage was no longer to be capable of being broken at the whim of either party and any breach of it must be regarded as adultery (11f).

In contrast to the usual biblical procedure, which uses the marriage relationship to illuminate the nature of God's relationship to His people, the passage from Ephesians (5:22–33) takes an opposite course and, with striking effect, makes of Christ's relationship to the Church an exemplary pattern for the relationship between husband and wife. Every Christian marriage, says the writer, should ideally be a reflection of the heavenly marriage, exhibiting the same harmony of mind and sense of common purpose. It ought to exemplify the self-sacrificing love on the part of the husband (vv. 25, 28, 33) and the sense of glad and affectionate dependence on the part of the wife (22–24, 33) which are the principal marks of the Church's relationship to Christ as his mystical Bride.

XXII. FAMILY LIFE

Genesis 47:5–12; Psalm 128; Proverbs 31:10–31; Ruth 1:14–22;
John 19:25–27; Ephesians 6:1–9; II John 1–6

It is not natural for human beings to live a solitary
life. The Bible tells us that God instituted marriage as
the normal means by which men can escape from solitude
and satisfy their hunger for companionship (Gen. 2:18).
But marriage is not just an end in itself; it results usually
in the creation of a new social group, the family. For the
the Bible, as for our race generally, the family is the basic
unit of human society and provides the environment
within which the life of the normal man is lived; it offers
to its members comradeship, affection, security, and abundant opportunity for self-discipline and mutual support.

Every family is a complex of different, but inter-
woven and ideally harmonious, relationships—those of
husband and wife, father and child, brother and sister—
each involving its own peculiar set of privileges and responsibilities which necessarily change with the passing
years. The duties of husband and wife are obviously con-
siderably different before the arrival of children than after;
the relation of child and parent is not the same when the
child reaches maturity as it was in youth. But though the
relationships change in character they never cease to exist,
and the changes result from the operation of certain natural and unchanging laws. The family, in other words, is
not a static institution, but a vital organism, pulsating
with an organic life of its own.

The Bible, especially the Old Testament, offers many pictures of the family at various stages of development, and, sometimes even, of dissolution. The selection from the Joseph story (Gen. 47:5–12) is particularly instructive because it pictures the restoration of a broken family relationship by the energy, courage and self-forgetful love of one of its members. Joseph was the injured member of the family, whom his brothers had callously sold into slavery in Egypt. But, once there, he was not happy until he had brought them there also, using the political power he had won by his merits to save them from want, rather than to satisfy a natural desire for revenge. Like the parable of the prodigal son (Luke 15), the story of Joseph was told—at least in part—to illustrate the power of redemptive love to nourish family life and heal its discords.

According to Psalm 128, a happy family life is one of the chief blessings which come from true religion ("to fear the Lord" and "to walk in his ways," v. 1). The picture of the father with his many children gathered around him at mealtime (v. 3) gives a pleasant glimpse into the joys of a simple family life, firmly anchored in the piety of the ancient Hebrew world.

One sees the nature of family life from a quite different point of view in the selection from Proverbs (31:10–31). This time attention is focused upon the mother, the "good wife" of v. 10 (RSV). She is by no means a mere drudge, but a responsible officer of the family (16), diligent, of course (13ff, 17ff, 27), but also charitable (20), wise and loving (26). In ancient Hebrew society as in our own, despite obvious differences of social custom, it was usually the mother who gave to the family its characteristic emotional and spiritual tone.

The good wife of Proverbs comes vividly alive in the character of Ruth, whose affectionate devotion toward the family into which she married survived even the death of her husband. There are few incidents in literature more genuinely moving than the account of Ruth's profession of loyalty to her widowed mother-in-law (Ruth 1:14–22), followed as it was by their return to the ancestral home and her devoted effort to rebuild the shattered life of her family. The story gains added poignance from the fact that Ruth was not a Hebrew by birth, but a despised Moabitess.

The few incidents related in the gospels of Jesus' childhood are sufficient to enable us to see the simple, idyllic nature of his own family life. In later years he never lost his love for associating with families, even though the nature of his vocation made it impossible for him to live that kind of life himself. So we see him in the home of Simon Peter (Mark 1:29ff) and, in another passage, finding special happiness in that of Martha and Mary (Luke 10:38–42). The Fourth Gospel represents him as showing, even on the cross, a concern for the integrity of the family into which He was born (John 19:25ff). Knowing how necessary is the relation of parent and child for the fullest kind of life, he bequeaths his best friend to his mother to be a son in his stead.

The description of Christian family life which began in Ephesians 5:22–33 with an account of the duties of husband and wife, continues in 6:1–9 for the other members. Children are reminded that their primary obligation, as stated in one of the ten commandments (Deut. 5:16), is to honor their parents by obeying them. But the parents likewise have an obligation not to deal harshly with their children and to train them in the fear of God (v. 4). A new element is introduced in vv. 5–9, which speak of the position of servants (i.e., slaves). In a Christian family they must be obedient, like the children, but must also be treated with the kindly justice which their master expects to receive at the hands of his own Master in heaven. The time would come, of course, when Christians would perceive that slavery in itself is inconsistent with the mind of Christ.

The little second epistle of John is ostensibly addressed to a mother and her family. This is probably just a pleasant way of writing to a church and its members, but it is significant that a congregation of Christians can be so naturally compared to an ordinary human family. The point the writer wishes to make is that Christian love is the only sound basis for corporate life; neither in the natural family nor in the parish family can there be any healthy living together until the members have learned at least in some degree to "love one another" (II John 1-6).

XXIII. THE STATE

I Samuel 8:4-20; I Chronicles 28:2-7; Deuteronomy 17:14-20; Mark 12:13-17; Romans 13:1-7; I Peter 2:13-17

Above the individual and the family stands the state. Since the state is not, of course, so basic an institution as the family, some primitive people manage to get along without it, but among civilized men it is always to be found in one form or another. Indeed, in some societies such as those of fascism or communism the state becomes so powerful that individuals, and other, lesser forms of social organization, are completely subordinated to it.

The attitude of the Old Testament toward the state is necessarily somewhat different from that of the New because of the different situation which then existed. In Old Testament times the people of God were a nation like other nations and needed, therefore, some kind of civil government. Although at first they experimented with a form of loose confederation (the rule of the "judges"), it was inevitable in the long run that they should adopt the institution of monarchy, the only practical and efficient form of government under the conditions of the ancient world. So the question of the attitude of the Old Testament toward the state really becomes a question of its attitude toward the king. Various positions are taken by different writers, but they can be easily reduced to three: *negative* (disapproval of kingship on principle), *positive* (enthusiastic approval of it as a divine institution), and *mediating* (a compromise which accepted monarchical rule as a practical necessity). Our three selections from the Old Testament exemplify these three different points of view.

The first (I Sam. 8:4–20) pictures the people asking for a king in order to be like other nations (vv. 5 and 19f) and Samuel indignantly protesting that to have a king is to reject God (7) as well as to expose the people unnecessarily to a useless and selfish tyranny (11–18).

The second selection (I Chron. 28:2–7) represents the other extreme view and puts expressions on the lips of David which glorify the monarchy as God's own deliberate creation (vv. 4–7)—although it is notable even here that the perpetuity of the dynasty is made conditional on its fidelity to God's Law (v. 7).

The third selection (Deut. 17:14–20) may be taken as representing the basic, considered opinion of the great men of Israel toward kingship, and therefore toward the state. For them it is a practical necessity which, one may infer, rightly commands the loyalty of its subjects. At the same time, it is not an end in itself; the king exists to serve his people, not himself (v. 16f), and is always subject to the higher law of God (18–20).

The Church in the New Testament was in a different position since it had no direct responsibility for civil government. Christians were a small group within the great body of the pagan Roman Empire. The question for them was whether or not they owed any loyalty to the actual "powers that be"—a government by unbelievers over which they had no control and of whose policies they must frequently disapprove. The answer which they gave was similar to that of Deuteronomy, at least in its practical good sense. Since civil government, whatever its form, obviously serves a socially useful function, it behooves Christians to support it, at any rate so long as it does not require them to violate the laws of God. The time would come when the Empire would ask of the Church something which it could not give; then it would resist to the death. But, until that point was reached, the good Christian had also the obligation of being a good citizen.

Although Jesus' pronouncement about giving to Caesar what is Caesar's (Mark 12:13–17) has been subjected to a variety of interpretations, it seems sufficiently clear that he spoke in opposition to those among his own people who advocated armed revolt as a religious duty. As long as Caesar does not arrogate to himself the things which belong to God, Jesus says, men should pay his taxes and accord him the respect which he demands.

The advice of Paul is quite unambiguous (Rom. 13:1–7). The empire, for him, is God's arrangement for the well-ordering of society, and Christians, like others, owe it loyalty (v. 5), financial support (6), and reverence

(7). Paul, himself a Roman citizen, had sufficient opportunity in his wide travels to experience the benefits of a
strong and stable government. The point of view expressed in I Peter 2:13–17 is the same. The believer's new-
found liberty in Christ should not lead to social anarchy,
but to a higher conception of the obligations of citizenship (v. 16).

The practical, common-sense attitude of the Bible
toward the state and the responsibilities of its citizens is
still the proper one and is one of the best safeguards in our
culture against the excesses of the modern state in certain
of its forms, particularly against the absolute and quasi-
religious devotion which it sometimes dares to claim. There
were kings in Israel, like Ahab, who claimed absolute
power over the lives of their subjects, but there were always religious leaders willing to challenge them to the
point of open rebellion. This is the spirit which continues
to animate the prophetic thinkers of the Christian tradition and explains why massive resistance to the autocracy
of the modern state often finds its most effective support
among the members of the Church.

XXIV. CORPORATE RESPONSIBILITY

Nahum 3:1–7; Obadiah 1, 8–14, 21; Lamentations 1:1–9;
Ezekiel 18:1–9; Revelation 17:1–6; 18:1–3

There is nothing in the Bible so alien to the modern liberal point of view as the way in which some of the
biblical writers condemn whole nations without making

any apparent attempt to discriminate between the guilty and the innocent among their citizens. This is, in part, a survival of a primitive view of man which saw him primarily as the member of a group rather than as an individual; and in part the result of a genuine and permanently valid insight which recognized that no individual can completely escape responsibility for the actions of the group to which he belongs.

Most of the prophetic books of the Old Testament contain considerable sections which consist of nothing but denunciations of the enemies of Israel (e.g. Isa. 13–23, Jer. 46–51, Ezek. 25–32). Needless to say, these are not the most profitable passages of scripture for meditation and study. Yet, since they constitute so large a part of the Bible, one must at least try to understand why they are there and what enduring message they convey.

There are two small books of the Old Testament which are entirely devoted to the passionate denunciation of a particular nation. The first (in order of time) is Nahum, which is simply a long exultation over the imminent downfall of the Assyrian Empire, represented by its capital city, Nineveh (Nah. 3:1–7). Since the capture of Nineveh occurred in 612 B.C., it is easy to arrive at an approximate date for the book. For over a hundred years the people of Israel and Judah had suffered under the tyrannical and often brutal rule of the Assyrians, so it is not to be wondered at that they rejoiced when Assyria was finally destroyed by an enemy as ruthless as itself. The poem—one of the most magnificent products of Hebrew poetic genius—rises above the level of mere nationalism to the extent that it sees the doom of Nineveh as the result of her indulgence in a policy of "lies and robbery" (v. 1).

When Jerusalem fell to the Babylonians in 587 B.C., the Edomites, neighbors and blood-relations of the Jews, instead of helping their brother nation, actually joined with the enemy in looting and taking prisoners. The Jews never forgot this treachery, and when, a century or so later, the Edomites in turn met with national disaster, the Book of Obadiah was composed to celebrate the event (1, 8–14, 21). The particulars of the indictment are given in vv. 10–14. Once again, what is condemned is not simply enmity to Israel, but the violation of the principles of brotherhood (cf. Amos 1:11). The book concludes (21) optimistically with a glimpse of the coming Kingdom of God in which the power of malicious human governments is to be eliminated forever.

The prophetic leaders of Israel were no less ready to apply these standards of moral judgment to their own people than to foreign nations, a fact which needs always to be kept in mind. The Book of Lamentations, written during the days of agony which followed the capture of Jerusalem, gives eloquent evidence of this capacity for self-judgment (1:1–9). There is no doubt in the mind of its author that the calamity was a punishment for Israel's sins (vv. 5 and 8), even though the magnitude of the disaster involved innocent girls (4) and young children (5). It was the nation as a whole which was corrupt, not merely her guilty leaders.

Eventually there set in a reaction against the rigorousness of this idea of corporate guilt and corporate punishment and Ezekiel was the principal proponent of a new, clearer idea of individual responsibility. The 18th chapter of his book is a kind of charter of individual rights (see vv. 1–9). When he says "The soul that sinneth, *it* shall die" (4) he means "The person who is guilty, *he,* and he alone, shall be punished." This was, of course, an important corrective to the one-sidedness of the older view. But it was by no means the whole story.

It still remains true that no individual lives entirely to himself. He is bound up in the bundle of life with others, and just as he shares in the benefits of a common life, he also participates in a common burden of guilt. It is significant that, even in the New Testament, where the main emphasis is obviously on the value and responsibilities of the individual, the persecuting Roman Empire can be denounced in undiscriminating language reminiscent of the older Hebrew prophets (Rev. 17:1–6; 18:1–3; "Babylon" in these verses is merely a cryptic name for Rome; note 17:18).

If the ancient world was inclined to overstress the idea of national and corporate guilt, it is certainly true that the modern world emphasizes too exclusively the absolute separateness of individuals. The truth lies somewhere between the extremes and the Bible contains a salutary reminder of an aspect of the truth we are much too likely to forget.

There is, of course, an important corollary to the principle of corporate guilt: the principle of corporate redemption. Without some understanding of these two related ideas, it would be difficult to make much of the Christian scheme of salvation, which sees man, involved by nature in the corporate guilt of his nation and his race, brought to newness of life by being incorporated in the mystical Body of Christ.

XXV. SOCIAL JUSTICE

Isaiah 1:10–26; Micah 3; Deuteronomy 15:7–15; 24:14–15;
Luke 16:19–31; 19:1–10; James 5:1–6

The chief sin of which nations are guilty is the toleration of injustice. Human society is properly organized to protect the rights of the weak, but too frequently it becomes merely a means of perpetuating the privileges of the strong. When this happens, from the biblical point of view it falls immediately under the judgment of God.

As we have previously seen, the Bible constantly asserts that justice is one of God's basic attributes; it regards it also as an essential mark of the godly man. But the assertion that *nations* must be organized to promote justice is an equally firm and fundamental element in biblical religion, particularly in the teaching of the Hebrew prophets. It is, for instance, characteristic of Amos that the opening chapters of his book show him sharpening the social conscience of Israel by directing her attention to the unjust actions of her neighbors. His audience readily agreed with him that these other nations deserved the wrath of God. Amos' real concern, however, was with righteousness in Israel itself and the climax of his address (Amos 2:6ff) is a passionate arraignment of the people of God for their own crimes against the law of justice.

Because of the almost monotonous intensity of his concern with this subject, Amos was in a special sense the prophet of justice. But the same theme occurs in some

form in most of the prophets. The opening chapter of
Isaiah contains a good example (1:10–26). The prophet
scathingly calls Jerusalem "Sodom and Gomorrah" (v. 10)
because its inhabitants imagine the splendor of their temple worship (11–15) to be an acceptable substitute for
justice to the oppressed and fatherless (16f). The familiar
words of v. 18 should probably be understood as a rhetori-
cal question: "If your sins are [in actual fact] scarlet, shall
they be [in my eyes] as white as snow?" Vv. 21–24 are a
lament over the city, which, polluted by injustice, is now
about to receive the punishment it deserves. In the end, it
is said, God by His own power will reconstitute her government and install officials after His own heart (25f).

Micah is, if anything, more violent than Isaiah (Mic.
3). He scornfully attacks Israel's rulers, those who should
be the protectors of the poor but are instead their worst
enemies, and accuses them, in gruesome imagery, of op-
pressing their helpless subjects (vv. 1–4). The spiritual
leaders, the prophets (5–7) and the priests (11), are no better, since they use their high office simply for self-aggran-
dizement and their religion is merely an opiate for their
consciences (11). A city—or nation—whose corporate life is
so deeply perverted is headed for inevitable, and irre-
trievable, disaster (12).

Views of this kind were not limited to a few fanatical
prophets. There was a real effort in the Law of Israel to
guarantee justice for the weak. This note is struck in all
the law codes of the Old Testament, but most consistently
in Deuteronomy, which is the closest of all to the prophetic
spirit. The passages here selected (15:7–15; 24:14f) deal
with three classes of people: first, the poor, whom every
citizen is commanded to help (15:7–11); second, slaves of
Hebrew origin, who are assured of fair and even generous
treatment (12–15); and, third, the ordinary employee, the

prompt payment of whose wages is made a matter of strictest obligation (24:14f). These provisions were not simply ethical ideals, but legal enactments with official sanctions behind them.

The New Testament, as we have noted, has less to say about social responsibility and national righteousness, because Christians of the New Testament age were a small group who had no control over the activities of government. Nevertheless the spirit of the Hebrew prophets is that of the New Testament also. The parable of the rich man and Lazarus (Luke 16:19–31), although told to teach another lesson, shows Jesus' instinctive sympathy with the sick beggar who at death goes immediately into Abraham's bosom, as against the conscienceless, self-indulgent aristocrat who goes directly to hell. The story of Zacchaeus, the Jericho tax collector (Luke 19:1–10), illustrates the strength of Jesus' influence for social righteousness, since it could compel even a corrupt, tough-minded public official to disgorge his unjust profits (v. 8).

The New Testament book which contains the clearest echo of prophetic teaching on social justice is the little epistle of James, as the selection given (5:1–6) illustrates. Verse 4 is a reflection of Deuteronomy 24:14f (as well as of Lev. 19:13).

While Christians cannot hope to *build* God's Kingdom of perfect justice—only God can do that—they have a powerful obligation, even under the conditions of present society, to apply its principles as effectively as possible. Christians of today are not the weak, ineffective little band of the New Testament period. While they may not have complete control over the agencies of government, they are in most Western countries the largest single group capable of exerting an effective voice in the affairs of human society. If their voice is not raised on behalf of the weak and helpless, for creating a just social order along the lines suggested by the Hebrew prophets, then they can expect only the judgment of which the prophets also spoke.

XXVI. INTERNATIONAL RELATIONS

Genesis 10; 28:10–14; Zechariah 8:20–23; Isaiah 19:23–25; Matthew 8:5–13; John 12:20–23; I Corinthians 12:12–13; Revelation 1:4–7

Such a phrase as "international relations" is, of course, a purely modern one. Because men of the Bible never used it and did not think in terms of the problem as we formulate it today, some would argue that the Bible can have nothing to say which is really relevant. But, even though the ancient world knew nothing of "nations" in our modern sense of the term and certainly nothing of the complexities which now characterize our global common life, the underlying problem was not so different as it might seem. It was simply the problem of how the people of the world, diverse in so many ways and similar in so many others, can live together upon the earth without destroying each other. The great leaders of both the Old and the New Israel, moved by the Spirit of God, were very much concerned with this matter and the basic affirmations which they were led to make at least suggest the lines along which a solution is to be sought.

The first passage to be considered (Gen. 10) is one of those which the casual Bible reader is likely to skip over rather rapidly because at first glance it seems like nothing except a list of names. But the names are those of the various peoples of the earth as the Hebrews conceived them and the striking fact is that they are all represented as descendants of a single common ancestor, Noah. Going back even further, they are all descended from the first man, Adam. As Paul said, God has made of "one" every nation of men (Acts 17:26 RSV). This assertion of the original, physical and metaphysical, unity of the human race is obviously an important presupposition for any discussion of international relations.

If the original unity of mankind is the Bible's first principle on this subject, God's intention to bring about its *final* unity is the second. To this end, God selected one man, Abraham, and one nation, Israel, to be the agents through which His blessing and unifying grace should come to "all the families of the earth." This promise, first given to Abraham (Gen. 12:3), was repeated to successive generations, last of all to Jacob, the father of the twelve tribes of Israel (Gen. 28:10–14).

Although this purpose was often forgotten in later times, when the "election" of Israel was interpreted in nationalistic terms, it reappears frequently with the greatest of her teachers. Zechariah, for example, sees men of all nations coming to worship the Lord of Hosts in Jerusalem (Zech. 8:20–23; cf. Isa. 2:1–4; 42:6; 49:6; 56:7; 60:1f; Dan. 7:27; Zeph. 3:9; Zech. 14:16).

The most remarkable of all passages of this type is the late oracle now found in Isaiah 19:23–25, which sees the future Israel, not dominating other nations by force or even by the power of her faith, but quietly fulfilling her long-promised role as a center of blessing in the midst of the earth (v. 24 RSV), serving as a bond of unity between her ancient enemies, Egypt and Assyria, now reconciled with her and with each other and acknowledged also as God's people and the work of His hands.

The New Testament sees the ancient promise beginning to be fulfilled in the work of Christ. When a Roman centurion comes to Jesus for help (Matt. 8:5–13), our Lord regards it as a foretaste of the time when "many shall come from the east and the west, and shall sit down with Abraham, Isaac and Jacob" (v. 11).

In the Fourth Gospel, the climax of Jesus' ministry is reached when "certain Greeks" express a desire to see him (John 12:20–23). Then he knows that the foundation of his work of reconciliation has been laid and the ingathering of the nations has begun. "The hour is come."

The remainder of the New Testament takes it for granted that Christ's work has obliterated for Christians all distinctions of nation, race or culture. This is explicitly stated in I Corinthians 12:12f (as well as in Gal. 3:28; Eph. 2:14; and Col. 3:11). It is true that these passages refer specifically to members of the Church, but it can hardly be doubted that Christians are also intended to see that all man-made distinctions are irrelevant in view of the original unity of the nations and God's purpose for their final reconciliation.

The last book of the Bible opens with a hymn-like passage (Rev. 1:4–7) in praise of him who is "the prince of the kings of the earth" (v. 5) and for whose sufferings on their behalf "all the kindreds of the earth" one day shall mourn (7). This last verse is an echo of Zech. 12:10 with the setting significantly transferred from Israel to the Gentile nations.

While the Bible offers no ready solution to our present international problems, it does contain the presuppositions with which a Christian must face them: belief in the basic oneness of men, faith in God's purpose finally to unite them, and assurance of Christ's ultimate dominion over all peoples. Certainly no world order which men may create, however effective it may be in some directions, is going to be equivalent to the Kingdom of God. But this must not lead Christians into a cynical indifference to the problems of the world with which they actually have to deal. Many of the perplexing questions which burden men today are capable of solution and will be solved best by men with the mature sense of responsibility and largeness of vision which come from complete devotion to Jesus Christ as the Prince of the kings of the earth.

BIBLIOGRAPHY

Books for further study. Those marked with an asterisk (*) are non-technical works intended for the general reader.

I. *The Theology of the Bible as a Whole*

Millar Burrows, *An Outline of Biblical Theology* (Philadelphia: Westminster Press, 1946)

*A. G. Hebert, *The Bible from Within* (New York: Oxford University Press, 1950)

*Alan Richardson (edit.), *A Theological Word Book of the Bible* (New York: Macmillan, 1951)

*J.-J. von Allmen (edit.), *A Companion to the Bible* (New York: Oxford University Press, 1958)

*Suzanne de Dietrich, *The Witnessing Community: The Biblical Record of God's Purpose* (Philadelphia: Westminster Press, 1958)

*Suzanne de Dietrich, *God's Unfolding Purpose.* Trans. from the French by Robert McAfee Brown (Philadelphia: Westminster Press, 1960)

*Louis Bouyer, *The Meaning of Sacred Scripture* (Notre Dame: University of Notre Dame Press, 1958). An important Roman Catholic Work.

*Robert Davidson, *The Bible Speaks* (New York: Thomas Y. Crowell, 1959)

II. *The Theology of the Old Testament treated separately*

Otto J. Baab, *The Theology of the Old Testament* (New York: Abingdon Press, 1949)

Paul Heinisch, *Theology of the Old Testament.* Trans. from the German by William Heidt (Collegeville: The Liturgical Press, 1950). A Roman Catholic work.

*H. H. Rowley, *The Faith of Israel* (Philadelphia: Westminster Press, 1957)

Ludwig Koehler, *Old Testament Theology.* Trans. from the German by A. S. Todd (Philadelphia: Westminster Press, 1958)

Edmond Jacob, *Theology of the Old Testament.* Trans. from the French by A. W. Heathcote and P. J. Allcock (New York: Harper, 1958)

Th. C. Vriezen, *An Outline of Old Testament Theology.* Trans. from the Dutch by S. Neuijen (Oxford: Basil Blackwell, 1958)

George A. F. Knight, *A Christian Theology of the Old Testament* (London: Student Christian Movement Press, 1959)

The two most important works in this field have not yet been translated into English:

Walther Eichrodt, *Theologie des alten Testaments*. Three volumes (Leipzig: J. C. Hinrich, 1933–1939)

Gerhard von Rad, *Theologie des alten Testaments*. Only the first volume has yet appeared (Munich: Chr. Kaiser, 1957)

III. *The Theology of the New Testament treated separately*

*Frederick C. Grant, *An Introduction to New Testament Thought* (New York: Abingdon, 1950)

C. H. Dodd, *According to the Scriptures: The Sub-Structure of New Testament Theology* (London: Nisbet & Co., 1952)

Rudolf Bultmann, *Theology of the New Testament*. Two volumes, trans. from the German by Kendrick Grobel (New York: Scribner, 1954–1955)

Ethelbert Stauffer, *New Testament Theology*. Trans. from the German by John Marsh (New York: Macmillan, 1955)

*Archibald M. Hunter, *Introducing New Testament Theology* (Westminster Press, 1957)

Alan Richardson, *An Introduction to the Theology of the New Testament* (London: Student Christian Movement Press, 1958)

INDEX OF SCRIPTURE PASSAGES